THE CONCEPT OF POLITICAL CULTURE

The Concept of Political Culture

Stephen Welch

150th YEAR

M

St. Martin's Press

© Stephen Welch 1993

First published in Great Britain 1993 by
THE MACMILLAN PRESS LTD
Houndmills, Basingstoke, Hampshire RG21 2XS
and London
Companies and representatives
throughout the world

This book is published in the *Macmillan/St Antony's Series*
General Editor: Rosemary Thorp

A catalogue record for this book is available
from the British Library.

ISBN 0–333–54534–6

Printed in Great Britain by
Ipswich Book Co. Ltd., Ipswich, Suffolk

First published in the United States of America 1993 by
Scholarly and Reference Division,
ST. MARTIN'S PRESS, INC.,
175 Fifth Avenue,
New York, N.Y. 10010

ISBN 0–312–09144–3

Library of Congress Cataloging-in-Publication Data
Welch, Stephen.
The concept of political culture / Stephen Welch.
p.   cm.
Includes bibliographical references and index.
ISBN 0–312–09144–3
1. Political culture.   I. Title.
JA75.7.W43   1993
306.2—dc20   92–38066
                                    CIP

To my father and in memory of my mother

Contents

Acknowledgements

The first three years of the research on which this book is based were funded by an ESRC Studentship. I wish to thank the following people for useful comments or conversations: Ralf Dahrendorf, John Goldberg, Joel Hellman, John Higley, Mary McAuley, David Priestland, Karl Rohe (and other participants in the Fifth Essen Conference on Political Culture, Essen, February 1989) and Joe Schull. Erica Benner and Martha Merritt read earlier versions of the manuscript in their entirety and made many good suggestions. Lakshmi Daniel helped me with some logistical matters. My D. Phil. examiners, Michael Lessnoff and Zbigniew Pelczynski, provided useful guidance and a singularly effective stimulus to many of the improvements contained herein. Mr Lessnoff went beyond the call of duty in making additional suggestions for the final revision, and could no doubt have made many more if time had allowed. I especially want to thank my supervisor, Archie Brown, for his support over the long haul. I used to think that the practice of sharing the credit while taking the blame was a paradoxical conceit; now I realize it is merely right.

Introduction

'Political culture is one of the most popular and seductive concepts in political science; it is also one of the most controversial and confused.'[1] Since this view was expressed in 1979, it has if anything become truer. Recent years have seen a recrudescence of theoretical debate about the concept and new applications in a variety of academic disciplines. In addition, its use has become quite widespread among journalists and television commentators; its appeal has even extended, in the most worrying development, to advertising copy-writers.[2] This state of affairs makes embarking on a general critique of 'political culture' and a survey of its uses daunting. It at first seems as though political culture research has ramified and expanded beyond the point at which it is useful even to refer to it under one heading. This first impression is to a degree accurate, in that whatever the conclusions of the present study, it is clear that there is something in the idea of political culture that will continue to attract political scientists, historians and pundits: like the early anthropological idea of culture itself, it threatens to absorb everything in its vicinity.

A second look reveals an opposite but equally off-putting problem. The categorization of different types of political culture research, if we notice the numerous attempts at this that have been made, turns out to be quite possible – indeed all too possible. The disposition to construct typologies that is endemic to political culture research turns out to afflict its summarizers also.[3] The existence of several typologies of political culture research already provides good grounds for not following that approach here. Further grounds are provided when we consider to what extent such typologies advance knowledge – raising thereby the important general question of the purpose of categorization.

When dealing with a large and complex domain of data, it is of course natural to attempt to give the domain some order by imposing categories upon it. It is something else, however, to make *a priori* assumptions about what these categories should be like, and to suppose, as many of these accounts do, that the act of categorization exhausts analysis. One of the studies we will consider makes the strong claim that a typology must 'produce a mutually exclusive and jointly exhaustive set of classes for the domain under consideration'.[4] But why? Moreover, whether or not such a result is feasible in the analysis of political cultures themselves (the aim of the study just referred to), there are

1

good reasons for doubting its feasibility in the analysis of political culture *research*.

These reasons follow from the fact that no useful criterion of distinction facilitates the creation of 'mutually exclusive and jointly exhaustive' categories. This claim rests on the meaning given to 'useful'. It is true that '*Any* criterion will organize data – will order items in classes – but only some classifications will be scientifically useful',[5] yet there is no need to assimilate usefulness to typological purity. Our goal in the following chapters is to assess political culture research, not simply to order it. Several criteria of ordering suggest themselves, but our argument will often take the form of showing how the distinctions they would establish are not hermetic and that the overlap or interference between 'categories' helps us to understand problems in political culture research. Thus it is one theme of the argument that noticing the *lack* of 'mutually exclusive and jointly exhaustive' categories helps us to understand the domain we are studying. The latter is to be considered the purpose of a 'useful' criterion of distinction. Indeed, the very term 'criterion of distinction' is somewhat rigid. Since we will be concerned with various forms of overlap, it would be better to regard the criteria as a range of polarities.

With this qualification in mind, we may go on to consider the 'distinctions' that will be employed below. One that prominently suggests itself is that between *behaviouralism* and *interpretivism*. The candidacy of this distinction for the subdivision of the political culture field is quite plausible. For one thing, the distinction has come to be at least one of the more important and common ways of analyzing political science as a whole, and polemics between the two camps have been going on for at least thirty years. More to the point, though, is the fact that political culture has itself provided an arena for that contest: in its hall of fame it contains major representatives from each side, and thus has served as a microcosm of the behavioural-interpretive debate in political science.

Behaviouralism, described by Robert Dahl as a 'mood' rather than a 'field', approximates in his view to a 'scientific outlook'. It had as its ultimate goal 'the development of a science of the political process',[6] 'a major step forward in the nature of political science as science . . . toward a probabilistic theory of politics'.[7] The optimism of these aspirations was of a piece with the optimistic attitude towards science and technology as a whole that was prevalent in America in the 1950s and early 1960s. But aside from this consonance with the mood of the times, behaviouralism drew strength from various sources. Dahl mentions specific factors such as the support for behavioural research given by various foundations and the hands-on experience of government by political scientists that occurred in the Second World War, as well as more general ones such as the influence of European sociologists who emigrated to the United States in the 1930s.

Bernard Crick, taking a more critical stance, has argued that the behaviouralist aspiration to 'value-freedom' is the result of a liberal 'belief in a natural unity and unanimity in American thought' which 'has cut itself away from the actual reasonings and experience that underlay the great political literature of the early republic'.[8] Crick's argument in turn has been contradicted by Gabriel Almond, who calls attention to the continuity of the behavioural movement with intellectual developments already underway in Europe, mediated by the fact of emigration, and argues that, therefore, 'the counterposition of a European and an American approach to social science around the issue of humanist vs. scientific scholarship will simply not bear the light of day'.[9]

Its philosophical roots aside, a sounder basis for distinguishing behaviouralism is perhaps that it combined the aspiration to make the study of politics scientific with a methodology that appeared to make the aspiration fulfillable: quantitative, and more precisely survey, methodology. The development of survey techniques, in other words, facilitated what had previously been seen as only a distant goal, because it enabled truly comparable and cumulative research. Nevertheless, we will discuss below the role of interpretation in survey methodology itself, justifying Anthony Giddens's contention that 'All so-called "quantitative" data, when scrutinized, turn out to be composites of "qualitative" – i.e., contextually located and indexical – interpretations produced by situated researchers, coders, government officials and others.'[10]

Another feature of behaviouralism, one clearly implied by its characterization by Dahl as a 'protest movement', is its attempt to transcend what were seen as the deficiencies of the previously dominant paradigm in the study of politics, the so-called 'legal-institutional' approach. This approach was held to have had an excessively narrow scope, restricting its attention to formal rules and institutions, and overlooking informal behaviour.[11] Behaviouralism may thus be seen as a stage in the territorial expansion of political science as a discipline; that is, the enlargement of its subject matter from constitutions to informal elite political behaviour, thence to voters' behaviour and, finally, to mass attitudes and behaviour beyond the realm of electoral participation.

The concept of political culture was in the vanguard of the behavioural revolution. Although the term had been used earlier (for instance by Herder in the eighteenth century and by Lenin in the twentieth),[12] Almond's characterization of political culture as the 'particular pattern of orientations to political action' in which 'every political system is embedded'[13] is generally regarded as an act of coinage. It played a key role in several subsequent studies which have assumed the status of classics of the behavioural tradition, such as Almond and Verba's *The Civic Culture* and Pye and Verba's *Political Culture and Political Development*. The concept of political culture offers itself as an ideal token of and catalyst for behaviouralism since it fulfils the two central aims of the approach: it can be defined so as to be measurable quantitatively, and it marks the ultimate expansion of the territory of political science. When Almond borrowed the term 'culture' from anthropology, he was thus trying to do two things. In subserving the goal of territorial expansion he was trying to make use of a concept that had historically had a very broad reference in its original anthropological setting. And at the same time, by asserting the 'autonomy' of political culture from culture in general,[14] he was trying to define a concept that would subserve the goal of quantification and cumulative research. These aims are, however, in conflict. It comes as little surprise that the aptness of the idea of 'culture' for the purpose of behaviouralist territorial expansion has enabled holistic conceptions of culture to come into play, thus undermining the behaviouralist explanatory aspiration.

Interpretivism, like behaviouralism, also has the character of a reaction; in this case, to behaviouralism itself. It is typified by the rejection, implicit or explicit, of behaviouralist standards of verification in favour of a criterion of plausibility. The intellectual sources of this approach are diverse. They are not completely distinct from those claimed as inspiration by behaviouralist writers on political culture. Any student of the kinds of differences between nations and groups which we now refer to with the term 'political culture', who thought and wrote before the advent of survey methodology, necessarily used interpretive methods, but at the same time can be seen as a precursor of those who today use surveys to characterize such differences. J. G. Herder, for instance, was one of the first to discuss systematically the differences between nations, the fact that 'human nature under diverse climates is never wholly the same'.[15] F. M. Barnard takes this as an early manifestation of political culture writing,[16] but Herder's speculative analysis has little in common methodologically with behavioural political culture research. Alexis de Tocqueville is another writer who might seem to be the epitome of an interpretivist. But he too has been claimed by the behaviouralists: 'One has to read the Tocqueville correspondence to appreciate how close that brilliant interpreter of American democracy . . . came to doing an opinion survey in his travels around the country.'[17] More specific to interpretivism are the methodological principles of *verstehende Soziologie* elaborated by Weber. But in terms of number of citations, the most significant influence on political cultural interpretivism is anthropologist Clifford Geertz, and in particular his notion of 'thick description', according to which behaviour is not usefully described 'objectively'; its meaning has also to be described.[18]

Thus within political culture research, the defining feature of interpretivism is a conception of political culture as the 'meaning' of political life, or the meaningful aspect of politics. This feature licenses a large range of methodologies, from the sweeping description and summary of a nation's history to the analysis of popular culture. The only common feature of interpretive methodology is, indeed, its distrust of quantitative analysis. The grounds for this distrust are well brought out in a seminal article by Charles Taylor.[19] The key terms in Taylor's approach, consistently with the central feature of interpretivism just identified, are 'intersubjective' and 'common meanings'. Intersubjective meanings are to be distinguished from 'common attitudes' of the sort whose presence survey methodology can expose. They are perceptible only in the social life to which they give rise, which they 'constitute'. Like language, they provide the fabric of social life, the criterion of a group being a society. Only when intersubjective meanings are present is there enough in common in a group for there to be shared attitudes, or for that matter disagreements. Some intersubjective meanings, moreover, do not just facilitate social life, but make it distinctive for the society's members. They express the society's values. These are 'common meanings'. Taylor illustrates the resistance of intersubjective and common meanings to empirical investigation with the example of children in missionary schools, who are taught the values and beliefs of a society that is alien to them. In this case, the values taught *are* capable of investigation as 'brute data' (that is, by surveys): their content is entirely captured in each child's individual expression of them. But that is because the ideas in this case are mere 'social "ideals"'. Where the missionaries come from, they are more than this; they are 'rooted in social practice' and hence cannot be fully captured by interviewing individuals, only by interpreting the social practice as a whole.

In accordance with its receptivity to a wide range of evidence, interpretivism employs a characteristically broad definition of political culture. Stephen White, for instance, defines political culture as 'the attitudinal and behavioural matrix within which the political system is located'.[20] There is an echo of Almond's definition in the implication that political culture provides some kind of context for politics, but the introduction of behaviour marks a big difference. The problem lies in differentiating the context from that which is located within it. The political system itself is, after all, from one point of view a 'behavioural matrix' or a 'pattern of behaviour'. To be sure, it is located within a larger behavioural matrix, the entire behaviour of society, but the latter is not what White goes on to investigate – his historical interpretation instead surveys Russian history. Other interpretivists have faced up to this difficulty more squarely, asserting that political culture cannot be analytically separated from politics itself, and hence seeing it instead as a certain *perspective* on politics. Alfred Meyer is one who has expressed such a view:

> in practice it is difficult if not impossible to maintain the separation between subjective propensities, actual behavior, and the framework within which behavior takes place . . . . And once culture is everything, what distinguishes it from other aspects of human behavior is not so much its contents as a manner of ordering or viewing the contents.[21]

It is therefore easy to distinguish behaviouralism and interpretivism in abstract terms. Behaviouralism is characterized by its scientific aspirations, including the aspiration to value-freedom, by its expansionist tendency and, within political culture research, by its use of survey methodology and its concomitant 'subjective' or psychological definition of political culture. Interpretivism makes use of tests of plausibility, and construes political culture as meaning; it is evidentially omnivorous, in keeping with its comprehensive definition of political culture. However, distinctions that seem clear when definitional and methodological preambles are compared evaporate or are reversed when attention is focused on political culture research itself. This is because the distinction between behaviouralism and interpretivism that we have just elaborated is somewhat limited, in what is not at first an obvious manner. It concerns the question of what political culture *is*, in the sense both of how it is defined and of what evidence is needed in order to describe it. This question might appear to be the only one we need to answer in categorizing political culture research, but it is not. The more important and useful question which will frame the discussion to follow is, how is political culture, once defined and described, to be *used*?

To be sure, the categories of behaviouralism and interpretivism have certain implications for the use of the concept, but these are not completely binding implications. We can thus speak of consistently behavioural or interpretive uses of political culture, and also of hybrid uses. Within the behavioural idiom, two uses of political culture may be identified, which we will refer to as the *comparative* and *sociological* uses.

As these labels imply, the uses we are distinguishing have characteristic disciplinary or sub-disciplinary settings: comparative politics and political sociology, respectively. That, however, yields only the most preliminary understanding of the point of the distinction, especially since it will be argued below that in many cases juxtaposition of the two uses occurs, with effects that we will analyze at length. By the comparative use of political culture is meant not simply the invocation of the concept in a comparison between nations, or any other units, but its invocation 'n a specific role in a specific type of comparison: namely, its use as an isolatable and comparable factor in the explanation of differences in national political outcomes and structures. The difference between this use and the sociological one is not one of methodology nor necessarily of definition. It is a distinction that can only be drawn clearly at a given *level* of putative explanation, or for given *units* of comparison. For instance, suppose we compare various nations and their political cultures, with a view to explaining divergent political outcomes in terms of the diverse political cultures. That would be a comparative use of political culture. If we then examine the relationship of variables *within* the political cultures, such as interpersonal trust and group-forming propensity, we are enriching the description of political culture, and arriving at a new explanatory theory, yet it is one in which individuals, not nations, are the units of comparison. Comparison and explanation are occurring at a lower level. The new theory would be a theory in sociology; it would not be a comparative use of *political culture*, even if the concept of political culture were to figure in it. A conflict between comparative and sociological uses of political culture arises from the fact that the more detailed and complex (therefore in a sense *adequate*) an account of political culture is, the less comparable it is. Sociological sophistication, as we will see in some detail, renders untenable the generalizations that are necessary for cross-national comparison.

One reason for concentrating on the use criterion in the discussion to follow is that in many cases there is a damaging juxtaposition of comparative and sociological uses. We will discuss some examples of this in Chapters 1 and 2, and will explore some of the reasons for it in Chapter 4. Another reason, more suited to discussion in this Introduction, is presented by the existence of what we called the hybrid cases. These cases render inadequate and confusing the putative distinction in terms of behaviouralism and interpretivism.

Hybrid cases occur when interpretive methodology and definition contribute to a characterization of political culture that is then *used* in either the comparative or the sociological manner just outlined as subcategories of behaviouralism. White's analysis of Soviet and Russian political culture is an example of this. Not only his definition, but his dismissal of 'futile attempts to import the methodology of the natural sciences into the study of human affairs',[22] suggest an interpretive outlook, but as the discussion of Chapter 3 will make clear, the use to which he puts the concept is explicitly comparative. Lucian Pye, a student of Asian political culture, employs a method with a large interpretive component, as Chapter 4 will show. But its overall purpose is comparison between nations in terms of their political cultures and the resulting political differences. As he puts it, 'probably no other skill is as sensitive to the parochialism of culture as that of the politician'.[23] Pye's pupil, Richard Solomon, has produced an account of Chinese political culture that is distinctive for its use of Freudian categories, as, for instance, in his assertion that 'Mao might be said to be an "anal" leader seeking to transform an "oral" society'.[24] This methodology makes Solomon's work seem the paradigm of an interpretive account. But although Freudian categories differ widely from those more normally used by comparative political culture researchers, they nevertheless have an important similarity, which is the assumption of their universal applicability. A different range and type of evidence is required to support a characterization of political culture such as Solomon's, and just like Freudian analysis in its original therapeutic setting the characterization has a large interpretive component. But the use made of these categories is reassuringly familiar: Chinese political culture explains certain outcomes in Chinese politics. Interpretive methods contribute to a comparative conclusion.

An interpretive specification of political culture can also be used in the sociological manner. Many of the 'sociologies of modernity' that will be discussed in Chapter 2 feature this combination. In the more speculative of these, evidence for the existence of some form of 'modern' or 'postmodern' culture comes from a variety of sources, with the notable exception of attitude surveys. The political culture thus interpretively specified is not, however, placed in a comparative framework, but is seen as an aspect of the modernizing process.

The categories of comparative and sociological uses of political culture will take us far in the analysis and critique of political culture research, but not as far as we need to go. It would be felicitous if interpretive political culture research offered itself for analysis in terms of contradictory uses as the behavioural variant does. Unfortunately for seekers of symmetry, interpretivism differs too much from behaviouralism for this to be the case. Indeed, one might say that the distinction between characterizing political culture and using it is itself hard to draw in cases of consistent interpretivism, if interpretive political culture is only a 'manner of ordering and viewing' certain phenomena. Nevertheless, an important distinction within interpretivism needs to be made. Instead of *uses*, it will be better to speak of tendencies, or even more vaguely of potentials. In particular, an argument will be made in Chapters 5 to 8 below that interpretivism contains an *idealist* tendency, as well as a *phenomenological* potential. Both of these labels require some justification.

The term 'idealism' comes heavily freighted with centuries of philosophical usage. We need only think of the related yet widely different 'idealisms' of Berkeley and Hegel to get an idea of its possible scope. Despite this, the core of content common to all of the term's philosophical variants already suggests its connection with the interpretive emphasis on meaning. In the analysis undertaken in Chapters 5 to 8, however, something more precise than an emphasis on ideas, or on the subjective, is intended by the 'idealist tendency'. We will be using the term to refer to analyses in which meaning for the analyst has taken priority over meaning for the participants. Idealist interpretivism, in this sense, manifests itself in a number of different ways, and to different degrees. We will argue, for instance, that it is to be found in the Geertzian notion of 'thick description', and that it is egregiously present in some recent analyses of political culture that have drawn on the anthropological structuralism of Claude Lévi-Strauss. In all such cases, for reasons that will become apparent, idealism is a deficiency. One possible means of avoiding it would be to avoid interpretivism altogether, but the argument below will suggest that idealism can be avoided within the interpretive framework by having recourse to the social theory of phenomenology. Phenomenology, and in particular the phenomenology of the social world elaborated by Alfred Schutz, we will argue, offers an antidote to idealism by insisting that the justification of the interpretive method lies in the interpretive practices of the participants themselves, which in turn are related to their social practices. In other words, phenomenology serves to anchor interpretivism to concrete social reality, while at the same time arguing that such reality is a construct needing to be continually reproduced. Since phenomenology has hitherto not been explicitly drawn upon as a basis for political culture research, we can hardly argue that there exists such a thing as the phenomenological use of political culture. But a phenomenological analysis of political culture, we will argue, both accounts for and avoids the deficiencies of behaviouralism and idealist interpretivism. Thus the *phenomenological potential* of interpretive political culture is the analysis upon which the argument of the following chapters converges.

Aside from distinctions of political culture research in terms of use of the concept, another polarity that will arise, though less explicitly, in the following discussion is between two categories of subject matter or focus of political culture research: *mass* and *elite*, where the latter usually refers to a political and sometimes to an intellectual elite. The initial impression that the concept, as originally defined within behaviouralism, is a necessarily mass-focused one, both because of its quantitative methodology and because of behaviouralist expansionism, is wrong. The same quantitative methodology that seems most applicable to the mass level has been applied also to the study of elite attitudes, pre-eminently by Robert Putnam.[25] Within interpretivism, analysts often concern themselves with issues such as ideology and political organization, issues that arise primarily in the study of political elites. We will see, in fact, that an interpretive use of political culture that left out of account the distinctive activities of political elites would be sorely deficient.

Before concluding this discussion of categories of and within political culture research, two further distinctions which, in contrast, are not going to figure largely in the following analysis should be mentioned. For an obvious reason, uses of the term 'political culture' that are *casual* will not be examined. Casual uses are by now in simple numerical terms the most common. They are not confined to journalists and commentators, but frequently appear in academic writing. They are distinguished by the fact that scholarly attention is elsewhere; the concept of political culture carries no explanatory weight. It is tantamount to 'historical background' or 'context' – concepts that themselves are potentially load-bearing, but are generally not so. Something analogous to what befell the concept of 'political system' has occurred. When it was first introduced, the latter concept was intended to bear much explanatory and descriptive weight.[26] Considerable controversy was generated by its introduction and by the attempt to define the concept. By now, however, the term is mainly used as a mere synonym of 'political structures' or 'political institutions'. In casual uses of political culture, explanatory claims are absent. It is merely, like the idea of 'political system', a convenient shorthand.

Uses of the term that are explicitly *normative*, having connections with the idea of 'culturedness' or 'civilization',[27] while they merit further discussion, are also largely outside the scope of this study. Explicitly normative usage is best illustrated by Soviet political discourse, where the concept became even more widely accepted than it is in the West, being frequently used by politicians as well as scholars.[28] Although reference will be made to this use, it will not be a major focus. (It is not intended, however, that the possibility be excluded that some of the uses we will be considering are, as some critics have alleged, *implicitly* normative.)

Some justification needs to be offered for the selection of examples in the analysis to follow. The desire not simply to reproduce at greater length existing typological approaches to the study of political culture research provokes an opposite reaction: emphasis on a small number of case studies. The examples we will consider have been selected for their representativeness of the issues raised in this Introduction. One of them, Almond and Verba's *The Civic Culture*, is an indisputable classic upon which much commentary has already been lavished. It will be argued in Chapter 1 that its critics have failed to do it justice, but also that a more powerful critique can be based on its conflation of the comparative and sociological uses of political culture. Chapter 1 also considers *The Civic Culture* as a basis for the evaluation of change in political culture in several of the nations studied. The aptness of the concept of political culture for the study of political change may thereby be assessed.

Chapter 2 pursues that question in relation to secular political change of the type referred to as 'modernization'. Here, again, a conflict between the comparative and sociological uses of political culture is revealed, the emphasis this time being on the latter. A variety of approaches to the process of modernization and the manner in which they use and construe political culture are considered, but particular attention is given to the most substantial study of the effects of secular change on political culture, a study ranking with Almond and Verba's as a contribution to political culture research in general, Ronald Inglehart's *Culture Shift in Advanced Industrial Society* (a continuation of his earlier *Silent Revolution*).

Chapter 3 pursues a different aspect of the issue of political change raised by Chapter 1, focusing instead on cases of sudden and radical political change, and looking at the use of the concept of political culture in the study of communist states. This body of research, which kept the concept alive through its period of greatest opprobrium during the 1970s, is occasionally mentioned by writers in the 'mainstream', but only one such writer, Almond, has paid it serious attention. The justification for doing so here (apart from that of novelty) is that communist states themselves, and the methodologies that, partly for logistical reasons, have been applied to the study of their political cultures, raise in a stark form some important issues in political cultural explanation. For the analysis of a political cultural explanation of political change, communist cases are doubly advantageous, both because of the imposition of communism, and because of its recent breakdown. Archie Brown and Jack Gray's colloquium, *Political Culture and Political Change in Communist States*, provides the main resource for the discussion of the first, and the chapter continues by attempting to assess the significance for political culture research of the events of 1989 and 1990 in Eastern Europe.

Chapter 4 draws together and reinforces the argument of the first three chapters, reaching sceptical conclusions about the adequacy of a comparative use of political culture, and presenting these conclusions in the light of the general theory of the 'comparative method'. It suggests that further development of the comparative use of political culture will have to involve not a perfecting of the techniques of measurement, but a radical contraction of explanatory ambitiousness.

In Chapter 5, we embark on a discussion of interpretive uses of political culture. Our starting point is the work of Robert Tucker on communist political culture, particularly on Leninism and Stalinism. But his analysis is amended, and supplemented by others that, while not explicitly using the term 'political culture', offer support for the cultural interpretation. At the same time, substantial qualifications are introduced, centred around the claim that an interpretive use of political culture, despite its apparent suitability (for reasons that will be made clear) to Stalinist politics, has the idealist tendency to abstract attention from concrete evidence, and to project on to the subjects of study the description made by the analyst.

Chapter 6 undertakes a more philosophical discussion of justifications and deficiencies of political cultural interpretivism. It approaches this by examining some developments in the way culture has been represented within anthropology, not in order to justify one or another definition of political culture,[29] but for the purpose of penetrating more deeply than is usually done in cross-disciplinary borrowing the theoretical issues that the donor discipline is contending with and learning from them. For a similar reason, the chapter refers to some historiographical uses of the concept of political culture and what will be seen to be related concepts, such as ideology. Common features of the use of culture in these diverse settings will expose the need for a phenomenological analysis of political culture. Chapter 6, accordingly, enters upon an account of phenomenological social theory, touching on related issues such as the relevance of ethnomethodology and 'social constructionism'.

As the discussions of East European and Soviet communism (in Chapters 3 and 5) suggest, there is a role for 'invention' in the elaboration of the interpretive context, the context of meaning. This observation indicates a focus on the elite sphere. In Chapter 7, the role of 'invented' meaning and its relationship to the phenomenological analysis are discussed in connection with the concept of national identity, itself a frequently mentioned but seldom examined component of political culture. Polish and German political histories provide examples. The phenomenological analysis of political culture is thereby expanded and further refined.

Chapter 8 returns to political culture research proper, specifically to its recent and somewhat distinct variants. Its first subject is the direct impact of anthropological structuralism on the use of political culture within political science. Structuralism is also the indirect source of an interpretive theory of political culture developed by Aaron Wildavsky and others from the work of anthropologist Mary Douglas. The theory presents a universal typology of 'viable' political cultures – a typology not only to end all others but, its authors claim, also to comprehend them. This theory is the chapter's second subject. In both cases, the phenomenological analysis of political culture is used as a critical tool. A more positive argument is made in the final section, in which it is found that political culture as used and developed within American historiography has begun to fulfil some of the promise of a phenomenological approach.

Enough has perhaps been said in this Introduction to justify the claim made at the outset that we are not dealing with a field which one can hope to divide up into neat, mutually exclusive categories. Our subject is instead best approached using categories that admit interpenetration and that offer insight precisely through that admission. Political culture research is a scholarly jungle, tangled and cacophonous. Accordingly, the concepts and categories we have elaborated provide a critical apparatus rather than an aesthetically pleasing typology. They comprise not so much a map of the complex terrain as a machete with which to hack a way through it. Representing the full complexity of the terrain would be impossible, and thus cannot be the aim of a study such as this. Instead, a single route across it has to be followed, a single sequence of chapters and arguments. That no other route exists is in this case a particularly transparent illusion. But it may at least be claimed, by the time the Conclusion is reached, that the following critical and constructive argument represents at least *one* viable route through this forbidding territory.

1 Political Culture and Democracy

One of the first questions to which Almond's newly-coined concept of political culture was applied was that of the relationship between political culture and democracy, and this has indeed continued to be a major area of political culture research. Gabriel A. Almond and Sidney Verba's *The Civic Culture*, published in 1963,[1] was the original entry into this field, and has remained a benchmark for much subsequent research. At the same time, it has provided an inviting target for criticism. Moreover, the substantial body of data it gathered has been utilized by other authors in arguments that diverge somewhat from Almond and Verba's. These are good reasons for according *The Civic Culture* some prominence in the present chapter, but, in view of its familiarity, not yet perhaps sufficient ones. Our argument will be that the study attempts to combine what were termed in the Introduction comparative and sociological uses of political culture. Critics have not noticed this fact, and their critiques have in consequence been somewhat partial. The aim of this chapter is, however, not simply to provide a more complete analysis and critique of *The Civic Culture*. It is to illustrate the effects of what we will argue is a characteristic combination of sociological and comparative uses of political culture. A perspective will thereby be developed that assists in the evaluation of the literature, critical and otherwise, that in one way or another has been provoked by Almond and Verba's study.

THE CIVIC CULTURE: TWO PROJECTS

To say that *The Civic Culture* deals with the relationship between political culture and democracy is accurate, but not very informative; to say exactly what relationship it establishes, or even tries to establish, is much more difficult. Rather than simplify and thus set up an easy target for criticism, this chapter takes the study's protean quality and the resulting diversity of the critical response as the major target of explanation. This quality is the product of the attempt to combine two distinct and not fully complementary projects. The comparative project, in summary form,

14

amounts to an attempted explanation of the presence of stable democracy in some countries and its absence in others in terms of pre-existing political cultural conditions. It is a comparative explanation with political culture as the independent variable. The sociological project consists in an investigation of the social conditions under which democracy functions. It is a contribution to the 'empirical theory of democracy' in which a range of sociological variables is taken to be explanatory. The way that these projects interact, and the tension between them, will be the main theme of this section.

The motivation behind the study is stated on the first page: it is anxiety, provoked by events in Europe in the first half of the twentieth century, about the future of democracy, and the resulting desire to understand the phenomena that sustain it (p. 1). The study gathers attitude data from five countries – the United States, Great Britain, Germany, Italy and Mexico – for a purpose expressed as follows: 'We wish to make statements, based on those separate interviews, about the general state of attitudes in these nations. And we wish to make statements about the relationship between these attitudes and the way in which the political systems operate' (p. 41). The authors note one difficulty of such an enterprise: the smallness of the sample of nations means that purely statistical correlations of attributes of political culture with attributes of national political systems are not possible. In response, the phenomena to be explained – those comprising stable democracy – are characterized much less rigorously than the putative explanans: 'a brief glance at history will tell us which of these are more stable, or an analysis of the party structures will allow a classification by type of party system' (p. 43).

Although a critique cannot be based on these introductory remarks alone, it is already possible to see in outline the tensions between the two projects which recur throughout the book. The comparative project argues that the civic culture is the type of political culture most conducive to stable democracy, and takes this argument to be verified by the fact, which much of the study is intended to demonstrate, that in the stable democracies of Britain and the United States political cultures most closely approximate to this ideal, while they fall somewhat short of it in countries where there has been recent instability or (in the case of Mexico) a deficit of democracy. The sociological project of developing a 'scientific theory of democracy' (p. 10) involves, as we will see, the description of the 'capillary structure' of democracy, that is, of its local or low-level manifestations in the democratic cases. Now a 'comparative political sociology' is not a patent contradiction. A theory which posited a certain political cultural phenomenon as being conducive to stable democracy would indeed receive support from the discovery that only stable democracies feature that phenomenon. However, the more complex the theory of democracy, the more difficult it would be to validate it in this manner; that is, the sociological part would be in tension with the comparative part. If a large range of phenomena were taken to be potentially conducive to stability, comparison among only five countries would be unlikely to be compelling. If, at the same time, quite complex relationships between the phenomena, and not merely their absolute values, formed part of the theory, it would begin to look impossible in principle to validate the theory comparatively. Just such a theory is developed in *The Civic Culture*, and just such a method is used ostensibly to validate it. When Almond and Verba write, in defence of the smallness of the national sample, 'This is no new problem in political analysis, and we are in fact five times as well off as most studies of this sort' (p. 43), they are expressing the very tension between a sociological theory of democracy and a comparative study. Does this statement mean that theories of democracy lacking a comparative element are worthless? If not, then we may ask whether the features that justify them might not be in tension with the requirements of comparison.

Let us now turn to some detailed examples of this tension. One is to be found in the authors' account of the prevalence of 'norms of participation' in local government (ch. 5). They find wide variation in this measure, and rank the five nations accordingly. The authors acknowledge that the wide difference in structures of local government, hence in scope for participation, between the nations may influence attitudes towards participation. But they argue that reciprocal influence of attitudes on government nevertheless obtains:

> The norms to which an individual adheres are largely determined by the role that the system allows him to play (though the fit between norms and structure will rarely be perfect); but these norms in turn have a feedback effect on the structure, reinforcing the structure if the fit between norms and structure is a good one; introducing strain into the system if norms and structure fit less well. (p. 125)

This admission suggests a particular instance of a criticism made by Brian Barry: that perceptions of government may be largely accurate, leaving no independent causal role for political culture.[2] Although, like many of Barry's criticisms, this is too general a claim (since some of the data gathered by Almond and Verba cannot be so plausibly explained by reference to variations in political structures), it certainly applies to the present argument, as Almond and Verba admit. But what we may note is that such circularity is damaging only to the comparative project. It is, on the other hand, a perfectly acceptable part of the sociological theory of democracy, which seeks to display the social 'micro-structure' of a democratic polity in the form of mutual inter-dependence between sociological variables. Hence, if one chooses at this point to emphasize the sociological theory, Barry's objection is rendered irrelevant. This is convenient, but perhaps a little too convenient.

Another example of the tension between a sociological theory of democracy and a comparative theory of political culture occurs in Almond and Verba's discussion of variations in political 'style' (ch. 9). Again, the authors discover wide variations, specifically in the extent of political co-operation – variations which are, in contrast with other variables (such as level of knowledge of politics) not eliminated by controlling for level of development. This is a finding, they note, consistent with Tocqueville's observation of the 'tumult' of political activity to be found in America, to which they counterpose contrasting observations about political style in an Italian village (pp. 216–218). Their method of arriving at these conclusions, the authors claim, while less 'colorful' than Tocqueville's, is, apart from being 'more reliable' and 'more precise', also superior for the possibility it offers of relating such behaviour to other variables (n. 5, p. 219). This is what they go on to do. It is found, for instance, that the propensity to discuss politics is correlated with group style (pp. 221f.), though the relationship is a 'mild one'. The uniformity of this correlation across nations compensates, the authors say, for its relative statistical weakness (p. 222). A relationship between group style and a preference for what Almond and Verba call 'outgoingness' (actually a measure combining approval of generosity and considerateness) is found to exist in Britain and the United States, but not elsewhere – indeed these variables are negatively correlated in Germany and Mexico (pp. 224f.). A similar pattern (though with the positive correlation strengthened) is found for the relationship of group style to a measure of 'trust in people' (pp. 227f.). Almond and Verba conclude that the 'buzz of political activity' is found in Britain and the United States for two reasons:

> it is not only that general social values and attitudes that would foster co-operation with one's fellow citizens are more widespread in Britain and the United States; beyond that, these general social attitudes are more closely related to political attitudes in these two nations than in the other three nations. (p. 230)

This formulation contains a peculiar mixture of interpretive and statistical reasoning. If the general social attitudes in question foster a political group style, we would expect the correlation between them to be uniform across nations. If, on the other hand, it is found that the correlation is not uniform, where is the evidence other than its plausibility for the claim that the social attitudes 'would foster co-operation'? There is an impression that Almond and Verba are having their cake and eating it, a trick facilitated by the scope for equivocation given by relating three variables: attitudes, group style and nationality.

Spelt out more fully, the authors' analysis at this point is as follows. Group style is demonstrably more prevalent in Britain and the United States than in the other countries. Social attitudes that are *plausibly* related to group style are also demonstrably more prevalent in these two countries. Furthermore, this plausible relationship is demonstrably present in these cases, although it is absent elsewhere, indeed is reversed in Germany and Mexico. The question that arises is whether it is the group style, the social attitudes or the correlation between them that is supportive of stable democracy. The answer 'all of the above', which is the answer Almond and Verba appear to give, is not justified by their data.

In fact, in this part of the argument it is not stable democracy that serves as the explanandum at all, but group style: 'The data presented . . . offer some explanation for the phenomenon of group formation noticed by Tocqueville and by many others since' (p. 239). As already noticed, this phenomenon might plausibly be related to stable democracy – although it is not difficult to imagine it reaching a level that would be destabilizing. The point is that the data and relationships presented by Almond and Verba here do not enable us to verify this claim, because of the lack of clarity in the putative explanation as to which of the three conditions is necessary. An explanation such as this, in which either absolute levels of variables or presence or absence (or degree) of correlations between them might be explanatory, and only five cases are compared, is sufficiently complex to be in principle impossible to verify: this is not mere lack of care on Almond and Verba's part.

The tension between the comparative and sociological projects thus has some damaging effects at the level of detailed analysis of data. Its effects can also be seen clearly in the overall structure of the argument, particularly in its concluding sections. Barry has identified a question posed by the authors as being particularly revealing of their intentions in the study: 'is there a democratic political culture . . . that in some way "fits" the democratic political system?' (pp. 337f.). This is indeed a crucial utterance, but its deficiency is not just the extreme vagueness of the notion of 'fit' to

which Barry draws attention.[3] The question equivocates between the two
projects we have been considering. On a first reading the question calls for
a comparative answer showing how American and British political cultures
differ from those of the other nations. On a second, and especially in the
mention of a 'democratic political culture', it suggests something broader,
a cultural perspective on democracy.

The most crucial findings for the purposes of the first question concern
the prevalence of what the authors term 'citizen' or 'political' competence,
on the one hand, and 'subject' or 'administrative' competence on the
other (the proliferation of labels is unfortunate). The former concerns
the respondent's level of political knowledge and confidence in his or
her ability to influence politics, the latter the respondent's expectation of
fair treatment by political authorities (as Barry notes, subject competence
does not actually require the respondent to be competent at anything).[4] The
relative weight of these two categories, as well as their absolute level, is
found to vary across nations. The explanation offered for this variation
is historical. For instance, the contrast in the proportion of citizen-to-
subject competence between the United States and Britain (65% : 37%
in Britain and 56% : 50% in the United States – p. 173) is attributed to
the absence in Britain of the historical competition between political and
administrative competence that is held to have occurred, primarily through
the revolutionary experience, in the United States (pp. 177–179). Similar
interpretive hypotheses are advanced for the other countries. So far as the
comparative project is concerned, the authors take the implications to be
clear. Of the Italian case, where both citizen and subject competence were
found to reach only 27%, Almond and Verba say: 'The current political
culture of Italy may be inappropriate for a healthy, functioning democracy'
(p. 184). But while the Italian case diverges from the American and British
in respect of these measures, the divergence is too complex to admit
comparative conclusions. Are high levels of both variables necessary, or
only one, or is the proportion of one to the other significant? We cannot
tell from these data.

Accordingly, the theoretical apparatus into which these centrally important findings are inserted is also lacking in support. This apparatus is seen
by the authors as a response to the theory they call the 'rationality-activist
model', which argues that widespread political knowledge and participation, of the sort espoused in high school 'civics' courses in the United
States, is necessary for functioning democracy. The unreality of this model
had already been amply demonstrated; Almond and Verba's contribution
is to argue that this state of affairs should not be diagnosed as a 'failure',
but as indicating the unnecessarily high standards of the model (p. 340).

Instead, they endorse a view expressed by Harry Eckstein, that the 'contradictory' nature of democracy requires a 'contradictory' political culture which is the attitudinal or subjective correlate of the balance between the effectiveness and responsiveness of the political system (pp. 341–343). This is just what the 'civic culture' provides, evidence coming from the data on citizen and subject competence in the five nations. But we have just seen that no such conclusion is warranted; indeed if 'balance' between citizen and subject competence is the crucial factor, Italy's score of 27% for each would appear to put it in the most favourable position.

Almond and Verba develop their alternative to the 'rationality-activist' model by relating it to the dimension of time. The authors assert that the 'contradictory' or 'balanced' nature of the civic culture is kept from leading to stress by the relatively low importance attached to politics. But if politics is made intense by some salient issue, 'the inconsistency between attitude and behavior will become unstable' (p. 349). Therefore, for long-term stability, a 'cycle of involvement' is necessary, in which increased tension leads to adequate government response and a renormalization of politics. Such cycles reinforce the civic culture, by providing evidence of the responsiveness of the political system, preventing the citizens' belief in their political effectiveness from 'fading away': 'For the democratic "myth" to be an effective political force, it cannot be pure myth. It must be an idealization of real behavioral patterns' (p. 351). For this to happen, elites as well as population must share in the ambivalence of the civic culture (p. 353). But if the theory of 'balance' is itself not comparatively well supported, the same is all the more true of this 'cycles of involvement' theory, which in addition would require time series data for its confirmation.

In further support of their comparative findings, as we have seen, Almond and Verba attempt to provide historical explanations for the 'alienated' political culture of Italy; the combination of alienation with aspiration in Mexico; that of political detachment with subjective competence in Germany and the respectively primarily 'participant' and 'deferential' political cultures of the United States and Britain (pp. 308–315). Ample evidence is thus provided to justify at least the positive half of W. G. Runciman's statement, 'History furnishes the explanation for their correlations, not their correlations for history.'[5] For Almond and Verba, of course, the findings are explanatory, in the sense of having predictive power. Divergent conclusions are drawn as to the prospects for democracy in the five nations. Though in different ways, German, Italian and Mexican political cultures are held to be 'incongruent with an effective and stable democratic political system' (p. 354). Moreover, 'unless the political culture is able to support a democratic system, the chances for the success of that system are slim' (p. 366). The gradual means by which the civic culture has emerged in British and American history are contrasted with the absence of such a process in the 'new nations' (pp. 368f.), and the possibility of education and other socialization agencies substituting for this historical process is held to be limited (p. 370). At this late stage a new idea is introduced: the necessity of a 'sense of common political identity', created perhaps by a 'symbolic and unifying event', such as a revolution, for the development of a civic culture (pp. 371f.). Only by this means, they assert, can the necessary evaluative and affective elements of the civic culture be created.

So far as the sociological project is concerned, the authors bring their findings together by relating political cultural variables to more general sociological categories. Education is shown to be the most influential of these – there are more attitudes that differ uniformly with education across nations than ones that do not change with education or upon which it has a varying effect. Some examples of 'strikingly uniform cross-national patterns' in the relationship of education to political cultural variables are found (pp. 317f.). Thus, 'the nature of political culture is greatly determined by the distribution of education' (p. 320). Gender is another important factor, mediated both through the degree of direct participation by women and by the role of women in family socialization: hence 'politically competent, aware, and active women seem to be an essential component of the civic culture' (p. 334).

It is in the findings about education that a link is drawn by Almond and Verba between the comparative and sociological projects, but the effect is by no means to vindicate either. The cognitive elements of the civic culture, it is found, are most strongly related to levels of education, and it is inferred that these are capable of being taught. Less easily inculcated are the evaluative and affective components. Hence the dim prospects for countries lacking a civic culture. But the finding, supported by comparative evidence, that only some portions of the civic culture are capable of being taught has only a secondary role in overall theory of the necessity of the civic culture to stable democracy. That theory, as we have seen, is not supported comparatively.

The Civic Culture, precisely because of its ambitiousness and the scope of its data, illustrates the mutually destructive effect of the comparative and sociological uses of political culture. Its data make possible and invite statistical analysis, both by Almond and Verba and by subsequent users, of a degree of complexity that prohibits comparison. From the point of view of the comparative project, Almond and Verba demonstrate a wide range of political cultural differences between the nations they study, but are unable to demonstrate which of these are crucial. Their version of the empirical theory of democracy, that is, the sociological project, presents a theory that does indeed seem more realistic than the one it is intended to supersede. But even though some of the components of this theory are comparatively validated, in the sense that some correlations are found to be invariant across national samples, the theory as a whole is not.

We now turn to discussion of the ample literature, critical and otherwise, that has spun off from *The Civic Culture*. Our analysis of the two projects serves to organize discussion of this literature also, suggesting that the juxtaposition of the two may be more than simply a product of insufficient care on Almond and Verba's part, and thus, as we have supposed, suggesting that their study teaches us some general lessons about political culture research.

THE COMPARATIVE PROJECT

As a theory in comparative politics, *The Civic Culture* makes certain predictions. An obvious test is to ask whether these turned out to be correct. The authors themselves have generously provided an edited volume – *The Civic Culture Revisited*[6] – whose contributors go some way towards answering that question, largely in the negative. Since the early 1960s, Britain and the United States have experienced, separately or jointly, the Vietnam War, the civil rights movement, Watergate, confrontations between government and trade unions, and the effects of the oil crises of the 1970s. Germany and Italy have not been immune to the more general of these processes, but have nevertheless experienced steady economic growth and, moreover, increasing distance from the events that made these countries such obvious cases of instability to Almond and Verba. The authors were not clairvoyant, and of course could not have predicted many of the events of the 1960s and 1970s; however, the differentiation in reactions to external and internal stimuli that might have been expected has not occurred. Germany provides the starkest contrast between prediction and reality, and its case merits more detailed investigation.

Writing two years after the original study was published, in 1965, Verba describes West Germany as 'a case study of the possibilities of the conscious manipulative change of fundamental political attitudes, in particular in the direction of more democratic attitudes'.[7] This differs from the position of *The Civic Culture* in treating it as an open question whether a supportive political culture could be generated, but the two positions have in common the idea that a certain political culture is supportive of stable democracy and is a necessary condition for it. Concern over the prospects for attitude change in Germany was not peculiar to Almond and Verba, or indeed to political scientists: assumptions about the significance of such change underlay a more widespread and quite understandable political concern over 'normalization' in Germany after the Second World War. Reflecting this concern, a particularly rich body of survey materials is available. Verba's conclusions from these data refer to a lack of intensity in attitudes towards politics, and a close connection between attitudes towards economic progress and democracy, revealing an overall pattern of 'apolitical attachment' that was also reflected in data on political participation. He also asserts the influence of the issue of national identity – going somewhat beyond the mere hint about this issue provided in *The Civic Culture* – whose unresolved nature, symbolized by the Berlin Wall, introduced volatility, he suggests, into the political culture.[8]

In his contribution to *The Civic Culture Revisited* (1980), David Conradt comes to somewhat different conclusions. Explaining Verba's finding of 'detachment' as a response to Germany's 'traumatic history', Conradt goes on to point to evidence of change: increased 'system pride', 'civic competence', 'participation' and 'mass interest' in politics, and a decrease in the family-oriented *Lagermentalität*, thus allowing German democracy to reach its 'take off' state. Conradt also asserts that acceptance of borders – between East and West Germany, and between East Germany and Poland – had greatly increased, and that it was correlated with support for democratic institutions and processes. Thus 'the question is now not whether there exists a consensus and strong support for political democracy, but *what kind* of democracy Germany will have' – apparently providing an affirmative result for Verba's case study.[9]

Geoffrey Roberts, surveying the literature on West German political culture in 1984, sees the differences between these two accounts in terms not of change over time in the data, but of differences in the analysts' evaluations. He characterizes the difference as a dispute over whether West German political culture is 'normal' or 'critical', a choice of terminology that reveals sympathy with Almond and Verba's original project. While agreeing that there is a tendency to normality and that West German political culture increasingly resembles that of other Western countries, Roberts notices some countervailing factors. The persistence of elements of the traditional, 'less democratic' political culture prevents any 'firm conclusion' about normality on the basis of survey data; and furthermore, persistent critical factors include the salience of 'new politics' issues, the existence of a large floating section of the electorate, the potential large support for 'alternative' political channels and the increasing gap between traditional political culture and 'alternative' political culture.[10]

These 'critical factors' are identified not through survey methodology but by analysis of democratic institutions and the operation of the political system. In particular, the nature and role of political parties is held to be crucially important, as indicators both of stability and of the persistence of 'critical factors': Roberts argues that all the accounts he cites 'demonstrate the importance of coupling analysis of political culture with examination of the party system if satisfying explanations of the West German "political miracle" are to be approached'. For Roberts, the necessity of this comprehensive analysis follows from the apparent paradox of the conjunction of West Germany's political stability with the ambiguous portrait of political culture drawn from surveys: 'one cannot with ease on the one hand acclaim the stability of the democratic system, and on the other criticize its political culture as fragile or non-supportive of such a stable system'.[11] This shift marks a deviation from the project of *explaining* stability *in terms of* political culture.

As Roberts' observations make clear, a large part of the problem here is with the meaning of the idea of 'stability', a problem that is an inheritance of Almond and Verba's comparative project. A distinction between stable and unstable countries that might have seemed obvious in 1963, as we have observed, is by now if not reversed then at least invisible. The absence of formal criteria for identifying stability has become a more serious problem. Indeed it raises doubts about the viability of the comparative project.

What is a stable democracy? Italy has suffered from frequent elections, but of course some democracies have fixed-term governments, so that is an unsatisfactory criterion. Resignations of Presidents or ministers, or other rapid changes in personnel, do not necessarily tell us anything about the stability of *democracy*, only about the stability of governments. It appears that only when we begin to consider the behaviour of the population – dramatic declines in electoral turnout, sharp increases in support for revolutionary or fascist parties, rapid escalation of protest, for example – are the relevant criteria approached. But then we also approach the problem of differentiating the explanans from the explanandum. Fully describing stable democracy seems to involve describing cultural attributes also. It is scant protection against this to fall back on a distinction between attitudes and behaviour, and to argue that these 'cultural attributes' are nevertheless behavioural and hence part of the explanandum. To do so would be to represent the problem addressed by comparative political culture theory as one of social psychology: the problem of discovering the conditions under which attitudes lead to action. We can put this another way. Suppose that attitudes hostile to democracy were widespread – would this be seen as *leading* to instability, or would it be seen *as* instability?

The impact of Almond and Verba's framework and of this particular deficiency of it can be seen also in works which are not direct follow-ups of *The Civic Culture*, such as in Walter Rosenbaum's survey, *Political Culture*.[12] Rosenbaum notes that a 'recurrent approach' in political culture writing has been to differentiate stable and unstable societies on the basis of their respective 'integrated' and 'fragmented' political cultures. In an 'integrated' political culture are found relatively consistent and hierarchical political identifications, low levels of political violence and the predominance of civil procedures for conflict management, diffuse political trust among social groups and reasonably strong and durable regime loyalties. A 'fragmented' political culture (found especially, Rosenbaum avers, in post-colonial areas, but also, for example, in Northern Ireland, and France), features the dominance of parochial political loyalties over national ones, the absence of civil conflict management procedures, the prevalence of political distrust between social groups and the tendency for national governments to be unstable in form and duration.[13] These descriptions for the most part would also suffice to distinguish stable from unstable societies – again, the separation of explanans from explanandum is not achieved.

Although the influence of *The Civic Culture* has been widespread, the deficiency we have just noted is not yet sufficient to justify a blanket criticism of the comparative use of political culture. In order to see how this problem might be overcome within the context of a comparative theory relating political culture to democracy, we may turn to the work of Ronald Inglehart. For some years Inglehart has been reporting findings based on a much larger body of survey research than Almond and Verba's, covering many more countries and extending over a considerable time period. His research largely concerns the relationship between values and the development of 'post-industrial' society, and as such will be considered at some length in Chapter 2. He has also used the data set, however, to address the same question as did Almond and Verba: the relationship of political culture to stable democracy.[14]

Inglehart's rescue bid for this comparative theory involves jettisoning some parts of it. He does not, for one thing, use Almond and Verba's definition of the civic culture, instead speaking of a 'syndrome' of attitudes that are hypothetically supportive of democracy, of which interpersonal trust and levels of 'life satisfaction' are the major components. His data demonstrate that life satisfaction levels do show enduring differences between nations that are not explained – although short-term fluctuations of them are – by immediate economic conditions. Long-term economic conditions, on the other hand, are hypothesized as the source of life satisfaction levels, as indeed, this time without evidence, are specific historical factors such as the defeat of certain countries in the Second World War. For interpersonal trust, similar enduring differences, and a high degree of consistency within nations over time, are found. In order to link these variables with stable democracy, Inglehart uses the duration of democratic institutions as the criterion of the latter. The evidence, though still not conclusive, owing to the fact that the most telling cases of transitions from non-democracy to democracy do not figure in the time series data, suggest that the original hypothesis relating the syndrome to stable democracy is correct.

The details of this finding are of some interest. In the first place, it has a large interpretive component, specifically with respect to the causal direction that correlations are said to indicate. Inglehart writes: 'It seems more likely that a global sense of well-being would also shape one's attitude towards politics than what is experienced in one relatively narrow aspect of life would determine one's overall sense of satisfaction.' [15] More important is the test Inglehart performs to assess the relative impact of cultural and other variables. Level of economic development (GNP in 1950) alone has little impact on persistence of democratic institutions: the two most important variables are political culture and social structure, the latter being measured by percentage of the population employed in the tertiary sector. Inglehart reports that 'over half of the variance in the persistence of democratic institutions can be attributed to the effects of political culture alone'. So far as social structure is concerned, Inglehart makes the argument that this factor's influence itself has a cultural component: 'commercial elites accept bargaining among equals, rather than hierarchical authority, as a normal way of dealing with people; these habits and skills are carried over into the emphasis on bargaining, rather than command, that characterizes parliamentary democracy'. [16]

This last point is of some significance, since it goes some way towards undermining the rigid distinction between cultural and other variables that is assumed by the statistical comparison of them. Economic development, social structure and political culture are separable up to a point, and their relative impacts thereby measurable. But if we probe more deeply, the boundary becomes hazy. Can a statistical test to determine the 'proportion' of the cultural element in the impact of the size of the bourgeoisie be conceived? Clearly not. This fact hints at something very important: that Almond and Verba's failure adequately to differentiate explanans and explanandum is a product not of lack of care, but of the fundamental inseparability of culture from structure. The example we have just considered is too meagre to support such a portentous conclusion, but it does at least suggest that the question of the separability of political culture from rival explanans and putative explananda is one worthy of more general investigation. Such will be undertaken in Chapter 4.

SOCIOLOGICAL CRITICISMS

The comparative project of *The Civic Culture* has a tendency, in construing political culture as an independent variable, to understate differences within nations. That Almond and Verba do, in fact, pay much attention to intra-national differences, invoking variables such as gender and education level, is an effect of their sociological project. Critics from the perspective of political sociology who accuse Almond and Verba of holding a 'consensus theory' are therefore half right; their objections illustrate the constraints that the comparative project exerts on the sociological one.[17] Where these objections are half wrong is in the claim that such an assumption is made by Almond and Verba: on the contrary, the authors explicitly disavow it (p. 13). They do admit that the extent to which they can provide cultural profiles of sub-national groups is limited by their sample size (about 1,000 in each country) and by concentration on attitudes towards the political system, not the ideological differences that might more clearly differentiate sub-national groups (pp. 307f.). Thus it is their comparative project that distracts their attention elsewhere, and necessitates looking at and comparing 'the' national political cultures, not any assumption about consensus.

Nevertheless the effect is the same, which is that sub-national cleavages receive less attention in *The Civic Culture* than its sociological critics think they merit. Michael Mann is one sociologist who has reused Almond and Verba's data for somewhat different purposes. On the basis of this and several other studies showing wide divergences and inconsistency in mass values he hypothesizes that 'only those actually sharing in societal power need develop societal values'.[18] Surveys of the attitudes of political activists add support to this hypothesis. He concludes by suggesting that it is the *lack* of consensus that keeps the working class docile and allows democratic stability.

Indeed, a substantial sociological debate has occurred over this question of which sector of society, the elite or the mass of the population, serves as the main locus of whatever subjective or cultural attributes are necessary to maintain stability.[19] One of the best-known contributions to this debate is Nicholas Abercrombie and Bryan Turner's critique of the Marxist 'dominant ideology thesis', the thesis that a dominant class produces the values found throughout society (a thesis that is, incidentally, implied by the radical critique of Jessop and Pateman). On the basis of a survey of English history covering, for instance, the degree of exposure of the medieval peasantry to the dominant religious and theocratic ideology, the temporal priority of individualism to capitalism, and the apparent irrelevance of 'Victorian morality' to the lower classes, they conclude that 'the dominant ideology has a greater impact on the dominant classes than the dominated'.[20] Bob Jessop's class-based theory of democratic stability, in which 'commitment to the dominant values is not equally distributed through society',[21] is a variant of this position. Jessop argues that *The Civic Culture* neglects the role of the elite in propagating democratic 'myths', and argues for a use of the concept of 'civic culture' and other studies of 'civility' as a means of describing dominant values, not an explanation of stability.[22]

Pateman's sociological critique is the sharpest and fullest. She redescribes Almond and Verba's 'subject competence' as 'apathy', a label with the opposite evaluative connotation. A degree of apathy may well, as *The Civic Culture* argues, lead to stability, but she takes issue with the description of this result as *democratic* stability. Pateman contends that not only is a degree of apathy on the part of the population caused by a straightforward perception of the unresponsiveness of the political system (as Barry has argued),[23] but access to political influence and hence perception of the responsiveness of the political system is unevenly distributed. Apathy is not equally balanced with 'citizen competence' within each individual; it is prevalent among women, the poor and other relatively excluded groups. Pointing to these cases Pateman asks, 'What is democratic about the civic culture? . . . Very little at all, except that it encompasses universal suffrage.'[24]

Pateman has also made explicit the location of *The Civic Culture* within the empirical theory of democracy, a body of political theory that attempted to come to terms with embarrassing survey research findings about the level of public knowledge of and interest in politics, such as those that made the 'rationality-activist model' look over-ambitious. The theory was a component of the behavioural revolution, not just in this reliance on survey data but also in its claim to be purely non-evaluative. This claim has been challenged on the grounds that a breakdown in consensus over what constitutes democracy, coupled with the commendatory sense now attaching to the term, makes its application by definition an ideological move, an act of commendation of a set of facts that could also be described by terms such as 'elitism' and 'oligarchy'.[25] Pateman more pointedly asserts that the theory is a rationalization of the state of affairs it purports to describe objectively, and is merely a reworking of Schumpeterian liberal theory, 'the theory of (ideology of?) the actual political institutional arrangements that have been part and parcel of the capitalist, liberal, "democratic" West, especially the United States and Great Britain'. She refers to an alternative, genuinely participatory, model of democracy, which she argues is obscured by empirical theory's claim to be *the* theory of democracy. The role played by the idea of political culture in this rationalization, Pateman argues, is further to reinforce the impression of the theory's 'reality' through the implication that the political system is 'embedded' in the political culture: 'The empirical theorists' defence would appeal to the existing political system and its political culture and therefore is . . . conservative.'[26]

The relationship of these critiques to Almond and Verba's sociological theory is complex. Mann, and Abercrombie and Turner emphasize the utility of culture for the cohesion and effectiveness of the ruling class. Jessop adds to this the suggestion that the civic culture contains myths whose propagation helps to maintain this class in its position of dominance. Pateman goes further, representing not just the civic culture, but *The Civic Culture*, as a contributor to dominance, through the 'empirical' rationalization that it offers. Yet although Pateman is the most critical, she also comes closest to agreeing with the description Almond and Verba offer, despite her revulsion at the rosy hue of their conclusions. Substituting 'apathy' for 'subject competence', and a skewed distribution for balance, she replaces Almond and Verba's complacency with censoriousness, while not disputing any of their findings. That this, and the many other reuses of Almond and Verba's data to different effects, may occur, tells us something about the supposed 'hardness' of statistical evidence.

We should not, however, at this observation flip over to the uninformed view that 'anything can be argued with statistics'. What is certainly true is that one's explanatory target necessarily introduces a degree of blindness to other issues. This applies *a fortiori* to *The Civic Culture*, for the reasons we have already elaborated. The comparative aims of the study entail a relative blindness to sub-national cultural variation. Yet its attempt to produce a 'scientific theory of democracy' yields a sociological theory of a degree of richness and complexity that not only is comparison prohibited, but an ample resource is offered for use by researchers not similarly constrained by the comparative goal, and possibly of somewhat distinct political persuasions too. Hence the peculiar misfortune of *The Civic Culture*: to have been most harshly criticized on the basis of information that the book itself provides.

2 Political Culture and Modernity

The Civic Culture was one of a group of studies published by Princeton University Press in the early 1960s together comprising the heroic phase of behavioural political culture research. While *The Civic Culture* concentrated on the relationship of political culture to stability, particularly stable democracy, others of these Princeton studies, such as Almond and Coleman's *The Politics of the Developing Areas*, and Pye and Verba's *Political Culture and Political Development*,[1] as their titles suggest, extended the use of the new concept to cover cases of political change. *The Civic Culture*, as we have seen, has implicit within it many of the ideas current at the time, for instance the empirical theory of democracy, and something similar is true of the studies that took political change as their main focus. Indeed, the similarity extends further, for their own implicit and sometimes explicit assumptions have also come to be seen as reflecting a Eurocentric or indeed Anglocentric bias. These assumptions concern the related ideas of modernization and political development.

However, this chapter has somewhat broader aims than the exposure of these assumptions, which has in any case been undertaken many times before. It takes the relationship between political culture and modernization not as the target of criticism, but as a starting point. The term 'modernity' is used in its title by way of implying not just the specific claims of modernization theory, but more generally those of perspectives such as 'postindustrial society' and indeed 'postmodernism' too. The theme of the chapter concerns the diverse ways in which political culture has been invoked in these perspectives. More specifically, we will observe the effect of the combination of the two uses of political culture within behavioural political culture research, as we did in Chapter 1. In this case, we are considering a number of studies rather than just one, and the two uses are not both present in all of them. But within the broad enterprise of relating political culture to secular change, a comparative and a sociological use of political culture can be identified. We will first consider the notion of 'cultural lag', a significant concept in the Princeton studies and their successors, before discussing the relationship of political culture to 'stages of modernity', variously conceived. We conclude by looking in detail at Ronald Inglehart's substantial contribution to the project of relating political culture to secular change.

CULTURAL LAG

The idea of 'cultural lag' expresses the claim that, while political culture may be created by political experience and hence by the structures of government, the latter can change much more quickly than the former. The creation of political culture is therefore not immediate. The idea plays a role in Almond and Verba's theory of stable democracy, both in their historical analysis of the emergence of the civic culture (and the persistence within it of earlier 'parochial' and 'subject' attitudes) and in their conclusion of the difficulty of creating a civic culture except in the long term. Cultural lag does not exhaust comparative political cultural explanation, because such explanation needs to demonstrate, as well as the stability of political culture, its subsequent influence. It is, however, a precondition of such explanation.

Cultural lag is linked theoretically with the process of socialization, the process by which, through childhood and adult experience, individuals come to learn the norms and habits of their society. If childhood socialization is emphasized, cultural lag operates in an obvious manner: it refers to the time difference between the period in childhood when norms and habits are learned, and the period in adulthood when they are put into effect in the political world, through voting and other forms of participation. However, even if the emphasis is on adult socialization, as it is, for instance, in *The Civic Culture*,[2] cultural lag comes into effect through the assumption that the process of learning is gradual. Thus, in both cases, changes in the political environment, from whatever source, take time to be registered in political culture and thus reciprocally to affect the political environment in the kinds of ways we have already discussed.

Evidence for the existence of cultural lag can take several forms. The simplest kind of evidence would be the 'persistence' of cultural attributes beyond the lifetime of their original stimuli. Evidence requiring more sophisticated measurement, not undertaken in all the studies we will consider in this chapter, would be the presence of generational differences in political culture or what statisticians call 'cohort effects'. Cohort effects are distinguishable from 'lifecycle effects' – differences which are related solely to age – only when time series data are available, when, if such effects are present, the cultural consistency of given cohorts may be traced. Evidence for cultural lag is, in other words, more convincing if its presence can be measured over time, where socialization theory would lead us to expect not only its gradual fading away in the aggregate, but its relationship to the arrival and departure of generations.

In most of the cases we will consider in this chapter, evidence of the latter type is absent; indeed evidence of the former type is not always present. Cultural lag is in these cases a somewhat speculative explanation for observable divergences in outcomes among cases supposedly subject to the same stimuli. In the present section the stimuli we will consider are a variety of processes grouped under the heading of 'modernization' and the related category of 'political development'.

Modernization has been defined as 'the process of change from an agrarian to an industrial way of life that has resulted from the dramatic increase in man's knowledge of and control over the environment in recent centuries'.[3] Political development theory posits links between this process and increased participation in politics, increased government 'capacity' and increased structural differentiation.[4] These ideas experienced their greatest popularity contemporaneously with the heyday of behaviouralist political culture research. As Raymond Grew writes:

> A short time ago almost any study of an industrial or industrializing society could be expected to make heavy use of the term [modernization]. Sociologists and political scientists were perhaps the most enthusiastic, but anthropologists employed it to evoke the sense of a world-historical process, historians (in introductions and conclusions) to show that they shared in scientific discourse.[5]

In more recent times, the theories of political development and modernization have been subject to opprobrium on the scale of their former popularity, suffering from a more general change of intellectual mood away from the optimistic, confident assertion of Western values and political and social structure of which they now appear to have been a part. For this reason, many subsequent writers have been careful to distance political culture from the concept of political development. While acknowledging a debt to the early studies, Archie Brown commends the subsequent separation of the two concepts, arguing that 'In the literature of the 1960s . . . the characteristics of a developed political system frequently bore an uncanny resemblance to the principal features of the American polity, though often in a somewhat idealised form.'[6]

However, this charge of value-laden teleology, characteristic though it is of critiques of both modernization and political development theory, confuses the two ways in which political culture was implicated in them.

These two modes of implication relate, as already suggested, to the two uses of political culture within behavioural political culture research that we discussed in Chapter 1. In the comparative use, political culture is relativized to nations, and is used to explain divergences in institutional implementation and outcome from the universal assimilating pressure of modernization. The sociological use is concerned not with the differences in outcomes, but with the similarities; that is, it considers political culture as an aspect or sometimes as an effect of the modernization process. In the latter use, to the extent that a typology of development is illegitimate, so too is the associated typology of political culture. Such guilt by association cannot, however, be asserted for the comparative use. In this use, as Grew notes, modernization theory draws attention to culture, and allows it some autonomy of the modernizing process. Or, as Almond has more strongly expressed it, political culture was in part a response to the *failure* of simplistic liberal theories of political development.[7] Such is the use to which the concept has been put by Black:

> Societies vary a great deal in their political culture, and these variations account for significant differences in the ways in which they react to common problems caused by the scientific and technological revolution . . . . Levels of achievement certainly tend to converge in developed societies, but due to differences in political culture, modern institutions are likely to vary considerably.[8]

Political culture, then, in its comparative use, has been invoked precisely to save modernization theory from accusations of illegitimate teleology. Cultural lag is the means by which this rescue is attempted. But of course it is one thing to distinguish the comparative and sociological uses analytically; it is another to separate them in practice.

The tension between them is illustrated by a recent revival of modernization theory undertaken by Lucian Pye, who applies it to what he calls the 'crisis of authoritarianism', not only in Eastern Europe and the Soviet Union, but also in China, East Asia, Southern Europe and Latin America.[9] He sees in these events a 'vindication' of modernization theory, suggesting that the only mistake of early writers on the subject (of whom he was in the vanguard) was to underestimate the extent to which 'factors of change' – 'economic growth, the spread of science and technology, the acceleration and spread of communications, and the establishment of educational systems' – would develop. Among the universalizing tendencies that have thereby been liberated, he asserts, are the movement into government roles of technocrats ('people who see governing as technical problem solving'), the demand of the 'information revolution' for 'decentralization and a diffusion of power throughout the society incompatible with centralized authoritarian rule', and the decreasing plausibility of 'the instinctive understanding that inferiors can expect benefits from yielding to the will of benevolent superiors'. Despite all this, Pye recognizes a

> fundamental clash between the culture of modernization (what I have called the world culture) and the various national cultures . . . . The outcome of this clash (and hence the outcome of any particular crisis of authoritarianism) will depend on the character of the political culture, and the extent to which it either moderates or accommodates the conflict or exacerbates it.[10]

Thus the 'vindication' of modernization theory is no more than a reiteration of the same equivocal claim that its more careful proponents always made: that modernization accounts for a growing similarity between societies, but also that the *deus ex machina* of cultural lag is waiting in the wings, ready to account for whatever exceptions might appear. Modernization theory states that, other things being equal, nations will tend to conform to the universal characteristics of modernity. Political culture provides the *ceteris paribus* clause. The combination, as we just saw in Pye's example, is a theory that could predict anything; that is, a scientifically useless one.

It is, of course, likely that advocates of this theory would assert that national and world political cultures could in principle coexist. This may be true, but to call them both 'political cultures' introduces a confusion that is far more than merely terminological. It implies similar origins for these cultures; a similar theory as to how they came into being. It is incumbent upon the advocate, therefore, not only to show how national and world cultures form distinct sets, but further to show what distinct socialization processes lead to their formation. This has seldom been attempted.

STAGES OF MODERNITY

As just observed, political culture has been implicated in modernization theory not just as an explanation of deviations from the outcomes the latter would predict, but as a means of characterizing the outcomes themselves. This is true, indeed, not just of modernization theory narrowly conceived, but of a number of different accounts of processes of secular change. 'Modernity', in its several versions, replaces the 'democracy' of our previous chapter as the social formation whose cultural aspects are exposed by the sociological use. Analogously, political culture is not in these uses ascribed the status of independent variable, nor indeed necessarily that of dependent variable either. The analogy with *The Civic Culture* may be taken even further, as we will see when we consider criticisms of theories of stages of modernity.

In one of the classic studies of modernization, Almond and Coleman combine the notions of cultural lag and the cultural impact of modernization ('traditional' and 'modern' components of political culture, as they term them) in the idea of 'cultural diffusion'. 'Traditional' components are 'diffuse, affective, particularistic, and ascriptive', while 'modern' ones are 'universalistic, specific, instrumental'. In fact, while differences in the 'particularistic' cultures – cultural lag – might be taken to account for differences in outcome, Almond and Coleman give an example that raises comparison to a higher level: they distinguish between Britain and France on the basis of the degree to which, in each country, 'traditional' and 'modern' components are 'fused'; in Britain there is 'a homogeneous political culture, secular and traditional in content', while in France there is 'a polarization of political culture, with some elements and regions manifesting traditionality and others manifesting rationality'.[11] But whatever the level of comparison (and there is obviously some scope for equivocation between these two levels), it is clear that political cultural description is being made not only of the setting for modernization, but of modernization itself.

This simple dichotomy of 'traditional' and 'modern' political cultures is of course only a rephrasing in political cultural terms of the dichotomous distinctions made by nineteenth- and twentieth-century sociologists such as Tönnies and Durkheim.[12] It is, however, only one of several typologies that relate political culture to levels or stages of modernization. An extreme example – extreme in the sense of maximizing the number of stages – has been produced by Stephen Chilton. Although his definition of political culture as mutually accepted 'ways of relating' differs from that used by the writers we have been considering, the categories he derives can be seen as a more elaborate version of Almond and Coleman's. He describes six 'stages' of culture – from 'Domination; physical compulsion; threats; seizure by force; extortion' through 'Mutual respect; rational debate; fair competition, and scientific testing' (the fifth stage, similar in some ways to Almond and Coleman's 'modernity') to the as yet unrealized sixth stage of 'undistorted communicative action; mutual care'. Various social and political institutions are associated with each stage, although, unlike the 'culturally universal sequence of organizing structures' ('ways of relating'), the variation of forms appropriate to each stage of culture means that 'there is no universal sequence of specific social forms'.[13]

More typically, culture has been related to the idea of 'industrial society'. An example is Alex Inkeles and Raymond Bauer's *émigré*-based study of *The Soviet Citizen*. While asserting that no unilinear path of development or specific government structures are implied, Inkeles and Bauer nevertheless conclude, 'The substratum on which the most distinctive Soviet features are built is after all a large-scale industrial order which shares many features in common with the large-scale industrial order of other national states of Europe and indeed Asia.' Accordingly, 'The patterning of values about the occupational structure, of opportunities for mobility, of the evaluation of education, of ideas about child-rearing, of communications behavior, and many other realms of experience is broadly similar in the Soviet Union and other large-scale industrial societies.' This 'suggests that the industrial social order carries with it certain inherent propensities which influence individual values relatively, if not completely, independently of the political setting'.[14]

The notion of industrial society is, as Margaret Archer has pointed out, one of several descriptions of modernity that have been successively advanced in the last several decades.[15] 'Postindustrialism' is another. This concept is most strongly associated with Daniel Bell and his thesis of the 'end of ideology', the latter indeed being the chief characteristic of this putative social formation. It is, of course, a cultural characteristic, but one that in Bell's account follows from the increased level of materialism and potential for its satisfaction, and the corresponding decline of utopian or revolutionary thought in modern society. As is well known, this thesis began to look somewhat implausible shortly after its appearance in 1962, amid the later upheavals of the 1960s; nevertheless, it has continued to be developed, by Bell and others. The distinct and somewhat more plausible variant developed by Inglehart will be examined in greater detail in the following section. A third example cited by Archer is the notion of 'information society', advanced primarily by Alvin Toffler, which emphasizes the scale of the changes being wrought by the development of information processing, telecommunications and cybernetics technology. Industrial society theorists point to the worldwide spread of General Motors; theorists of information society to that of CNN. The former would cite East European enthusiasm for the market as a motivator of the collapse of communism in that region; the latter would allege an avalanche effect caused by uncontrolled public knowledge of the breakdown in adjacent states, giving Nicolae Ceauşescu's downfall as the most graphic illustration of the power of the media.

As Archer observes, what is common to all of these sociologies of modernity is their 'impoverished' view of culture, which 'consists principally in the progressive subordination of culture until it becomes an epiphenomenon of structure'. She also observes that criticisms of these accounts, in concentrating their attacks on the structural claims, have perpetuated this impoverishment: 'what was remarkable for its absence was an extended discussion of culture as an independent variable in the modernization process or the relative autonomy of culture to direct industrial societies in different ways – not just at the beginning but in perpetuity'.[16] This diagnosis appears simply to recommend a return to the comparative use of political culture; its phrasing very much recalls Black's. However, this is not the main form her reaction takes. Instead, she emphasizes that the impoverishment of culture has removed a basis, other than their own 'instrumental rationality', for criticizing these modernization processes. In response, she proposes that sociology regain a connection with moral philosophy, with the idea of the 'Good Life', and set itself up not as 'value-free' recorder of modernization processes, but as critic of them. To this end, she suggests that the notion of culture as an integrated whole be abandoned. This notion, she alleges, conceals critical resources within culture itself, and hence the fact that 'cultural contradictions make just as important a contribution to social change as anything going on in the structural domain'.[17]

Here we can observe a sociological response to a sociological use of political culture that follows the same contours that we traced in Chapter 1. Attempted empirical descriptions in terms of culture – in this case of modernity, in the previous one of democracy – are countered by challenging their claim to value-freedom, and exposing their mobilization of the concept of culture in support of that claim. And like the sociological critics we discussed in Chapter 1, Archer responds by pointing to cleavages in culture. Thus, far from rejecting the notion of political culture, Archer, like Pateman, Jessop *et al.*, reappropriates it for critical, rather than 'empirical', purposes.

The notion of 'postmodernism' is a recent entry to the ranks of the sociology of modernity. It differs from the ones criticized by Archer in its origin, which is not only 'cultural', as opposed to 'structural', but is indeed aesthetic. John Gibbins points out that the term itself was used first in architectural criticism to denote a 'deconstruction' of Le Corbusian modernism with 'an eclectic usage of old and new styles involving pastiche, nostalgia and an awareness of citizens' real needs'.[18] This architectural prototype of postmodernism is amply suggestive of the sociological meaning of the concept. It suggests the postmodern emphasis on play and hedonism, and in rejecting the modernist architectural premise that form should follow function it metaphorically dissociates culture from the basis in class politics it supposedly had in the now defunct 'modern' period. Rejecting architectural modernism also means, for instance, rejecting bleak, high-rise public housing, and hence, by implication, social homogenization and social engineering, and possibly even the welfare state – all of which are reactions characteristic of the politics of the 1980s in many Western countries. The architectural metaphor is therefore a fruitful one, and it is not surprising that it has extended across a wide field of cultural criticism into sociology. There, we find 'postmodern culture' pictured as 'fragmentation, multidirectional change and a psychedelic collage of contemporary attitudes, values and beliefs'. Postmodernism, we are told, 'does not recognize a gradual change in value priorities in the contemporary world but a turmoil of values and preferences, the byproduct and waste of centuries of the modernizing process'.[19]

It is also easy to see how the aesthetic origins of the postmodern perspective have contributed to excesses in its sociological formulation. The bright colours, redundant shapes and playful historical allusions of postmodern architecture have their analogues across the entire range of aesthetic activity; in pop music 'sampling', in music proms, in haute couture. Wandering into a video arcade it is difficult to avoid a sense of being drawn into a dizzying techno-hedonistic vortex; and such wandering, metaphorically speaking, is what postmodern cultural critics engage in. It is unsurprising that they identify only 'turmoil' and a 'psychedelic collage'. However, apart from momentarily wondering whether such reactions are not typical of people who have reached an age at which they might write and publish academic papers, we cannot avoid serious doubt when this perspective is made into a fully sociological one. Even in Gibbins's own formulation we may notice a contradiction between the denial of gradual change and the claim that postmodernism is the product of 'centuries of the modernizing process'. Perhaps, instead, these disturbing phenomena, many at the level of popular culture, have always been present, but have only just become the subject of academic attention. Such, certainly, is the implication of Bryan Turner's observation that postmodern culture has much in common with the culture of the Baroque, which featured '"kitsch" cultural frivolity' and an awareness of 'the crisis of religion, the differentiation and fragmentation of culture, the emergence of new sensibilities, the erosion of an overarching ideology, and the necessity to discover a new basis for moral order'.[20]

Whatever the degree of novelty of postmodern culture in aesthetic terms, the attempt to relate it to the traditional concerns of sociology necessarily introduces a sense of more gradual change. Many critics have indeed doubted that postmodernism is so very different from modernism itself. Gibbins's response that such claims of 'faulty periodization' may be countered by noticing the distinctive self-consciousness of postmodern theorists,[21] amounting as it does to no more than the claim that postmodernism exists because some analysts say so, is not of much help. Indeed it hints that the danger of postmodernism descending into self-referential self-absorption may not be confined to architecture. Gradual change is suggested both by Turner's attempt to relate postmodernism to Bell's analysis of postindustrial society and by the attempt to integrate it with Inglehart's concept of 'postmaterialism'. Neither of the latter analyses admit to anything like the degree of disorientation posited by postmodernism.

The sociological extension of postmodernism provides a good illustration of the argument by Archer that the holistic view of culture derived from anthropology has had a detrimental effect on sociological uses of the term. While that argument, as we will see in Chapter 6, ignores debates within anthropology over precisely this issue, its suggestion that the result was an attempt to 'grasp' cultures as wholes in the manner of aesthetic appreciation is partly true. The idea of postmodernism is in a sense the limiting case of this approach, where not only aesthetic methods, but aesthetic objects, have been used to characterize culture and by extension society. The attempt to achieve such 'grasp' exposes the analyst to the danger of 'psychedelia', with effects on the analyst's sociological conclusions opposite to what the true meaning of that word would suggest.

POSTMATERIALISM

Many of the approaches we have considered so far in this chapter have the character of 'speculative sociology', particularly in regard to their treatment of culture. In contrast, the work of Ronald Inglehart has a solid foundation in survey research.[22] Moreover, this foundation consists of the largest database so far used in political culture research, covering a large number of countries and a lengthy time period. As such, Inglehart's work merits more extended discussion.

The findings of *Culture Shift* are many, and are given persuasive and sometimes elegant support from the statistics. It is unnecessary to mention all of them here. The thrust of Inglehart's argument is as follows:

> The values of Western publics have been shifting from an overwhelming emphasis on material well-being and physical security toward greater

emphasis on the quality of life. The causes and implications of this shift are complex, but the basic principle might be stated very simply: people tend to be more concerned with immediate needs or threats than with things that seem remote or non-threatening . . . . Today, an unprecedentedly large proportion of Western populations have been raised under conditions of exceptional economic security. Economic and physical security continue to be valued positively, but their relative priority is lower than in the past. (p. 5, quoting from p. 3 of *Silent Revolution*)

This claim – essentially that materialism declines as material security increases – is combined with a second major thesis, that the effects of improvement in material security are not immediate, since the relevant values are learned during 'pre-adult' years (p. 68). The combination of these 'scarcity' and 'socialization' hypotheses yields a theory that may be tested by observing the rise of 'postmaterialist' values, and moreover their gradual movement through the population in the course of generational replacement. Inglehart's data, unusually in political culture research, are sufficient at least to draw preliminary conclusions regarding the latter, which is part of what gives his findings their weighty plausibility.

Culture Shift, like other behavioural studies we have looked at, makes both a comparative and a sociological use of political culture. This claim needs some qualification, because throughout the book the term 'political culture' is reserved for the comparative use only; it is invoked when national deviations from the general patterns associated with increasing postmaterialism are found. But we cannot overlook the book's title; and moreover 'values' are, of course, a central part of most definitions of political culture. Thus to reserve the term 'political culture' for national cultural variation and to speak elsewhere only of values is somewhat artificially to suggest that no problem of conflict between comparative and sociological uses exists. The conflict, such as it is, is less apparent than the one we identified in *The Civic Culture* and in many versions of modernization theory. This is because the comparative element is largely recessive. Emphasis is on common trends and outcomes, not, as in the explanation of stable democracy, on differences. The comparative use arises in the explanation of divergences, but these are rather few in number, and are paid relatively little attention when they arise. (Chapter 1 of the study is an exception, concentrating on national differences in an attempt, which we evaluated in our first chapter, to reassess Almond and Verba's comparative theory.) Thus *Culture Shift* deserves to be evaluated primarily as a contribution to the sociological use of political culture. Even so, this does not mean that no problem of conflict arises; indeed we will argue later that the very recessiveness of the comparative element is a serious weakness.

Postmaterialist values are measured by questions inviting respondents to list a range of national goals in order of importance – sometimes twelve choices were given, more often a subset of four of these, namely 'maintain order in the nation; give people more say in the decisions of government; fight rising prices; protect freedom of speech' (pp. 74f.). The results indicate, firstly, that respondents did tend, as expected, to group the first and third, or the second and fourth, of these goals together, and similarly with the twelve-item question, demonstrating the existence in most of the countries surveyed of a materialist/postmaterialist dimension in values. This dimension is then used as a variable which is statistically compared with many other measures in the course of the study, in an attempt to discover both the source of postmaterialist values and their effects.

So far as the source of the materialist/postmaterialist dimension is concerned, the scarcity and socialization hypotheses are confirmed by the discovery of cohort effects and of a relationship between postmaterialist values and what Inglehart calls 'formative security', a measure derived from the occupational and educational level of the respondent's father, the educational level of the respondent's mother, and the respondent's own educational level (p. 122) – a measure, in other words, of the economic security experienced by the respondent in the pre-adult period.

Inglehart reports several effects of the growth of postmaterialism. Postmaterialists, while coming from secure backgrounds and thus being likely themselves to be economically successful, in fact underachieve economically relative to materialists, as their values would lead one to expect. Postmaterialism is found to be correlated with declining 'traditional' religious observance, and with what might be termed 'progressive' attitudes regarding social issues such as homosexuality, abortion and divorce. Postmaterialism is also found to dispose people towards the appeals of the so-called 'new politics', which emphasizes issues such as nuclear power, disarmament and the environment, and to lead them away from allegiance to the traditional economic or class concerns of existing major political parties. Accordingly, postmaterialists have both the ability (deriving from their higher educational levels) and the disposition to participate in political movements such as the European peace movement of the early 1980s and more generally to engage in 'elite-directing' rather than 'elite-directed' political activity.

As might be expected of survey research (since we, of course, have an unscientific exposure to other people's opinions in everyday life), some of these findings are unsurprising. Some of them, on the other hand, are quite surprising, such as the finding that 'yuppies' are actually less materialistic than the population as a whole. A study such as Inglehart's does not in general rely for its force on the novelty of its findings, but on the firmness with which they can be demonstrated, and in this respect it is difficult to find fault with it. Furthermore, it interconnects with other political cultural observations we have recorded, such as Roberts' and Lemke's of the rise of what they call 'alternative political culture' in the former West and East Germany. Whereas Bell's 'end of ideology' thesis was thrown into doubt by the events we group under the label of 'the 1960s', Inglehart's thesis provides some explanation of these events and indeed would predict that such unconventional forms of political activity would continue whenever the political context demanded them. To the argument that the relatively conservative 1980s do for his thesis what the 1960s did for Bell's, Inglehart points out that, in Europe, the reaction to the installation by NATO of new theatre nuclear weapons followed the 'new politics' pattern, and further argues that the rise of the 'moral majority' in the United States is best seen as a reaction to the relentless emergence of postmaterialist values by an increasingly isolated, and ageing, *minority*.

In emphasizing value cleavages, Inglehart also escapes to some extent the charge of using empiricism to justify the status quo – indeed his thesis is a radical challenge to that part of the status quo that is constituted by the traditional political parties. The empirical theory of democracy, according to which political elites contend for the allegiance of passive voters in a political marketplace, using the techniques appropriate to the marketplace, describes just that 'elite-directed' politics that Inglehart claims is undergoing terminal decline. Where perhaps the kind of complacency that the radical critics object to can be identified is in Inglehart's argument that redistributive policies are becoming less attractive to voters precisely because of their success in the past, and hence of their diminishing returns. It may be true that the majority no longer stands to benefit from the growth of government and the welfare state and from the resulting increased taxation, but the inference from this that the continuing needs of certain substantial minorities will fall out of consideration is questionable – especially when one considers the impact that the allegedly beleaguered minority of materialists had through conventional political action in the 1980s.

To some extent this is a question of timescale, since postmaterialists have not yet penetrated certain key sectors of society, such as corporate business and political leaderships (as contrasted, for instance, with the media). When they do, such backlashes may be more difficult to organize, and the postmaterialist world will have dawned. At present, however, as we observe various election campaigns following their customary course, and despite the formidable evidence marshalled in *Culture Shift*, the dawn seems hard to discern. Indeed, it is a significant problem of the study that when it descends to the particular it does not always seem on target. A minor example is Inglehart's treatment of British politics in the 1980s, which identifies the breakaway Social Democratic Party as postmaterialist and the Labour Party as traditional leftist. This has some truth, but it is worth noting that it was the Labour Party that adopted unilateral nuclear disarmament and most strenuously opposed modernization of the NATO nuclear arsenal – and which later abandoned that policy in the face of its obvious unpopularity. The SDP's popularity was short-lived, and the party no longer exists.

Part of the explanation for such events may be deviation on the part of Britain from the general trends Inglehart records – such deviation is noticed, for instance, in the British relative lack of enthusiasm for European integration (pp. 418f.). This brings us to the general problem of the explanation of such deviations – the problem of the recessive comparative element of the study. It surfaces at several points. For instance, it is noticed that in Japan, an item that in Western countries is found to be one of the components of the postmaterialist syndrome (in the twelve-item measure), dealing with 'a less impersonal, more human society' (translated into Japanese as 'a society with harmonious human relations') is given priority by everyone, not just postmaterialists. The proposed explanation for this is the persistence in Japan of *preindustrial* values, which emphasized a sense of belonging: 'the transition from preindustrial to industrial values has been superimposed on the shift from Materialism to Postmaterialist priorities' (pp. 146f.). Low Japanese anxiety about crime is traced to the low crime rate in that country, which is in turn explained by reference to traditional culture (p. 150). In general, 'Items that have one consistent meaning throughout the West sometimes have a quite different significance in Japan' (p. 151).

Another example is Belgium, which somewhat unexpectedly stands out as an exception to several of Inglehart's generalizations (e.g. on p. 410). In Denmark, uniquely, the percentage of people claiming to 'be religious' is higher than the percentage who believe in God, suggesting that the former question possibly had a distinct meaning there (pp. 190f.). But outside the opening chapter, national variations come most to the fore when Inglehart (ch. 7) sets out to address two problems: why does greater wealth not lead to greater happiness, and why do nations vary in overall levels of happiness? The first problem is answered by the thesis that 'aspirations adapt to situations', supported by the finding that those situational factors that are most susceptible to rapid change account for the greatest amount of variation in levels of life satisfaction and happiness, income not being such a factor. An exception to this is however the variable of nationality, which is a highly stable characteristic that nevertheless produces wide and consistent variation in happiness levels – indeed it is the strongest predictor of such variation. Inglehart's explanation is that 'given societies may have different cultural baselines for the normal response to questions about how well one is doing' (p. 243). Some other evidence is presented to justify this claim, including the stability of national suicide rates. But this 'enduring cultural component' (p. 246) is not further explained: the second of the 'problems' Inglehart set out to address is far from solved.

Inglehart is, of course, quite open to the idea of national cultural variation; indeed his first chapter is aimed at demonstrating it, so these findings do not represent contradictions in his theory. But the way they are handled reveals that, for all the sophistication with which the sociological project of describing the origins and consequences of the rise of postmaterialism is handled, political culture as a national, comparative, attribute is treated just as it has been in modernization theory, as a catch-all residual category. The crucial problem of what accounts for 'enduring cultural components' is not addressed.

This chapter has further demonstrated the utility of analyzing political culture research in terms of use, in that the deficiencies of many of the examples considered have been traceable to their combination of comparative and sociological uses. Broadly speaking, when modernity is examined in conjunction with political culture the problem arises of whether the latter is to be regarded as a *context* for the former (the comparative use) or as an *aspect* of it (the sociological use). Resolving this problem would not necessarily involve excluding one or the other use; but recognizing the tension between them, and accounting for the contradictory etiologies of political culture that they suppose, is necessary. Perhaps, however, the frequency with which each use contaminates the other tells us that something is fundamentally wrong with political cultural explanation. Chapter 4 presents theoretical arguments to this effect, while the next chapter discusses attempts to relate political culture to cases of more rapid political change.

3 Political Culture and Communism

Following the initial surge of interest in political culture research in the early 1960s, the concept fell relatively out of favour, a fact which is partly explained by its 'guilt by association' with the theory of modernization, whose decline in popularity was precipitous. In the 1970s, however, the concept underwent something of a revival, this time in the political science subfield of communist studies. This subfield was always somewhat isolated from the mainstream of political science, and for this reason its use of political culture, although occasionally noticed, was seldom paid serious attention as a contribution to the theoretical development of the concept (Gabriel Almond, as we will see, is an exception to this statement). But, in the 1970s, in this out-of-the-way scholarly environment, the concept was indeed not only being preserved but also developed. In the hands of some authors, this development took political culture beyond the constraints of its behavioural use, whether comparative or sociological, and into interpretivism – an outcome that it is difficult to avoid at least partially attributing to the relative scarcity of attitude survey data in communist states, and the difficulty of conducting surveys there.[1] That development will be pursued in Chapter 5. This chapter will instead concentrate on uses of political culture that continued to mine the comparative vein. As such, it will continue and enhance the critique of the comparative use that has been presented so far. But even within this vein, the peculiarities of the communist cases led to peculiarities of use, as well as to certain deficiencies. One significant peculiarity of the communist context is that the political change that took place there was revolutionary, not gradual, making these cases distinct from the instances of secular change discussed in Chapter 2. Another is that communist states were the sites of a self-conscious attempt by political authorities to change political culture directly. And a third is provided by the recent collapse of communism in Eastern Europe, offering the chance to assess a political cultural explanation of sudden political change. In view of these circumstances it is indeed surprising that political culture research within communist studies has not been more closely examined from a theoretical perspective. The first section of this chapter elaborates the theoretical significance of these circumstances in connection with the comparative use of political culture, while the second looks closely at two settings for political cultural explanation: the Soviet Union and Czechoslovakia. The third considers the prospects for and problems of a political cultural explanation of the collapse of communism.

THE CONSONANCE/DISSONANCE THEORY AND RESOCIALIZATION

The absence of an adequate general theory relating stability and change to political culture has been pointed out by Harry Eckstein.[2] Noting that, in political culture theory, 'continuity is an expectation akin to that of inertia in the Galilean conception of motion', he suggests that the 'window' for contingent explanation opened by this approach allows varieties of *ad hoc* adjustments – such as emphasizing adult rather than childhood socialization, and de-emphasizing the need for consistency of individual outlooks – that weaken the theory. Eckstein's proposed 'culturalist theory of change' considers three types of political change: 'pattern-maintaining change', 'social trauma' and 'political transformation', and discusses these in relation to political culture. In the first case, orientations are adjusted minimally, or come to fit the new circumstances; or if change is frequent, they become more abstract and flexible, turning into 'forms' rather than 'contents'. In the case of social trauma, Eckstein states that rapid general reorientation is prohibited by cultural theory, and that 'ritual conformity' or 'retreatism' (into family life) are likely initial reactions, suggested by research on children's reaction to novel experience. Political transformation is a special case of social trauma, having a more deliberate and planned quality. Here 'brute power' or 'legalism' can compensate for cultural formlessness, with the expectation, through family resocialization, of a long-term return to the pre-transformation culture: 'the short-run effects of attempted transformations are greater than the longer-run effects'. But of these three cases, the first two are accounts of the impact of political change *on* political culture; only the last case is a true 'culturalist theory of change'. It gives political culture an independent role in cases where rapid political transformation has been attempted.

Unlike the case of West Germany, where the transformation was perhaps, a defender of this theory might say, not rapid enough for such a cultural lag to come into effect, in communist states it was rapid and radical. In addition, they were states in which overt and extensive attempts at 'resocialization' of the populations were made, through education, the activities of youth organizations, workplace agitation and propaganda; thus providing useful test cases for the theory. The theory, in a slightly different form, has indeed been the main vehicle of comparative political cultural explanation in these cases. For instance, Samuel Huntington and Jorge Domínguez write: 'Political change is not likely under conditions of congruence between political culture and political structures . . . [it] occurs when congruence between political culture and structures erodes or breaks down.'[3] Barbara Jancar, in a discussion of the literature on communist states, goes further: she proposes 'operationalizing' the study of political culture by *defining* political change as the movement towards congruence between political culture and political structure.[4] Archie Brown provides a more careful formulation. At any time after a revolutionary change in the political system, he writes,

> there can be dissonance between the political culture and the political system . . . . In such cases, a crisis triggered off by other stimuli (frequently but by no means always economic) may produce a more open political situation in which the strength and direction of political change may be strongly influenced by the dominant – and no longer dormant – political culture.[5]

We will term this version of comparative explanation the 'consonance/dissonance theory'. Adopting it has implications for the definition of political culture that have occupied a good deal of debate in this field. A definition of political culture that, like Almond's, is 'subjective', that is, psychological, has been proposed by Brown and justified on the basis that it facilitates the analytic distinction between culture and structures that the consonance/dissonance theory requires.[6] Brown, however, while allied in this regard with the mainstream in political culture research, has found himself in a minority in its communist subfield.[7] Those who employ a 'comprehensive' or what is usually called, misleadingly (because the subjective definition is more clearly connected with behavioural*ism*), a 'behavioural' definition, incorporating patterns of behaviour as well as subjective factors, have formed the majority. We noticed above that the circumstances of communist states led some analysts to eschew comparative explanation altogether, and adopt interpretivism. The situation is, however, not so clear cut, because some authors have produced what we termed in the Introduction 'hybrid' analyses, combining an interpretive *rubric* with a comparative *use* of political culture. This exposes them to Brown's criticism, and to some others that we will consider shortly. We can illustrate this somewhat confusing situation by referring to two arguments for a comprehensive definition. Richard Fagen, who has been cited to this effect by several authors, argues that a subjective definition misses the essential content of resocialization, namely mass mobilization, by construing 'the efforts of the regime as a kind of political advertising'.[8] A strict distinction between attitudes and behaviour, in other words, presents a 'thin' picture of the resocialization effort. This interpretive use of political culture predominates in Fagen's study, though it is worth pointing out that scope for the consonance/dissonance theory is offered by his conclusion that a modification in the value system is 'perhaps the most important long-term consequence of attempts to transform the political culture' and that 'the revolutionary environment makes considerable disjunction [between behaviour and attitudes] both possible and probable'.[9] Stephen White's monograph *Political Culture and Soviet Politics*[10] illustrates a similar ambiguity, but much more obviously. While espousing a comprehensive definition White nevertheless directs a good deal of attention to resocialization in the narrow sense (what Fagen would call 'political advertising'), noting low levels of interest on the part of the population in official political education, inappropriate reasons for attending ideological classes and general popular scepticism about official values.[11] Not only that, but White elsewhere, as we will soon see, makes clear the comparative aims of his study. White therefore comes much closer than Fagen to a position that makes him vulnerable to Brown's argument. These conclusions, with their emphasis on 'dissonance', would justify Brown's argument in favour of a subjective definition. However, what is most apparent from these disputes is that the decisive issue is not the definition itself, but whether the comparative use which a subjective definition facilitates is viable. That is our present concern.

White's account of the failure of the Soviet resocialization effort introduces the question of the contribution of this particular kind of dissonance to political cultural explanation. Gabriel Almond has emphasized this finding of failure in studies such as White's. He asserts that, hence, an attempt to 'falsify' political cultural explanation has been refuted. Needless to say, communist leaders did not initiate the resocialization programme in order to falsify any theory of Western political science; nevertheless, had their attempt to inculcate new values been successful, the claim that political cultures persist and exert a pull on the more quickly changed political structures would indeed have been undermined. Political culture would have become 'a weak variable at best'. Instead, the failure appears to show that 'a prior set of attitudinal patterns will tend to persist in some form and degree and for a significant period of time, despite efforts to transform it'.[12]

However, there is an important distinction between showing that an out-come that would invalidate political cultural explanation has not occurred, and validating such an explanation. The failure of the resocialization effort is a necessary condition for the validation of the consonance/dissonance theory, but not a sufficient one. Unfortunately, in much of the writing on communist states, the distinction is elided. To be sure, the finding is a useful corrective to earlier assumptions, connected with some versions of the 'totalitarian model', of the success of resocialization or 'brain-washing'. Indeed that assumption is not confined to the 1950s, when the totalitarian model was most prevalent. Huntington and Domínguez, who define political culture subjectively as 'empirical beliefs about expres-sive political symbols and values and other orientations of the members of the society toward political objects . . . a society's central political values', assert that politics in the Soviet Union became 'participatory', so that the Soviet Union presented a 'successful case of planned pol-itical culture change', in which 'a consummatory value pattern, linking all spheres of life, is . . . established in a modernizing polity'.[13] No evidence of attitude change is presented to support this claim. Within the polemical environment of communist studies, therefore, it is easy to understand the stress which has been placed on findings such as White's. But, again, they do not demonstrate the causal efficacy of political culture. To pre-empt somewhat the detailed discussion below, the example may be given of Almond's comment that Czechoslovakia provides 'the strongest support for political culture theory' among com-munist states.[14] This exceeds the more reticent causal claim made by Brown and Gordon Wightman, whose findings contribute to Almond's conclusions: 'the dominant Czech political culture came much closer to changing Czechoslovak Communism than Czechoslovak Commun-ism came to procuring acceptance of its official political culture'.[15] Since, as Brown and Wightman demonstrate, communism came nowhere near procuring acceptance, that is not making much of a causal claim.

We noted above that the scarcity of attitude survey data prompted many of the peculiarities of the analysis of political culture in communist states. This observation needs some qualification. While in many cases, such as the Soviet Union, official admissions of the inadequacy and poor results of attempts to inculcate new values were available, these provided only characterizations by default of the attitudes that were, in fact, present. Such admissions could, until recently, be supplemented in the Soviet case only by surveys applied to *émigrés*, of which several examples exist.[16] In other cases, notably Czechoslovakia, but also Poland and Hungary, conditions in the communist period facilitated the publication of somewhat richer survey research. Political culture analysts thus had an easier time in some communist states than others adhering to the requirements of the consonance/dissonance theory. The Soviet Union, as we have seen, presents difficulties in this regard, while Czechoslovakia is perhaps the case where the consonance/dissonance theory has its most straightforward application. These two cases therefore provide a good basis on which to assess the viability of the comparative use of political culture.

THE SOVIET AND CZECHOSLOVAK CASES

White's historical survey is not designed to be a new contribution to historical scholarship; indeed, as he frankly admits, 'if anything it reflects too faithfully the mainstream of scholarly consensus'.[17] It is intended to expose the main themes of Russian 'historical experience'. One such theme, according to White, is the 'absence of institutions in any way constraining the exercise of monarchical power' and a 'highly personalized attachment to political authority, and in particular to the person of the Tsar', which was apparent in the lack of a clear distinction between the Tsar's ownership and rule. Government was distinctively centralized and bureaucratic, with a wide scope of responsibility that extended to its citizens' moral and material welfare. Church and state were integrated, as expressed by the slogan 'Autocracy, Orthodoxy, Nationality'.[18] As continuities in the social fabric, White stresses the underdevelopment of industry, commerce and the bourgeoisie, and the prevalence of the village commune as a social organization. An analysis of the redistributive and regulatory functions of the commune prompts the conclusion 'it would be surprising if [the commune] failed to reinforce the disposition of its members to resolve their affairs in a collective, consensual and broadly egalitarian manner'.[19]

A wide range of evidence concerning political institutions, social structures and ideology contributes to this description of Russian political culture. White's conclusion from it is that 'there was much in an inheritance of this kind which the Bolsheviks could adapt for their purposes'. However, 'there was much . . . at the same time, to which the new Soviet government could not but take exception'.[20] The remainder of the monograph discusses these two parts of the Bolsheviks' 'inheritance'. *Emigré* surveys show widespread support for state ownership, a degree of egalitarianism, approval of state action in social and cultural affairs and approval of political institutions. This is the 'adaptable' residue of Russian political culture. 'Exceptionable' elements are those that official resocialization efforts have failed to eradicate, such as low interest in politics and surviving religiosity.

The inconsistency between White's historical methodology and his methods for assessing 'contemporary political culture' has been noticed by several critics. Jancar argues that White's conclusions 'relate not to continuity and change in political culture under the impact of a revolutionary ideology, but to the legitimacy of the regime and propositions regarding the strengths and weaknesses upon which its claims to legitimacy rest',[21] while Mary McAuley asserts

> authors who claim that today's dominant . . . political culture – as discovered in surveys – is *not* the offspring of existing government practices can in no way suggest that it is appropriate to seek an earlier period's dominant political culture in that period's political practices.[22]

There does indeed seem to be a lacuna between White's historical survey and his focus on the resocialization effort in the remainder of the book. Moreover, these two components produce different, indeed opposite, conclusions when plugged in to the consonance/dissonance theory.

That White intends his findings to be so used is not hard to demonstrate. His first contribution to this subject was to the colloquium *Political Culture and Political Change in Communist States*, published in 1977. Although it was not clearly expressed in every contribution, the main explanatory thesis presented by the collection was the consonance/dissonance theory. The comparative purpose was established in the editorial commentary, and, of course, by the very fact of juxtaposition. White, moreover, defending his account against criticism of its accuracy by McAuley, has emphasized its comparative intent by making explicit comparisons between political developments in Russia and elsewhere in Europe, concluding, despite an acknowledgement that the original contrast may have been drawn too sharply, that Russian historical experience was indeed distinctive.[23]

The consonance/dissonance theory would lead us to conclude that the Soviet Union was, in view of White's historical account, a case of political stability. Such a conclusion was implied by Brown, who pointed (in 1984) to the existence of three 'cultural supports for the status quo' in the Soviet Union: the fear of chaos, patriotism, and agreement on the identity of national heroes, notably Lenin.[24] Continuity even in the face of attempts at resocialization has indeed been stressed by many writers, suggesting, as Stephen Burant does, paraphrasing Marx, that 'the traditions of all the dead generations weigh like a nightmare on the brain of the living, even if they have been exposed to intense ideological re-education'.[25] Others, attending more to the Soviet period itself and its impact on political culture, have written of a 'Stalinist' or 'communist' political culture, in which elements of traditional authoritarianism are compounded and reinforced by the Soviet, particularly Stalinist, experience.[26] Brown writes:

> Because political cultures are historically conditioned, the long-term authoritarian character of the Russian and Soviet state constitutes a serious impediment to political change of a pluralizing, libertarian, or genuinely democratizing nature . . . . Such elements as acceptance of strict political hierarchy; the taking for granted of political police powers, administrative exile, and restrictions on travel; great deference to the top leader; loyalty to a person rather than to political, and particularly legal, institutions; and reluctance to engage in autonomous political activity could only be strengthened by the Soviet experience and, above all, by what happened in Stalin's time.[27]

As we will see, the consonance/dissonance theory produces a sharp contrast in the case of Czechoslovakia, where no such agreement or continuity obtains. This would appear to demonstrate its utility as a comparative theory. But in this interpretation, White's account of the failure of official resocialization plays no useful role. Whereas in the Czechoslovak case (and other cases of dissonance), findings regarding the penetration of official values have the same implication of instability that historical analysis might suggest, in the Soviet Union they do not. Incorporating them therefore necessitates a more complex theory than that of consonance and dissonance.

White's solution is to make use of Inkeles and Bauer's distinction of support for the Soviet *system* from that for the *regime*, his evidence pointing, he avers, to a high level of the former combined with a low level of the latter. This is not equivalent to the distinction often made in accounts of the legitimacy of liberal democratic states between support for the democratic process and support for a particular government. Such a distinction was not available in the Soviet Union and other communist states, where, instead of the process legitimating the power of a party, the party's power was justified in ideological terms and all other political processes were legitimated with respect to it. The objection that this was only an official claim may well be valid, but this would still not make it possible for political institutions to be assessed by the population in abstraction of the party dominance to which they were so obviously subject. White, indeed, counts institutions, as well as ideology, as part of the 'regime'. On the other hand, the attributes of the 'system' for

White include 'public ownership of the means of production and the comprehensive provision of welfare'. On the basis of this distinction, he concludes:

> Liberal democracies, buttressed by the 'come rain or come shine' legitimacy which their political institutions confer upon them, may find it possible to survive a period of static or even falling living standards; a regime whose legitimacy is based rather more narrowly upon 'performance' criteria may find it rather less easy.[28]

Thus while from the consonance/dissonance theory we would predict stability in the Soviet Union, as several writers did, consideration of the failure of resocialization leads White to a conclusion of at best fragile stability. The theory seems to allow the explanation of either outcome, which, to say the least, undermines its plausibility.

In fact, in the course of *perestroika* and its aftermath, the Soviet Union did turn out to be unstable, to the rather dramatic extent of self-destructing. The loosening of constraints on free expression, organized protest and formal political opposition opened a Pandora's box of contending parties and factions, expressions of economic discontent such as strikes, and centrifugal national tendencies. The anti-communist sentiments that were manifested first in elections and then by prohibition of the Party and republican secession would appear to indicate that failure to instil widespread belief in Marxist–Leninist values and in Soviet political institutions was indeed decisive. But while such alienation was revealed by political culture researchers' examination of the resocialization effort, the phenomena provoked by Gorbachev's reforms can hardly be claimed as a vindication of political culture theory. And in view of the ambiguity to which we have just drawn attention, a conservative reaction to these reforms such as occurred in August 1991, and cannot for that matter be ruled out for the successor states, would not decisively validate the theory either.

Yet more ambiguity is introduced when some of the more optimistic prognoses of Soviet writers, asserting the possibility of change in the political culture and thus of escape from its constraints, are considered. Brown cites Fyodor Burlatsky's view that 'a new Soviet political culture has begun to be formed to a significant degree before our eyes'. Brown wrote, in 1989:

> although political cultures do not change overnight, or even within a year or two, they are not immutable. From the perspective not only of

the continuing reality and prospects for success of the reform process now under way in the Soviet Union but also from the standpoint of the deeper imprint it might make on Russian political culture, it is of crucial importance that *glasnost'* be maintained and developed. If openness becomes 'not a campaign, but a norm' [Gorbachev's phrase], that in itself will constitute change in the Soviet political culture and pave the way for other changes – institutional as well as cultural.[29]

Thus the consonance/dissonance theory was not taken to be falsified by the transition from stability to instability in the Soviet Union. The incompatibility of recent events with earlier predictions of stability has simply been ignored, and Russian/Soviet political culture given a new role as a brake on the process of change and, indeed, a locus of blame for its slow pace under Gorbachev. Opposition to reform undoubtedly came from conservatives who had not abandoned the old values, particularly the fear of chaos (which was voiced in justification of the August 1991 coup attempt), as well, of course, as from those who felt it to be moving too slowly, or to have been heedless of national aspirations. Once, however, the values of these diverse social and possibly occupational groups are invoked, political cultural explanation in the simple form of the consonance/dissonance theory is invalidated. Yet no attempt to devise a more sophisticated form of political cultural explanation has accompanied the recent uses of the concept.

We can gain a further understanding of the deficiencies of the consonance/dissonance theory by looking at the cases to which it applies paradigmatically – that is, where describing the failure of resocialization has not led to contradictory conclusions – namely the states of Eastern Europe. The Czechoslovak case is a useful one not just for the reason Almond gives – that the failure of the communist attempt to 'falsify' political cultural explanation by resocialization can be demonstrated – but also because it offers evidence that can yield a very clear picture of the attitudes and values that the regime failed to replace. As in the Soviet case, historical analysis has been used in characterizing Czechoslovak political culture; but this evidence, distinctively, has been supplemented by attitude surveys taken in relatively free conditions in 1946 and 1968, enabling a limited comparison over time.

The 1946 surveys pre-dated the communist takeover, while the 1968 ones were applied in the aftermath of the Prague Spring, within the period when 'political conditions in Czechoslovakia were such that people could be relied upon to answer honestly the most sensitive political questions'.[30]

A survey on the 'relationship of Czechs and Slovaks to their history' conducted in Autumn 1968 provides the main resource for Brown and Wightman's account of Czechoslovak political culture. The survey found, in the Czech case (where the results could be compared with a similar 1946 survey), considerable continuity in evaluations of the 'most glorious period', one notable discontinuity being the move from fifth to first place of the interwar First Republic, a move counter to the direction pressed for by the communist authorities. The Slovaks in 1968 were somewhat less positive towards the First Republic (they put it in fourth place), but they shared with the Czechs a hostility towards the 1950s period and the Soviet invasion of August 1968. Support for the 1968 reform programme was expressed in surveys tracing support for various politicians who were identified with reformism or conservatism.[31] The symbol of Thomas Masaryk (President of the First Republic) was powerful, especially among Czechs, in both 1946 and 1968 – indeed his popular esteem (according to the 'history' survey) increased in that period. Slovaks placed him fourth in a list of esteemed personalities in 1968 – behind various Slovak figures including Dubček.[32] Results recording the extent of identification with other nationalities (again from the 'history' survey) show the destruction of the goodwill Czechoslovaks had previously shown to the Soviet Union as a consequence of the Second World War.

For all the richness and specificity of the 'history' surveys, issues of interpretation still arise. H. Gordon Skilling has pointed out that the political experience of the First Republic was by no means unambiguously pluralistic: that pluralism was distorted by authoritarian or bureaucratic tendencies, and that nationalism was a 'corrosive influence' upon it, often leading to the subordination of dissident elements.[33] David Paul has placed somewhat more stress than Brown and Wightman on the distinctiveness of the interwar political experience of the Slovaks.[34] Brown and Wightman argue, on the basis of analyses by Czechoslovak historians and politicians of both the reformist and conservative persuasions that, whatever its possible range of connotations, 'Masarykism' was construed by all sides in Czechoslovakia as expressing 'social democratic' values.[35] The fact that 'Masarykism' and, in general, the interwar period as a symbol, have a range of possible values, from the 'normative assumption of pluralism'[36] to what might be seen as the oligarchy represented by the almost permanent dominance of the group of five coalition parties, the 'petka', indicates that the values expressed in 1968 involved a degree of reconstruction of the past. This reconstruction, to be sure, bore some connection with historical reality, but at the same time it was pushed in a certain direction by the political circumstances of the time of its expression. As Brown and Wightman put it, 'the timing of the 1968 survey (two months after the armed intervention in Czechoslovakia . . .) doubtless added to the emotional appeal of the First Republic'.[37]

At a first glance, the failure of the Czechoslovak communist authorities to suppress values inimical to their rule seems to open the way for the occurrence of 'deviations' from communist rule such as the Prague Spring to be explained on the model of deviations from the universal process of modernization; that is, in terms of cultural lag. But any of the several theories of socialization on which the notion of cultural lag depends imply only that attitudes change gradually; hence that older ones will only gradually fade away. The Czechoslovak evidence, looked at more closely, rather than demonstrating the mere resilience of values, can be read as demonstrating their responsiveness to political circumstances (though certainly within the constraint of the ways in which the interwar period could *plausibly* be evaluated, a constraint which the government's resocialization effort exceeded). Support for this point may be gained from surveys conducted in Poland. In their summaries of this survey-based work, both Stefan Nowak and Janina Frentzel-Zagorska[38] argue that the communist regime had considerable and diverse effects on values, in one respect reinforcing them – 'the lack of any opportunity to articulate the dominant political culture on a day to day basis adds to its "moral orientation"' [39] – but in other respects weakening them. Nowak speaks of an 'almost random statistical aggregate of values', that is, the dissociation of values from their expected correspondence with social classes and groups, a result, he avers, of the rapid social changes of the Stalinist period.[40] Frentzel-Zagorska endorses this 'social vacuum hypothesis'. Where Nowak speaks of 'latent values', she speaks of 'recessive' ones, which may 'sink into the unconscious or semi-conscious'. In the 1980–81 Solidarity period, recessive values re-emerged, and intermediate affiliation also began to appear. The crushing of Solidarity again impinged on values, increasing apathy and resignation, but at the same time creating a myth, which 'may serve to organize the social imagination on a very wide scale'.[41]

In the Czechoslovak case, Brown argues that no explanation of the events of 1968 could avoid mentioning the dissonance between popular perceptions and official norms that the surveys reveal.[42] But, as we have seen, looking closely at political culture as measured by surveys makes a simple model of cultural persistence seem questionable. Some proponents of political cultural explanation have acknowledged the element of creativity, but have not seen it as problematic for such explanation. For instance, regarding the creative element in evaluations of the First Republic, Kristian Gerner has written:

The point is that when utopias and ideological blueprints of the future are hopelessly discredited by the actions and policies of the communist rulers, the peoples have sought inspiration and guidance in the past – that it is an idealised and even romanticised past seems likely, but this does not affect the validity of the assertion. People can be mobilized even with the help of pure myths and historical symbols.[43]

But these admissions – valid ones, we have seen – surely do make a difference to political cultural explanation. The straightforward transmission of attitudes and values from one generation to another (which even White, despite his comprehensive definition of political culture and his account of 'institutional continuity', takes to be the main mechanism of political cultural persistence)[44] is rendered inapplicable. And the more general claim of the consonance/dissonance theory, that through the influence of political culture, nations that have undergone rapid political transformation eventually return to the pattern of their past, is put in doubt by the question: which past?

THE COLLAPSE OF COMMUNISM AND THE MULTIVALENCE OF HISTORY

The question 'which past?' becomes even more significant in the face of the events of 1989 and 1990 in Eastern Europe. Having failed to inculcate new values, the communist party regimes found themselves toppling, to be replaced, in the new, more open situation (for which the withdrawal of support by the Soviet leadership for repressive measures must be seen as providing much of the explanation), by a belated 'eruption of genuine history'.[45] The process of collapse and replacement was achieved at different speeds and with varying degrees of disorder and violence, and the immediate outcomes also showed wide divergences, from the electoral victory of a broad anti-communist coalition in Czechoslovakia to the continuation of the former communists in a new guise as the National Salvation Front in Romania.

The notion of an 'eruption of genuine history' as an analysis of events in Eastern Europe is appealing because it draws attention to the obvious 'falsehood' of the claims to legitimacy upon which the Soviet-backed regimes rested. The speed with which the regimes crumbled once the ending of Soviet support for repressive reaction was signalled (in 1988)[46] lends plausibility to the claims of dissident writers, who caricatured this fragility in metaphors such as the 'emperor's new clothes' or the outbreak of laughter at a funeral.[47] It is true that some writers also emphasized the penetration of the regimes into society. Václav Havel, for instance, has characterized communism as a system in which everyone was implicated, by virtue of the necessity of each member of society's 'living under a lie', that is, publicly manifesting his or her subjugation by means such as the display of blatantly false slogans.[48] Havel's claim, though, is that truth corrodes falsehood; that despite universal complicity, the system and its psychological effects could be thrown off in an instant. Thus the penetration, although socially comprehensive, was psychologically shallow, just as the metaphors of fragility would have it. In terms of morale and self-esteem, the utility of this position for those who, like Havel, suffered considerable hardship for their attempts to preserve 'truth' is obvious. Whether it is a correct analysis is a different matter, not least because the very notion of a single truth must soon come into question when the single falsehood in contrast with which it is defined ceases to be promulgated. Thus it is possible to see the related ideas of 'genuine history' and 'living within truth' as responses to – that is, products of – a moral environment that was radically simplified by the communist experience, especially in its later stages, when the bankruptcy of ideological claims and dependency on Soviet military power were most apparent.

In fact the continuity between events since the fall of communism and the pre-communist history of Eastern Europe is somewhat limited. Calls for democracy have been voiced throughout the region, and democratic governments widely, though not universally, established. Little in the interwar experience of Eastern Europe would lead one to expect this. In what he correctly describes as a generous estimate, Cyril Black counts as 'experience with free competition among political parties under reasonably stable conditions' '1918–23 and 1931–34 in Bulgaria, 1918–26 in Poland, 1918–19 in Hungary, 1918–34 in Yugoslavia, 1925–28 in Albania, and 1918–37 in Romania', Czechoslovakia providing the only example of a less ambiguous experience of democracy.[49]

In the immediate aftermath of the communist collapse, 'the West' has become the 'single truth' of East European political culture. Hostility to the Soviet Union has been accompanied by a desire to join the supranational structures of Western Europe and a widespread endorsement, at least in theory, of capitalist economics, particularly the redemptive power of the market. Enthusiasm for the latter is reflected both in popular demand for Western consumer goods and in the somewhat uncritical endorsement of market economic solutions by East European economists. Increasing scope for free expression among East European (and Soviet) scholars in recent years has yielded ample illustration of this tendency. For instance, summarizing the results of a 1986 conference on the Yugoslav economic crisis, Dennison Rusinow observes: 'The need for a genuine market economy in solving the economic crisis and mitigating internationality conflicts went virtually unchallenged, although the Yugoslav participants were more optimistic about its potential contribution than most of the Americans. Perhaps this is because the viewpoint of the Yugoslavs . . . is entirely theoretical.'[50] Rusinow's suggested explanation may well be applicable to many of the Western enthusiasms currently on display in Eastern Europe; and if it is valid, the very opposite of political cultural explanation – that lack of experience of the political and economic structures now being created accounts for their creation – is suggested.[51]

Upon travelling to Eastern Europe, as Karen Dawisha has observed, 'It is impossible not to be impressed by the richness of culture and historical tradition binding the peoples of Europe together despite its division after 1945.' Moreover, quoting a phrase of Milan Kundera's, she continues, 'It was not just Americans or West Europeans but also and even primarily the East Europeans themselves who regarded their region as having been "driven from its destiny".'[52] But she also notes the claim of communist leaders in the Soviet Union and Eastern Europe to have rescued the region from its history of despotism, and endorses Hugh Seton-Watson's claim that, before the communist takeover, 'the social structure of Eastern Europe more closely resembled that of Russia, or even of Asiatic countries, than that of France, Britain, or Germany'.[53] According to the latter view (and notwithstanding the claims of communist ideologues), the communist phase in Eastern Europe marks a continuation of the region's history. Such a claim has been made by several writers, sometimes explicitly in terms of political culture. Black writes, 'The success of the USSR in establishing an orbit of predominant influence may also be attributed in considerable degree to the political culture of this region.'[54] Joseph Rothschild, while asserting that diversity was preserved in that 'at a minimum, the citizens of each East Central European nation perceive their particular state as having a moral and historical significance far beyond being a mere unit in a supposed "socialist fraternity" of states and peoples', nevertheless concludes that 'The Communist apparats have inherited, adopted, refined and intensified a deplorable tradition of conducting domestic politics not as an exercise in compromise and consensus building among fellow citizens, but as a mode of warfare against enemies.'[55]

It was probably in order to escape such uncomfortable conclusions that a tradition of dissident writing quite distinct from Kundera's, asserting instead East European exceptionalism, arose during the communist period.

The values of this tradition are summarized in terms of political and economic programmes by the idea of the 'Third Way' (the title of a book by leading Prague Spring reform economist Ota Šik), and in terms of political culture by the idea of 'Central Europe'.

The third way – or 'socialism with a human face' – is the rather vaguely defined and far from even imperfectly realized path upon which Czechoslovakia was thought by its reformist leaders to have embarked in 1968. Whether its programmes are economically feasible or politically consistent is an interesting question, but more relevant to the present discussion is the critical element that the idea contains. Its critique of the failure of East European command economies and political systems is apparent enough from its origin, but its critique of the West should also be noticed. The individualism, materialism and consumerism of the West, as well as its social problems, were phenomena from which some reformers and dissident writers of Eastern Europe recoiled. Their aspiration was to create systems in which both these social ills and Soviet totalitarianism would be avoided. Frequently, dissidents approached this goal by eschewing political activity altogether. Havel, for instance, declared that 'traditional political activity' was irrelevant to the East European situation, that political protest had to be freed from utopian and Western categories, and that the confrontation of truth and lies had to be addressed directly.[56] George Konrád's appropriately titled *Antipolitics* goes furthest in this direction. 'Antipolitics' consists mainly of opposition to the nuclear arms race and profound cynicism about politics and politicians. In a typical passage, Konrád writes: 'The career of Adolf Hitler was an extreme paradigm of the politician's trade . . . . there lives in every politician more or less of the delirium that was Hitler's demon.'[57]

These ideas were historically grounded in the traditions allegedly characteristic of 'Central Europe'. Timothy Garton Ash has examined the expression of this idea in the work of several writers.[58] He quotes Havel's characterization of the Central European mind as 'skeptical, sober, anti-utopian, understated' and Konrád's description of Central Europe as a 'cultural-political anti-hypothesis'. Geographically, the notion was somewhat problematic. One of its main deficiencies was its implied exclusion of Germany, whose historic links with its Eastern neighbours – expressed not least by the presence throughout the region, until the forced migrations of the immediate post-war period, of a large German-speaking diaspora – would appear to necessitate its being counted part, perhaps the centre, of Central Europe, if the concept is to claim historical accuracy. Historical accuracy, however, has very little to do with it, as Garton Ash makes clear. The idea was a rhetorical response to that of 'Eastern

Europe' – a toponym that was seen as expressing Soviet domination over the region.

It is not implausible to see in the notions of the third way and Central Europe an attempt to put a positive gloss on the fact of Eastern Europe's economic and political backwardness relative to the West. Be that as it may, it is noteworthy that (even though the labels 'Central' and 'East Central Europe' have become fashionable among western analysts) both have somewhat faded from view amid recent events. Their nature as an artifact of the communist period, rather than as an expression of regional traditions or 'genuine history', is thereby implied.

There can, it is clear, be no doubt as to the accuracy of Dawisha's conclusion that 'a fundamental problem always has been manifest in the political culture of these states, in so far as there has never been any consensus between the communist leaders and the people regarding whether or not they are indeed "beyond" their history'.[59] Indeed the dissensus is far more complex than one between elites and populations. This is very far from suggesting the irrelevance of history to East European politics: the contrary is instead suggested. But the manner in which history intrudes on current political developments is not adequately captured by the consonance/dissonance theory. Historical experience does not provide a single tendency to which the liberated polities of Eastern Europe may now return. It is multivalent. We can illustrate this fact at a more specific level with an example from Polish politics of the divergent appeal to history by political actors.

Kristian Gerner has described the use made of the historical symbol of Joseph Piłsudski, Prime Minister and leading progenitor of the independent Polish state of 1918–39 by Solidarity leaders and activists in 1980–81.[60] In his first public appearance as leader of Solidarity, Lech Wałęsa had a portrait of Piłsudski on the wall behind him. In 1981, the anniversary of the Republic's founding on 11 November was marked by a speech given at Piłsudski's tomb in Cracow, and the Solidarity weekly newspaper featured on its front page a facsimile of his decree of 1918 founding the Republic. A shipyard in Gdansk was unofficially renamed after him by its workers. Piłsudski, however, is a highly ambiguous historical symbol. While his positive legacy includes the creation of the Republic and his leadership of the successful war against the Soviet Union in 1920, he was also responsible for the coup of 1926 which brought the brief period of democracy to an end and installed him as leader of an increasingly authoritarian regime. It is therefore as a symbol of the assertion of Polish nationhood against Soviet aggression, and not as a representative of democracy, that Piłsudski most plausibly serves.

At the same time, the virtual military coup of December 1981, which had been presaged by increasing military domination of government, recalls, as Gerner notes, the Piłsudski precedent. Indeed, the latter takeover was justified by Wojciech Jaruzelski in terms of the preservation of Polish national identity. He made this justification explicit and invoked another resonant symbol from the Polish past when, in 1982, he told a Central Committee plenum that, in the Solidarity period, 'The spirit of *Liberum Veto* triumphed, the times of lone wolves returned . . . . The authorities announced that they would not hesitate to use the constitutional measures of defending the state if this were inevitable.'[61] Here Jaruzelski made reference to the collapse of the fragile democracy of the Polish-Lithuanian Republic, which had been paralyzed in its time of greatest danger by the practice whereby a single member of parliament – a 'lone wolf' – could bring its proceedings to a halt. That Russia was one of the partitioning powers which benefited from this paralysis was for Jaruzelski's audience also, presumably, a resonant fact: again, he was implying, national survival was being risked because of an obsession with democratic procedure at the expense of prudential action.

Thus two contending parties claimed to be the representatives of Polish identity, and marshalled highly potent symbols accordingly. Of course, in the end it was Solidarity's appropriation of history that prevailed (though one might speculate that Jaruzelski's was plausible for some of the population, since the external threat was indeed quite palpable). But since both sides were making essentially the same appeal to historical symbolism – the struggle of Poland to maintain or regain statehood – the outcome cannot be explained on the basis of the greater historical accuracy of one claim or the other.

Explanation of political developments in Eastern Europe in terms of political culture within the framework of the consonance/dissonance theory is rendered impossible by such historical multivalence. Its effect on political cultural explanation is illustrated by Paul's attempt to incorporate qualifications of his earlier diagnosis of Czechoslovak interwar politics as 'pluralistic' into the description of political culture itself. His revised opinion is that 'Czechoslovak political culture, in both its Czech and Slovak variants, is both pluralistic and unpluralistic, both democratic and authoritarian', so that 'the predominant character of the political culture is incoherence'.[62] This state of affairs, with all the difficulties it creates for comparative explanation, is not unique to Czechoslovakia, we have argued.

This chapter has looked at a body of political culture literature whose existence but little else has been noticed by writers in the 'mainstream'.

Application of the political culture approach to communist states has offered the possibility of testing the assertion that political culture exerts a 'pull' on rapidly changed institutions or structures – what has been termed the 'consonance/dissonance theory' of political cultural explanation. Confirmation is indeed available for the claim that mass values are not readily changed by government re-education and resocialization efforts. Evidence for this striking failure has often, however, been taken to support the wider claims of political cultural explanation, instead of merely establishing a necessary condition for it. The failure of resocialization plays a role too in the collapse of the communist regimes of Eastern Europe in 1989 and 1990, but again this lends support only to the most minimal of political cultural explanations. Many factors speak against the viability of the consonance/dissonance theory even in this apparently most propitious context: the ambiguity and multivalence of historical experience and the diverse manner in which it has been invoked by political actors, as well as the obvious impact of present circumstances on the way in which history is perceived, revealed as clearly by surveys as by any other method. Communist states therefore appear to offer little help to the attempt to establish political culture as a tool of comparative politics. In the next chapter, that attempt will be examined from a more theoretical perspective.

4 Political Culture and Comparative Explanation

The preceding chapters have attempted to show, by examining in detail some classic attempts at comparative political cultural explanation and the cases to which they have been applied, in what ways political culture falls short of its putative comparative use. The present chapter aims to summarize and reinforce this critique of 'comparative political culture' as a subfield of political science by addressing the same problems at a more theoretical and general level. Apart from exposing more clearly the common threads of the earlier more detailed discussion, this chapter will introduce some further examples of political culture research, and will discuss several existing theoretical critiques of the concept.

CAUSE AND EFFECT

Stated briefly, the comparative use of political culture is to place the concept in a theory which asserts that variations in political culture cause variations in political outcomes, where the latter may take the form of structures (as in the comparative theory of *The Civic Culture*) or events (as in some versions of modernization theory). To be sure, this theory is usually hedged around with acknowledgements of the reciprocal influence of events and structures on political culture, as in Almond's assertion that political culture is 'both an independent and a dependent variable'.[1] But such statements are caveats, if important ones, to the main proposition, that political culture has causal and hence explanatory power.

As we saw in the Introduction, the concept of political culture was a leading token of the 'behavioural revolution' in political science, a revolution, we suggested, whose chief features were aspirations to the status of a science and to the territorial expansion of that science. Several critics have used the first of these aspirations as a basis from which to criticize political culture research as failing to live up to the promise inherent in characterizing political culture as an independent variable. For instance, in a critique of *The Civic Culture*, Brian Barry suggests that, as the 'beginnings of an answer' to the question 'what is the connection between attitudes such as [those described by Almond and Verba] and the existence of democratic politics in a country?',

> We should first need an hypothesis relating the prevalence in a country's population of the 'civic culture' (to a specified extent) with [*sic*] the existence in that country of (a certain amount of) democracy. (The criteria of 'democracy' would, of course, have to be spelt out.) Then we should have to test this hypothesis by seeing whether the two kinds of variable – 'cultural' and 'institutional' – were related in the data in the way required by the hypothesis. And finally, we should have at least to face the question of causality . . . . [E]ven if the relationship does exist, is this because the 'culture' influences the working of the 'institutions', or is it merely that it reflects them?[2]

Mary McAuley, in the course of her critique of Stephen White's study of Russian political culture, poses the question 'what might be the significance of the views expressed in response to surveys?', and gives the answer:

> We could advance some predictive hypotheses whose testing would enable us to see whether they are a critical set in influencing activities. For example, the existence of a particular set of views at time A will lead to a particular pattern of disturbance at time B if official policy offends these views. The testing of such a hypothesis would be very complicated – it would have to be done comparatively and this in turn would engender the cross-cultural problem – but it could be set up now, for the future. It obviously could not be asked of the past.[3]

The mere statement of these putative explanatory programmes emphasizes not just how far existing political culture research has fallen short of the behaviouralist promise, but also how it must fall short. There is an obvious impracticality in the proposals, arising, as Brown has noted, out of the complexity, unpredictability and lack of controllability of events.[4]

Are these critiques too demanding? We might suspect that their status as critiques enables them to seize the methodological high ground, not themselves being burdened by any data. A distinction introduced by Arend Lijphart in 1971, and much cited since then, might be invoked in defence of the theory we are considering.[5] Lijphart locates the comparative method between two methodological poles. At one pole lies the case study method, whose chief deficiency is its lack of contribution to theory-building. At the other are the experimental method and the slightly softer statistical method, deficient, Lijphart thinks, for the difficulty of ensuring experimental control and of collecting adequate amounts of data, given limited resources. Characteristic of the comparative method is the problem of 'many variables, small *N*' – a problem which can readily be seen to obtain in most of our examples of political culture research. Numerous innovations aimed at mitigating this problem have subsequently been made, such as the use of a greater number of cases,[6] focusing on more closely comparable cases (in effect introducing a scientific control), focusing on widely different cases, with a view to highlighting their common elements, and reducing the number of proposed variables.[7]

We will see below that some of these responses have indeed been made in political culture research (Inglehart's work, we can already see, is an example of the first response). But though Lijphart's distinction offers some protection for political culture research against the more extreme of behaviouralist demands, it is not by any means the end of the story. Even under the 'comparative method' so defined, the causal claim to which we alluded at the outset is made; as David Collier in a review of Lijphart's article observes, new accounts of the goals of comparison notwithstanding, assessing hypotheses remains a paramount goal of comparative politics.[8] The viability of this causal claim is what we need to focus attention on.

We can begin to do this by looking at what for our purposes seems to be the aptly-titled article 'A Cause in Search of its Effect, or What Does Political Culture Explain?'[9] Its authors, David Elkins and Richard Simeon, define political culture as 'assumptions about the political world'. They provide a list of such possible assumptions, and discuss various means by which political culture might be measured. They argue that the 'unconscious' or 'taken for granted' quality of political cultural 'assumptions' prohibits their direct measurement, while at the same time making short-term deviation less likely. Therefore the investigative methods they recommend are the study of 'specialized respondents' – politicians, artists, malcontents – and of emigrants and immigrants, as well as the ways in which societies as a whole appear to differ in political cultural terms, and even, on the model of demonstrations of the cultural origins of optical illusions, the carrying out of laboratory experiments to test for the effects of cultural assumptions.[10]

Elkins and Simeon also set out a methodology by which 'cultural explanation' may be compared with 'structural' and 'institutional' explanations of political outcomes. A phenomenon, they argue, has a cultural explanation when, by 'controlling', structural and institutional factors can be ruled out. This procedure identifies the 'culture-bearing unit' for each variable; that is, where the data reveal variations that are not eliminated when structural or institutional factors are controlled, the geographic or ethnic units in which these variations inhere are taken to be 'culture-bearing', or to have distinct cultures that explain the variations. Examples of this procedure are given, based on data drawn from *The Civic Culture*.[11]

Where Elkins and Simeon's account is deficient is in effecting a link between its descriptive and explanatory facets, the definition of political culture and the method for identifying 'culture-bearing units'. No evidence is given to demonstrate that the culture-bearing units, defined through the purely formal method of positing them as the substrate of a variation for which non-cultural explanations have been ruled out, possess distinctive 'political cultures' in the sense derived from the definition and method of investigation. Rather, it is *assumed* that these will overlap; that political cultures, specified as certain sets of political assumptions, will be what formally-specified culture-bearing units actually bear. What they call the 'explanatory' component of their methodology does no more than identify the need for 'cultural' explanation by demonstrating the inadequacy of 'structural' explanations. There is a large gap between this and the description or 'measurement' of political cultural 'assumptions'. Elkins and Simeon's title is, therefore, not an entirely accurate guide to the content of their argument. Not only is political culture, as defined by them, a 'cause in search of an effect', certain effects are also in search of a cause. Far from depicting this longed-for coupling, Elkins and Simeon show cause and effect poignantly passing each other by.

This argument merits such detailed examination because it contains, in microcosm, two essential problems faced by the attempt to develop a comparative theory of political culture: we will term them the problems of the 'retreating cause' and of the 'retreating effect'. In political culture research, we will argue, when investigation begins by specifying the effect, it becomes difficult to discern the cause; and when it begins by specifying the cause, it is hard to discern the effect. These generalizations need to be illustrated with examples.

Elkins and Simeon's recursive method for identifying 'culture-bearing units' is in fact a formal variant of a way of looking at political culture that is quite common, namely treating it as a residual category, an 'explanation' for variations for which no other explanation can be found. The variables with which, in this usage, political culture is in competition are in general more accurately and easily specifiable and measurable. This means that they are more readily controlled, in the scientific sense. To be sure, the variable 'nationality' can be controlled too, but doing so would contradict the whole purpose of gathering cross-national data: to control for nationality is simply to undertake an intra-national, non-comparative investigation. In comparative research, therefore, political culture will typically play a secondary role in the competition between variables. The role becomes not just secondary but residual because of the fact that such research, when it cumulates, tends to discover further socioeconomic or structural factors, pushing political culture further into the background. The concept comes to serve as a place-holder for an anticipated explanation in terms of more easily specified factors, or as Fransisco Moreno has aptly if inelegantly put it, 'A political phenomenon explained on the basis of the cultural forces motivating it is often the same as stating that an explanation for it is not available.'[12]

Even as sophisticated a study of political culture as Inglehart's, Chapter 2 made clear, manifests this problem of the retreating cause. The problem accounts for the 'recessive' nature of the comparative element of the study. Inglehart's account of national differences in life-satisfaction levels, we saw, illustrates this best. The fact that levels of happiness and life satisfaction vary in a stable manner across nations was not so much explained as restated, receiving scanty treatment compared with the 'sociological' theory that 'aspirations adjust to circumstances'. The very term 'political culture', we observed, is reserved in *Culture Shift* for use in such cases, adding to the implication of its residual status.

Another good example of this mode of specifying political culture is found in Geert Hofstede's study, *Culture's Consequences*.[13] His study is not specifically of *political* culture, but his definition of 'culture' as 'the collective programming of the mind which distinguishes the members of one human group from another'[14] suggests an affinity with the comparative studies we have been considering. It differs in that cultural explanation is arrived at not by a progressive exclusion of competing factors in a series of statistical operations but in a sense all at once, by examining an environment in which all the relevant 'controls' are already present; in other words, taking the second of the routes we noted above to be ways of escaping the constraints of 'many variables, small *N*'. Hofstede uses survey methods, but instead of trying to ensure statistical representativeness of a whole population, he selects his respondents only from particular job categories within a certain multinational corporation. He thereby controls not only for general factors such as level of education, but also for highly specific ones such as job description and position in the firm's hierarchy. He assesses responses in four 'dimensions': 'power distance', 'uncertainty avoidance', 'individualism' and 'masculinity'.[15] From statistical analysis of the data he derives a set of 'country clusters' or 'culture areas'.[16]

Despite Hofstede's ambitious-sounding title, his conclusions are very modest, not seeking to go beyond the highly limited scope of his evidence. He argues for the 'cultural relativity' of organizations and the need for a 'cultural' or relativistic approach in organization theory. He makes no argument for the more general relevance of his 'culture areas', and little attempt to characterize these areas other than in the terms provided by his data. Like Elkins and Simeon's 'culture-bearing units', his 'culture areas' are formally or statistically derived. Now these findings are undoubtedly suggestive in the sense that one is tempted to generalize beyond them and speculate, for instance, about the sources of these distinct cultures, or their other implications beyond the operation of a multinational corporation. One might even be tempted to regard political systems themselves as universal structures on the model of Hofstede's corporation, in the manner of David Easton's 'systems theory', and to infer the effect on them of Hofstede's culture areas.[17] But as they stand, Hofstede's findings represent culture purely residually. Thus we cannot assume that findings such as this will necessarily cumulate, giving us a progressively clearer and fuller picture of the political cultures of the world. That Hofstede's areas are 'country clusters', not countries, gives us one indication of this, suggesting that different sets of controls will yield different sets of 'culture-bearing units'. Perhaps Hofstede's corporation is a stimulus that provokes responses that vary at a certain level; other stimuli might provoke a different set of responses. Each new stimulus, if this is true, would represent a new experiment in cultural relativity. The mere juxtaposition of Hofstede's and Inglehart's findings, with their different levels of cultural variation, should alert us against the assumption of cumulation.

A more specific example of the retreating cause is provided in the field of communist studies by John Miller. The variation for which he wants to consider a political cultural explanation is the deviations of Kazakhs and Balts from the norm among Soviet republican nationalities whereby high levels of party membership are correlated with various indicators of socio-economic development. The latter factors having in these deviant cases been ruled out, a speculative explanation would point to 'cultural' factors – the individualism of the Baltic Protestant tradition, the tribal, nomadic traditions of the Kazakhs. But Miller points out that equally plausible 'explanations' could have been adduced had the pattern been reversed – Protestant political quietism, the politically engaged Islamic tradition of *Jihad*. A better explanation relates differential membership levels to different perceptions of interests, on the basis of differing degrees of disadvantage for the titular nationalities in access to sought-after professions. Such an 'index of perceived opportunity' does correlate with the party saturation difference between Kazakhs and Balts. However it fails in the case of a third group, the Uzbeks, who suffer even greater disadvantage in career access than the Kazakhs, but show no corresponding excess of party saturation beyond what the socio-economic criteria would suggest. Miller's explanation for *this* disparity is that the Uzbeks, being, unlike the Kazakhs, a majority in their republic, 'feel relatively relaxed about their position in Uzbekistan and feel no need to compete for their place in it'.[18]

Although this explanation forsakes the concept of individual self-interest, and eliminates some putative structural explanations, it is some way from vindicating comparative political cultural explanation. It focuses, as Miller asserts, on the structural circumstances that help to maintain a certain pattern of values, not on the values themselves. Political culture as an independent cause drops out of contention at an early stage in this procedure owing to the vagueness with which it is specified. The suspicion necessarily arises that it could meet the same fate in many of the other cases in which it has been employed in this residual manner, if they were subject to the same careful examination.

A mode of investigation that might seem to escape the problem of the retreating cause is that which has been termed 'inductive' or 'heuristic'. This approach also begins with the observation of effects that seem to call for a political cultural cause, but it does not arrive at the latter by a process of elimination. It considers the central problem to be what Lucian Pye has called the 'bountifulness' of survey data and the difficulty of showing that attitudes that are revealed in surveys are actually the 'critical' ones in determining the nature of political life.[19] Arguing from the assumption that political culture gives meaning to the political system,[20] Pye suggests that research should proceed by hypothesizing orientations that would provide meaning for a given political system, and then trying to find them. A method similar to this has been used by Bradley Richardson in a study of the political culture of Japan. Richardson's 'inductive approach', as he calls it, 'seeks out the political culture patterns or attitudinal correlatives of actual behaviour in a particular place, and endeavours to link identifiable correlations with socialization processes or historical experience'.[21] Recognizing that this approach requires guidance in targeting 'attitudinal correlatives', Richardson recommends developing hypotheses from extant research.

The problem here, as Miller's discussion brings out clearly, is that hypotheses, as well as attitude survey data, are bountiful. More than one set of values and attitudes might be thought to provide 'meaning' for the observed phenomena: how are we to decide between them? As Glenda Patrick has put it, 'Pye ignores . . . the mode or process for the construction of the model and especially the whole issue of "validating" the model itself.'[22] In fact, writers using this approach usually present only one hypothesized 'meaning', for which evidence is then gathered from the bountiful range available. If more than one alternative were presented, then deciding between them would necessitate a more scientific form of comparative study, with the consequences we are in the course of describing.

The problem of the retreating effect, we suggested, arises when attention is focused first on the supposed cause. What this rather vague statement means is that the investigative effort is stimulated by a perception of some fairly obvious and comprehensive distinctness or individuality. In its most extreme form, this perception leads to the adoption of a holistic definition of culture and hence to interpretivism, an outcome whose ramifications will be discussed in the next two chapters. This outcome, we will now argue, is in fact impossible to avoid; the attempt to avoid it, to continue, in other words, to see political culture as a separable factor in comparative explanation while beginning with an account of cultural differences, is doomed. The more fully cultural differences are specified, the less easy it is to separate them from their putative effect.

In one form this point merely reiterates the debate over the definition of political culture that has been prominent in theoretical discussions of the concept among students of communist societies. Stephen White is the best example of an analyst who wants to claim the advantages in terms of evidential omnivorousness of 'thick description' while nevertheless adhering to the comparative consonance/dissonance theory. This combination is not feasible. Another example, more clearly illustrating the phenomenon of the retreating effect, is based on a study of American political cultures by Daniel Elazar.

Elazar's theory, first set out in his *American Federalism: A View From the States*, describes three subcultures, which he labels 'individualistic', 'moralistic' and 'traditionalistic', and whose geographical distribution he accounts for by migrations of the early colonial groups in which they originated.[23] What is interesting from our present point of view is not that account itself, but a more recent attempt by Ira Sharkansky to 'test' its explanatory potency. Sharkansky constructed the three types as a scale and located each state on the scale using Elazar's account of the types' geographical distribution. He then tested the correlation of this scale with '23 dependent variables that are likely correlates of political culture', for instance 'percentage of voting age population voting for Governor', 'number of state and local government employees per 10,000 population', and 'percentage of citizens' personal income that is paid in taxes to state and local governments'. Fifteen of the twenty-three variables did indeed 'pass a test of statistical significance', and, moreover, many of these relationships were independent of socio-economic variations in personal income and urbanism.[24]

Sharkansky's is a careful statistical analysis using a simple typology of political culture. Its deficiency arises, however, in the initial specification of the typology, rather than in any point of detail. Elazar's three subcultures are not derived from survey data but from observation and interpretation. They describe differences. The problem lies in ensuring that the differences that contributed to the original descriptions are distinct from the ones held to be the 'effects' of these subcultures.[25] Since Elazar's original descriptions were somewhat abstract, we cannot tell exactly what differences contributed to them, which makes it impossible to ensure the necessary separation. The effects retreat from view *as effects* in proportion to the fullness of the description of the cause. No amount of mathematical sophistication can compensate for this deficiency.

That the comparative use of political culture is subject to the dilemma of the retreating cause and the retreating effect has one quite obvious implication. If neither cause nor effect can be given primary attention without the other fading from view, the explanation that the two are not in fact distinct presents itself rather forcefully. We will return to this claim shortly.

CULTURE AND CONTEXT

An experience familiar to all academic students of politics is of the mention of 'political culture' being accompanied by a deprecatory and apologetic phrase such as 'for want of a better term'. Despite many times having been pronounced dead by purportedly comprehensive and conclusive critiques, the concept apparently refuses to lie down. The familiar situation is this: the impact of a common event, a general trend, or a proposed policy is being discussed, and almost ritualistic, but apparently necessary, obeisance to national variation is made via the concept of political culture. It is impossible, it would seem, to avoid the elementary observation that events, trends and policies work out differently in different settings, an observation that, as was pointed out in the Introduction, initially provoked the coinage of the term.

The general appeal of the concept is aptly summarized by Judith Shklar:

Political culture is a notion that serves policy-makers well even if its scientific standing is poor . . . . Political culture as a concept may not explain social conduct, but it can be used by an informed political observer to devise intelligent questions about what the likely and unlikely consequences of political actions will be.[26]

A similar view is expressed by John Miller's suggestion that political culture is more appropriately seen as a teaching aid than as a research tool,[27] and it is indeed likely that a large proportion of uses of the term nowadays are in the introductory chapters of area studies and comparative politics textbooks.

There remains, however, something disconcerting in the claim that a concept whose 'scientific standing is poor' could 'serve policy-makers well'. Policy-makers are, after all, usually confronting much more directly than political scientists the brute facts of causal relations: they are not people who will for long remain vulnerable to the seduction of metaphor or a fashionable-sounding phrase. They are, in fact, a species of engineer. Surely, then, the 'usefulness' to them of the concept of political culture is inconsistent with its poor standing among political scientists. This section will provide an explanation of this puzzling state of affairs.

The dilemma of the retreating cause and the retreating effect can be diagnosed from another perspective as the result of conflict between the two aspirations of behaviouralism, scientific explanation and territorial expansion. The latter aspiration, reaching its maximum fulfilment in the concept of political culture, comes to contradict the former. Political culture was coined as a means of describing an important part of the environment in which political systems operate, namely the attitudinal environment. As a behaviouralistic concept, it was to be construed as a variable. The problem has been that territorial expansion has progressed beyond the point at which it makes sense to regard political culture as a variable, a progression facilitated by the concept of culture itself. If the utility of political culture was suggested by the observation that the practice of politics differs widely across nations, the attempt to limit the concept to one part of the context that accounts for these differences was bound to be somewhat artificial.

When a political scientist labels that which leads to differential outcomes after a common stimulus (event, tendency or policy) the 'political culture', the implications within the behaviouralist framework of so doing are these: that the same *type* of factor or factors, though of course with different *values*, is found across the range of cases, affecting the outcomes in the same types of ways; and that the same types of factor are applicable to the explanation of outcomes across the range of possible stimuli. The tension that is fundamental to political culture is that the idea of culture, in amply and intuitively satisfying the expansionist tendency towards the broadening of coverage, offers itself as a label for the entire context, without these commitments necessarily being met. We must suppose that these connotations of the concept of culture were originally found to be suggestive. But Almond, in 1956, uncorked a genie whose appetite was far too voracious to be held in check by the feeble constraint of his insistence upon the 'certain autonomy' of political culture from the 'general culture'.[28]

'Sensitivity to context' has come to be widely recognized as a virtue in political science and elsewhere since the 1950s. The concept of political culture has been the political scientific manifestation of this virtue. From the point of view of the scientific aspirations of behaviouralism, the dilemma of the retreating cause and the retreating effect casts serious doubt on the usefulness of the concept. But when 'political culture' is recognized as being useful to policy-makers, what is in fact being commended is an undefined 'sensitivity to context'. Similarly, it is helpful to writers of textbooks, and increasingly to journalists, because of its implications of comprehensive difference. No amount of scientific embarrassment is likely to deter the use of such a handy term.

Hofstede's investigation of 'cultural relativity' in a multinational corporation is, of course, pitched at a level that is of the greatest interest to policy-makers. If they seek to impose some stimulus that is closely related to the one Hofstede considers, his findings might be of direct relevance. But even if the stimulus is different, the fact that Hofstede had any findings of cultural relativity at all is significant. It demonstrates the need for 'sensitivity to context', which, at its broadest, involves not the expectation of a specific variation at a specific level, but simply the expectation of *some* variation, and preparedness for it. We suggested above that studies such as Hofstede's do not necessarily cumulate; but if the policy-maker approaches foreign countries and regions in the spirit of conducting a similar experiment to test for cultural relativity, then whether or not the results tally with existing research and thus contribute to a cumulative description of political cultures, the requirement of sensitivity to context will have been met. Thus political culture research may be useful less as a set of findings for the policy-maker than as a model for his or her conduct.

PROBLEMS OF COMPARABILITY

We may conclude this chapter, and our treatment of the comparative use of political culture, by reviewing the various barriers to comparison in terms of political culture that this and preceding chapters have exposed. We will first consider three problems of comparability, which will be labelled the problem of complexity, the problem of salience, and the problem of indexicality, before discussing how these and previously discussed issues relate to the problem of the separation of culture and structure.

The problem of complexity is an exacerbated case of the problem of 'many variables, small N'. It is exhibited by Almond and Verba's *The Civic Culture*, where, as we saw in Chapter 1, the sociological and the comparative uses of political culture are in tension. The sociological use develops a theory of democracy in which many factors, such as levels of citizen and subject competence, a group-forming style of political behaviour, and the notion of 'cycles of involvement', are combined. Not only are many variables involved in this enterprise, but degrees of correlation between some of them are held to be significant, giving rise, in effect, to a second order of variation. We have seen how this sociological theory can be challenged on its own ground, but our point here is that the comparative element of the study provides no refuge from such challenges, since the possibility of useful comparison is eliminated by the complexity of the phenomena to be compared. A theory of democracy such as this is not validated by comparison of the sort undertaken by Almond and Verba; all that is achieved by such comparison is to make clearer the politicocentric relativity of the theory to the American and British cases.

The problem of salience also has some manifestation in the work of Almond and Verba and in other political culture studies that have used their framework. It refers to the fact, to which Moshe Czudnowski has drawn attention, that politics and political objects themselves have varying 'salience' across nations, which means that attitudes towards them cannot be directly compared.[29] In their contribution to *The Civic Culture Revisited*, Ann L. Craig and Wayne A. Cornelius give two examples of this problem in relation to the measurement of Mexican political culture. One is that Almond and Verba's measures of political knowledge are based on questions that in the Mexican context would be somewhat esoteric, owing to the regional nature of political conflict there. Another is that measures of ability to influence political outcomes ignore the fact that, in Mexico, influence is usually directed to the 'rule application' rather than the 'rule making' stage.[30] A point very similar to the latter one has been made in connection with the study of Soviet political culture. Frederick Barghoorn had characterized Soviet political culture as 'subject-participatory', a modification of Almond and Verba's typology designed to draw attention to the combination of low levels of 'subject competence' combined with 'participation directed ultimately from the political center at the top of the [Communist Party] command structure'.[31] Taking issue with this characterization, Wayne DiFranceisco and Zvi Gitelman, on the basis of *émigré* survey evidence, demonstrate the use of informal channels and means of influence, such as the use of connections and bribery. Local rather than state agencies were seen by the respondents as being more responsive to these techniques, again marking the inappropriateness of the Almondian categories.[32] Outside the Almond and Verba framework, Richardson's 'inductive method' encounters the same problem. Regarding one of the attitudinal dimensions he examines he notices that 'Ambivalence may have quite different consequences in different countries as a result of different backgrounds and varying intensities in both idealism and cynicism that may not be reflected in our measures.'[33]

Czudnowski's response to the problem of salience is to formulate what he calls an 'index of salience' by which attitudes towards political objects may be weighted according to the salience of these objects. The index would thus provide a 'filter variable' enabling comparison to proceed.[34] Such proposals, apart from applying the term 'variable' to categories that are clearly not variables, and thus unjustly appropriating the term's scientific aura, overlook the depth of the problem.[35]

Czudnowski's quantitative talk of 'weighting', in particular, assumes that differences of salience are merely differences of degree, whereas we have seen that they can be qualitative, and involve differences of the *meaning* of notions such as 'participation'. It is true however that, when such differences have been identified, comparison can proceed at a higher level, with 'levels' of participation being replaced by 'forms' of participation, for instance. Indeed, Inglehart's theory of postmaterialism, for one, very much depends on such distinctions being made. But it is not true that the mere recognition of the problem of salience enables it to be overcome simply by some kind of statistical adjustment. A theory of which levels of participation counted as an independent variable would have different explanatory targets than one in which forms of participation had this role; for the latter would not simply be a more quantitatively accurate version of the former.

The problem of indexicality is a particularly severe form of the problem of salience. In philosophical logic, 'indexicality' refers to phrases such as 'my hat', whose denotation is indexed to the utterer, and possibly to the time and place of utterance also. Indexical responses to questions clearly necessitate, on the part of the inquirer, an act of contextualization if they are to be understood. We will use the term 'indexicality' in a somewhat extended sense, to refer to responses that require a degree of contextual interpretation that threatens their comparability. For instance, a response that indicated a high level of participation in politics would, as we just saw, need to be contextualized in order to make it comparable; we would need to know whether the decision-making stage or the implementation stage was the more usual target for participation in the context we were studying. But suppose that response to a question refers to a specific event or figure from, say, Mexican history. Then the problem becomes one of indexicality. An even larger, potentially prohibitively large, amount of interpretation is necessary in order to render such responses comparable.

Because of the difficulties presented by indexical responses, for comparative purposes questions are usually phrased in such a way as to avoid them. But by the same token, indexical responses can yield the greatest insight into the peculiarities of the context to which they refer, that is, to which they are indexed. A good example from the research that we have looked at is provided by Brown and Wightman's analysis of Czechoslovak political culture. The surveys on which Brown and Wightman drew, on 'the relation of Czechs and Slovaks to their history', immediately suggest indexicality. One of their key findings, that of Thomas Masaryk's ranking as the most esteemed figure from Czech history (among Czechs) is used to demonstrate not only the failure of the government's attempt to eliminate him from history, but also the prevalence, in 1968, of 'social democratic' values.[36] With this claim some degree of comparability is achieved, but of course arriving at it requires a large interpretive effort; one not, as we saw in Chapter 3, invulnerable to challenge.

'Indexical' measures of political culture, therefore, provide the richest information but *ipso facto* require the greatest amount of interpretation and are most subject to challenge. They provide a more substantive characterization of political culture than that yielded by more rigorously comparative methods, which, we saw, in specifying political culture formally lead to the problem of the retreating cause. Thus we find, even in *The Civic Culture* and *Culture Shift*, repeated examples of *ad hoc* historical, and hence indexical, explanations being inserted to account for otherwise unaccounted-for national variations: an attempt to give substance to formally-derived national political cultures. Such interpolations, whether concerning the heritage of the Mexican revolution or the impact on Germany of defeat in the Second World War (to give examples from each of these studies)[37] are, by virtue of their indexicality, not testable comparatively.

Indexical descriptions or measurements of political culture, moreover, bring to our attention the issue of the contestability of history and historical symbolism, discussed in Chapter 3. This is an issue of a quite different type to the problems of comparability that we have been discussing in this section. It is not a methodological problem, but an ontological one.

As such, it is a further manifestation of the fundamental issue unearthed in this chapter: that of the separation of political culture from its supposed explanandum.

By way of elucidating how political culture can be both a dependent and an independent variable, Stephen White draws an analogy which is of some interest here. The relationship between political culture and political structure, he suggests, parallels that within Marxist theory between the categories of superstructure and base.[38] This analogy is, in fact, more apt than he realizes, when we take into account the debate in Marxist theory that the latter distinction has provoked. A contribution to that debate by Raymond Williams throws light on our current topic. In Marxism, the idea of temporal lag has been invoked in the explanation of the relationship between superstructure and base, in particular the imperfect correlation between them, just as cultural lag has been invoked in political culture research. But Williams asserts that 'superstructure' was a metaphor intended by Marx to express relation, not separation, and that subsequent usage which emphasized separation was indeed attacked by him. What is damaging about this translation of analytic categories into substantive descriptions, in Williams's view, is that it makes the categories seem fixed, concealing their own internal contradictions.[39]

In just the same way, the separation of culture and structure simplifies the relationship between them and underemphasizes internal contradictions within each. The hypothesis of cultural lag, for instance, suggests that the whole of political culture, originally a reflection of the whole of structure, is left behind when the structure shifts, changing only at a slower pace. But the East European examples of the reconstruction of indexical values, and the multivalence of 'historical experience' that we saw to be revealed by its use by contending political actors, suggest both a more dynamic relationship between culture and structure and one complicated by the cleavages within each. Historical experience and the attitudes and values associated with it do not, it appears from these examples, merely 'survive' *en bloc*; they are recreated to serve specific purposes in political conflict. That a historical fact has a certain meaning in current politics does not mean either that all contemporaneous historical facts are equally well remembered (which no one actually claims, although the hypothesis of cultural lag would imply it) or that only one meaning can or did attach to it.

Evidence that culture and its 'effects' cannot easily be disentangled comes also from the sociological use of political culture that we have been examining in tandem with the comparative one, especially from its critical variant. In the latter, as we saw, cleavages in both culture and society are emphasized in several different ways. In some views the utility of cultural consistency for the internal cohesion of the political elite is asserted; in others, the nature of the civic culture as a 'mystification' of elite hegemony. What these views have in common, whether or not they are mutually consistent, is a refusal to represent political culture as separable from political structure.

For reasons presented in this chapter, the comparative use of political culture is likely to continue, and indeed to predominate, if not always in the most scientific form, despite the inevitable difficulties it encounters. The ultimate source of these difficulties is the reification of the analytic distinction between culture and structure, which diverts attention from the relationship between the two. So far, however, we have seen only the symptoms of that relationship, and have diagnosed them only as problems for the comparative use. In the following chapters, a more positive view will be adopted, offering pointers and not just warning signs to future political culture research. We will argue that the concept of political culture contains the potential to transcend the dichotomy of culture and social structure, a dichotomy which we have hitherto presented only as the source of many of the deficiencies of existing uses of the concept. Arriving at that conclusion will necessitate turning our attention more directly to the interpretive use of political culture, and particularly to what was termed in the Introduction its idealist tendency and its phenomenological potential.

5 Political Culture and Stalinism

If a large variety of ways of operationalizing the concept of political culture is found within the behaviouralist idiom, the same is all the more true within interpretivism. While the stringent scientific standards of behaviouralism are not always adhered to in political culture research, at least standards exist. Interpretivism begins, as we saw in the Introduction, by denying the need for such standards. Accordingly, a wide range of uses of political culture could be marshalled as examples of interpretivism, from historiography as well as political science. But rather than beginning with a broad survey, we will follow a procedure similar to that adopted in earlier chapters, of looking in detail at a representative example. In this case, however, we need to go further; we will examine a use of political culture that to some extent has to be inferred and constructed from a number of sources. The initial and main source for this use is Robert C. Tucker's political cultural interpretation of Stalinism. However, the use we will develop and assess goes beyond Tucker's in some ways and limits it in others. Our purpose in so doing is twofold: to present interpretive political culture research in its most persuasive light, and to distinguish it clearly from the hybrid uses with which, the Introduction argued, it is often intertwined, as it is in Tucker's work. Although vulnerable to criticism, the interpretive use that we will develop is, therefore, far from being a straw man.

One respect in which we will limit Tucker's analysis is to exclude his explicit and implicit commitments to the project of comparison. He has, for one thing, correctly observed that the activity of theorizing itself has comparative implications.[1] For another, in one of his first contributions to this field he observed that the typical use of the concept of political culture had been comparative, and far from differing from that precedent, suggested the formulation of the idea of 'Soviet political culture' as a 'paradigm concept' and the tracing of the 'diffusion' of this 'donor political culture' to 'receiving political cultures'.[2] We will also see that his analysis sometimes includes implicit comparative claims. But our interest in Tucker is in his elaboration of an approach to political culture which denies that it is an isolatable phenomenon and instead regards it as a context for interpretation. In common with many of those who have used political culture as an interpretive tool, Tucker declares a debt to Clifford Geertz and his method of 'thick description'. Tucker, in turn, has been widely cited by political culture researchers in support of a 'comprehensive' definition of the term. His own understanding of the implications of this use would appear to prohibit the project of comparative explanation:

> Might not the central importance of a concept like that of political culture be that it assists us to take our bearings in the study of the political life of a society, to focus on what is happening or not happening, to describe and analyse and order many significant data, and to raise fruitful questions for thought and research – without explaining anything?[3]

There is, of course, a quite conventional meaning of 'explanation' that would see it as tantamount to 'description, analysis and ordering of data'. What Tucker must have in mind is the sort of explanation using political culture that has been criticized in previous chapters; explanation in which political culture appears as a *variable*. Just what sort of explanation remains possible when this has been ruled out will be exemplified in the following discussion and elaborated in succeeding chapters.

THE 'PREFIGURATION' OF STALINIST POLITICAL CULTURE

In the same article in which he endorses Geertz, Tucker makes use of another anthropologist, Ralph Linton, and his distinction between 'ideal' and 'real' culture. The notion of an 'ideal', we will see, is of central importance to Tucker's analysis. However, the label, rather than Linton's specific definition of it, is what Tucker borrows. Linton's 'ideal culture' referred to 'consensus of opinion on the part of society's members about how people *should* behave in particular situations', as opposed to their real behaviour.[4] Utilizing the concept in this form would of course necessitate finding evidence about the ideals held by society's members – but this is just what is impossible for most of the period Tucker proceeds to discuss. A major theme of *our* discussion, therefore, will be what sense of 'ideal' Tucker has in mind, and what its implications are.

Tucker's description of communist political culture begins with an analysis of Lenin's revolutionary writing. He construes Lenin's Bolshevism as a 'culture in the making', arguing that Lenin's *What Is To Be Done?*

(1905) was not simply a treatise on party organization, as it has usually been considered, but in fact expressed 'an implicit design for the new socio-political world, the party-state political culture'.[5] Lenin's 1917 *State and Revolution* asserted: '*only* socialism will be the beginning of a rapid, genuine, truly forward movement, embracing first the *majority* and then the whole of the population, in all spheres of public and private life'.[6] Lenin, according to Tucker, 'was putting into words the central, sustaining myth of Soviet society, laying the foundation of Soviet Communism as a culture. In the Leninist canon, to be a Soviet citizen was to be a member of a goal-oriented all-Russian collective of builders of socialism and communism.'[7] Thus communist revolutions are 'cultural revolutions', 'attempted transformations of national cultures';[8] in this respect they differ from coups or palace revolutions.[9] Another idea central to Tucker's analysis of Leninism is that of a 'movement'. A movement is, for its participants, a 'culture', consisting of 'organizational structure, doctrine, ideology, ritual, on occasion uniforms and insignia'.[10] Also of importance is the idea of a 'sustaining myth', 'a notion or concept of that society as a common enterprise'.[11] 'In a certain sense the myth *is* the society; or to put it otherwise, the society has its real existence in its members' minds.'[12]

Tucker argues that it was the comprehensiveness of Lenin's aspiration to cultural revolution that placed him in opposition to the more class-based position of Bolsheviks such as Alexander Bogdanov and Anatoly Lunacharsky.[13] Bogdanov emphasized the necessity and possibility of radical change in the ideological or cultural superstructure (he used the terms 'spiritual culture' and 'ideology' interchangeably). According to Zenovia Sochor, he 'expressed dismay at the "startling tenacity" of ideological forms that had long since lost their meaning in the life of society'.[14] Lunacharsky's organization of radical artists, Proletkult, announced similarly:

> In questions of culture we are *immediate socialists*. We affirm that the proletariat must now, immediately, create for itself *socialist forms of thought, feeling, and daily life*, independent of the relations and combinations of political forces. And in that creation, *political* allies – the peasantry and the petty bourgeois poor – cannot and should not control its work.[15]

Several scholars have drawn the contrast between Lenin and these opponents in terms of pragmatism *versus* radicalism.[16] Lenin's pragmatism interacts with what Alfred Meyer diagnoses as 'a tendency in Marxist usage to endow the term "culture" with a meaning of achievement or culturation reminiscent of the use which the Enlightenment made of it'.[17] Thus, Meyer asserts, 'The "culture" Lenin had in mind when he preached the cultural revolution entailed technological skills, political maturity, and other aspects of *westernization*.' Furthermore, 'The adjective "uncultured" was . . . used very often to characterize the rough-shod methods of Soviet and party bureaucracy, its authoritarian degeneration and its corrupt abuses.' In 1927, *Pravda* was using the idea of cultural revolution in this sense as a *critique*:

Industrialization – our general course – is unthinkable without rationalization. But rationalization, in its turn, is unthinkable without a raising of the cultural level: both the cultural level of 'cadres' and the cultural level of the masses. The demand to raise the cultural level of the worker-peasant masses, the demand to carry out a broad and profound '*cultural revolution*' in the country is evident: it is now really 'in the air'.[18]

But whether the emphasis is placed on the unorthodox non-class comprehensiveness of Lenin's proposed cultural revolution, or on its relative pragmatism, it is clear that at the time of these debates cultural revolution remains just an idea in the minds of political elites, not an actual social process. This implicit elite-level focus is maintained in Tucker's account of the events of the 1920s. He writes of 'weighty testimony' that 'the militarist, voluntarist political culture and mystique of War Communism lived on [through the NEP period] among many Communists'.[19] Other writers, too, have stressed the cultural impact of the civil war and War Communism on the political elite. Jonathan Adelman refers to the isolation of the Bolsheviks, to their lack of national appeal (in contrast with the Chinese communists who were allied with the largest social class, the peasantry), and to the consequent greater role of the secret police.[20] Sheila Fitzpatrick has referred to the increasing importance to the Bolsheviks of their Russian identity through the Civil War in general and the Polish campaign of 1920 in particular, although she qualifies the impact of the events themselves by noting their consonance with existing Bolshevik principles, concluding that the Bolsheviks 'had the formative experience they were looking for in the Civil War'.[21]

The NEP period is regarded by Tucker as a culture in its own right,[22] and a model of gradualist reform that was available to Gorbachev and his supporters.[23] However, it is an ambiguous model, as is attested to by Stephen Cohen's assertion that 'The atmosphere of relaxation fostered in the country by NEP triggered an opposite course inside the party'

– an 'uncertain economic policy' was concurrent with 'an increasingly authoritarian, bureaucratic pattern of decisionmaking'.[24] At the same time, Tucker asserts, the 1920s saw the 'breakdown of revolutionary culture', post-Lenin disputes being best seen as 'divergent offshoots of Lenin's Bolshevism as a culture'.[25] Here we should pause again to ask what role the idea of 'culture' is playing. It appears, once more, as if the debates Tucker is referring to are debates over what *ideal* should be asserted. So his use of the term 'culture' shades over the distinction between real and ideal. Moreover, if the NEP was short-lived, anomalous and ambiguous, does it even merit the denomination 'model', let alone 'culture'? Does the interpretive use of political culture allow for a distinction between the two? These questions will recur.

THE 'REALIZATION' OF STALINIST POLITICAL CULTURE

It is in the period after Stalin's consolidation of power in the late 1920s that the comprehensive social movement Tucker sees as having been prefigured in Leninism comes into existence. In Tucker's analysis, the collectivization of agriculture, the drive for industrialization under the five-year plans, and Stalin's attack, in the late 1930s, on the Party itself, are aspects of the 'society in movement'. To avoid confusion, it should be noted that in recent scholarship the label 'cultural revolution' has tended to be restricted to the period 1928–31. Largely under the influence of Sheila Fitzpatrick, the outbreak in that period of radicalism in academia and of attacks on 'bourgeois specialists' (the trial of several such in 1928 – the 'Shakhty trial' – was the trigger of this outbreak) has come to be seen as a 'class war' in which a new generation of radical Bolsheviks displaced the residue of the old regime whose participation Lenin had deemed vital to the success of the revolution. The ideas put forward in this ferment similarly reflected the radicalism of Bogdanov and Proletkult. There was talk of abolishing academia itself and of the merger of town and country, education and industry (Fitzpatrick writes that 'these predictions were a kind of running commentary on contemporary processes of institutional disintegration and social flux'),[26] and a proletarianization and politicization of education, including the appearance of the idea of the 'withering away of the school'.[27] In law faculties, Pashukanis's critique of law as a regulator of commodity exchange which would wither away under socialism became prominent, and opponents were purged (as was Pashukanis himself, more conclusively, in the authoritarian reaction of the 1930s).[28]

Construing the phenomenon of cultural revolution mainly in terms of this 'class war' and as an instance of rapid 'upward mobility', in Fitzpatrick's phrase,[29] would imply that when its 'excesses' were criticized by Stalin in 1931, leading to an abrupt cessation of the activity of radicals, some kind of normal, non-revolutionary condition was restored. That would be to take the condition of academia and the activities of intellectuals as representative of society at large, and also to construe 'radicalism' as the preserve of left-wing Bolsheviks. But since 1929, when collectivization and the First Five-Year Plan got under way, Soviet society had been convulsed across its entire spectrum, and it would continue to be (not exempting intellectuals and academics) after the 'cultural revolution' narrowly defined had been called off, the convulsion reaching into the upper levels of the Party itself by the time of the 'Great Purge'.

In this broader, more Tuckerite, sense, the Stalinist cultural revolution was characterized, in the countryside, by the elimination of the wealthier peasants and by the impoverishment of the remainder, especially, though not exclusively, the uncollectivized *edinolichniki* (individual peasant farmers), through coerced procurement and punitive taxation. 'Impoverishment' could result in starvation and death, or migration to the cities. By 1933 peasants had been denied mobility by the internal passport system. Influx into the cities up to 1933 resulted in their 'ruralization', reflected in high labour turnover and low levels of discipline, themselves provoking further harsh responses from the authorities.[30] Conditions in the cities were economically severe, and in the workplace the institution of *edinonachalie* (one-man management) gave managers autocratic powers in the enforcement of discipline. The initial, already implausible, targets of the First Five-Year Plan (1928–32) – which included increases of 250 per cent in industrial and 150 per cent in agricultural production[31] – were repeatedly and substantially revised upwards: the Plan, Moshe Lewin has said, was a plan in name only, in reality being an agglomeration of implausible exhortations, falsifications and *ad hoc* responses to failure.[32] Throughout society, new forms of hierarchy were created or imposed, having (as Fitzpatrick claims) a purely Stalinist, and neither Bolshevik nor traditional character.[33] The scale of repression and terror, affecting the peasantry, workers and the party and non-party intelligentsia, was also novel, as were the tactics and technologies that facilitated it.

In the realm of the arts and sciences, following the 'cultural revolution' of 1928–31, a more stable period set in; but that revolution had facilitated the extension of central control, and the stability was of a new type. In science, fundamental assumptions were made to conform to the political emphasis on rapid and comprehensive transformation, amounting, as Tucker puts it, to the 'projection of totalitarianism upon nature'.[34] Many tokens of this projection can be found, for example the supersession of Darwinism by Michurinism (a doctrine that posited the adaptation of the individual organism to its environment in place of adaptation by natural selection) in genetics,[35] and the shift to an emphasis on organic disorders and the transition to Pavlovianism (again implying the malleability of individuals) in psychology.[36]

'Culture as myth', Robert Williams writes of the avant-gardism of early post-revolutionary Bolshevism, 'sought to transcend reality; under Stalin culture as science sought to transform it entirely.'[37] But myth was, in fact, a salient feature of Stalinist politics also. In the doctrine of 'socialist realism', promulgated in 1934, we can observe a further manifestation of the Stalinist claim to totality. Max Hayward writes that the common denominator of socialist realist canonical works was

> their authors' attitude to the historical process. It did not matter whether they were Marxist, or even whether they wrote from inner conviction (some probably did not), as long as they presented the course of events and the development of society in such a way as to lead the reader to conclude that ultimate victory was certain.[38]

Similarly, Katerina Clark argues that the central theme of socialist realism in literature, underlying its 'biographical master plot' of heroic victory against various forms of adversity, is the struggle between consciousness and spontaneity. Through consciousness, often acquired from a mentor, the hero is able to overcome the 'elemental', the spontaneous, which is represented in numerous ways, for instance by the forces of nature or by natural symbols, or by ignorance, backwardness and other politically undesirable phenomena. Additional, secondary, themes include ritual sacrifice, both of the hero himself and of the personal, non-heroic aspects of his life, the idea of society as a family, and (part of the developing cult of personality) the appearance in the role of mentor of Stalin.[39] The *form* of the socialist realist novel was also distinctive. Clark relies on Bakhtin's theory of the distinctness of the novel and epic forms of literature, and identifies socialist realism as containing a preponderance of epic elements.[40] As such, the genre is distinguished by the absence of self-consciousness (not to be confused with political consciousness), an underlying heroic sense of 'Great Time' to be compared with the present 'profane time' and, in its fully developed state, by its complete resolution and lack of doubt and by the hagiographic treatment of its heroes.

Literature, and the arts in general, thus provided through socialist realism a mythic rendering of the movement towards communism that was actually taking place. Concomitantly, real political events had an obviously heroic quality. Moreover, the sense of 'closure' of Stalinist politics, reinforced by its co-option of science and indeed historiography (through a degraded Marxist historical materialism according to which Soviet communism was seen as the end point of world history), recalls Bakhtin's distinction of the epic and the novel. Stalin's appearance as a character in many socialist realist novels is significant in this respect. No doubt it contributed to the Stalinist cult of personality, but the cult, as Graeme Gill has argued, served not just to glorify Stalin but as a direct channel of communication and authority from the leadership to lower administrative strata, in a situation where normal, hierarchical channels would have been overwhelmed.[41] Thus along with the politicization of myth marked by Stalin's appearance as mentor in socialist realist novels, there occurred the mythicization of politics: mass mobilization was effected not just through conventional political means but also through mythic representations.

But although the Stalin period appears to offer support for Tucker's broad conception of cultural revolution, in his writings on Stalinist politics several new factors are introduced that complicate the political cultural account Tucker is offering. One of these is his assertion of continuity between Tsarist and Stalinist political practice. He sees Stalinism as a combination of the 'culture' of the Bolsheviks, including Lenin's ambition to absorb the whole of society into a movement and the 'Bolshevik *mores* of War Communism', with the Stalinist elements of construction and state building, themselves having precedents in the Tsarist period. Tucker argues that the first phase of Stalinism, the frenetic period of the First Five-Year Plan, served to absorb the peasantry (through collectivization) and the proletariat (though rapid expansion of industry) into the state's constructive purposes; and that the second phase, of which the Great Purge of 1937–38 was a novel element, extended this process of the 'binding of society to the state' to groups closer to the centre: the intelligentsia, and the party itself.[42] Thus, 'the Stalinist revolution of 1929–39 yielded an amalgamated Stalinist Soviet culture that, paradoxically, involved at once the full-scale Sovietization of Russian society *and* the Russification of Soviet culture'.[43]

Tucker's assertion of continuity between Tsarist and Soviet politics is one of many such assertions, not all of them compatible or equally plausible. Stephen White, for instance, despite asserting continuity, largely ignores Stalinism,[44] while Edward Keenan's thesis is that the true nature of pre-revolutionary political culture was oligarchic rule, which was 'destabilized' by the process of industrialization, making Stalinism part of an 'aberrant' period: 'Stalin's brief disturbance of that balance may be considered a vestige of the period of turbulence'.[45] Both views clearly contradict Tucker's claim that Stalinism represents continuity.[46]

The usual basis for a claim of cultural continuity such as Tucker's and its competitors, as we saw in Chapter 2, is the idea of cultural lag. But this notion requires an analytic separation of culture and structure, which Tucker in his theoretical preamble was careful to avoid. Perhaps there remains in Tucker's account an implicit acceptance of the idea of cultural lag, and if so his account is vulnerable to some criticisms that have been made in previous chapters. However, the only mechanism of cultural continuity about which he is explicit provides another of the distinctive features of Tucker's account: the role of Stalin himself.

Tucker attempts to render an emphasis on Stalin's personality compatible with his political cultural approach by drawing on the work of the 'culture and personality' school of anthropology, by which cultural and personal explanations may supposedly be assimilated. Whatever the fate within anthropology of this now rather outdated perspective, its introduction by Tucker is problematic. On the basis of Stalin's political 'coming of age' in the period of War Communism,[47] Tucker argues that his personality was the mechanism by which its 'Bolshevik *mores*' were combined with a Tsarist heritage of state building with which Stalin identified himself.[48] This emphasis on personality, an unsurprising one from Stalin's biographer,[49] contains highly dubious assumptions. One is contained in the idea of 'coming of age'. Tucker does not provide any justification for its use from psychology, and in view of the brevity of the period involved (three years, when Stalin was aged 38–41), it would be surprising if any could be found. An alternative justification might be that War Communism was the kind of experience that would *bring about* a coming of age. This claim encounters the objection that the other leading Bolsheviks do not seem to have been similarly affected (despite their similarity of age), as the debates of the 1920s show. Although Stalin's personal role in the politics that go under his name clearly should not be downplayed, Tucker's desire to account for this role in terms of a somewhat underdeveloped psychological theory merely exposes his argument to obvious counter-examples. Therefore, this part of Tucker's argument also needs to be set aside if we are to focus on his interpretive use of political culture – his attempt to provide a 'thick description' of Stalinist politics.

It is, of course, a somewhat ungenerous procedure to knock away from the part of Tucker's argument we are most interested in, and will shortly proceed to criticize, the props of his continuity and biographical claims. But these, we have argued, are unsound props; and in any case we do not have to follow Tucker's assimilation of what in fact are a number of quite distinct arguments. On the contrary, for the purpose of analysis it is necessary that we do the opposite. We can, moreover, offer some compensation by way of reinforcement of Tucker's argument that Stalinism marked the realization of the Leninist ambition to incorporate the whole of society into a single movement. This reinforcement takes the form of pointing out the ways in which Tucker's analysis is consistent with others'. It is, firstly, consistent with the theory of totalitarianism advanced by Hannah Arendt. For Arendt, the idea of a 'movement' was also of central importance:

> a movement . . . can have only a direction, and . . . any form of legal or governmental structure can only be a handicap to a movement which is being propelled with increasing speed in a certain direction . . . . [I]t is not accurate to say that the movement, after its seizure of power, founds a multiplicity of principalities in whose realm each little leader is free to do as he pleases and to imitate the big leader at the top . . . . The direct dependence was real and the intervening hierarchy, certainly of social importance, was an ostensible, spurious imitation of an authoritarian state.[50]

For Arendt, therefore, the idea of a movement leads to a distinctive view of the resulting organizational form, which is in fact a form of permanent *dis*organization. This view is echoed by T. H. Rigby, who argues that the Stalinist political system had an 'organic mode of operation' which differed from the 'classical bureaucratic model' in featuring parallel hierarchies and the blurring of roles, the irrationality and inconsistency of demands and the salience of mobilizational methods. In such a situation, politics becomes 'crypto-politics', masquerading as the performance of assigned roles. Where a system is operating 'organically', Rigby asserts, its 'organizational culture' can become crucial to successful performance, with, in this case, the construction of communism in the role of all-embracing 'basic' goal.[51]

These phenomena, however, manifest themselves only within the administrative mechanism. So far as society as a whole is concerned, Arendt's portrayal makes use of the idea of 'atomization', a precondition of the incorporation of society into a movement. She argues that 'totalitarian movements are mass organizations of atomized, isolated individuals',[52] and a 'mass' can only be created from 'a highly atomized society whose competitive structure and concomitant loneliness of the individual has been held in check only through membership in a class'.[53] Disorder is thus exactly what the imposition of totalitarian rule demands and creates:

The totalitarian ruler must, at any price, prevent normalization from reaching the point where a new way of life could develop . . . . [otherwise] totalitarianism would lose its 'total' quality and become subject to the law of nations, according to which each possesses a specific territory, people, and historical tradition which relates it to other nations – a plurality which *ipso facto* refutes every contention that any specific form of government is absolutely valid.[54]

This passage indicates Arendt's conviction that totalitarianism is not only novel but necessarily cuts itself off from tradition, a view that is clearly at odds with Tucker's claim of continuity between Tsarism and Stalinism. Her view, at the same time, closely parallels Tucker's claim of the 'binding' of successive layers of society to the Stalinist state. Moreover, Arendt's idea of 'atomization' receives some apparent support from observations such as Lewin's that the chaotic circumstances of the First Five-Year Plan created a 'quicksand society', and Daniel Brower's that 'In conditions of disorder, the meaning that individuals give to power relations, to notions of truth and good, to their very identity, can change rapidly and substantially.'[55]

Thus, by bringing to bear other writings on totalitarianism and on the social history of Stalinism, Tucker's perspective on 'cultural revolution' may be amplified and refined. The link between social historical observations of chaos and Tucker's 'binding' is Arendt's claim that the very prevalence of chaos *exposes* society to incorporation into a single movement destined for a single all-embracing goal. In Tucker's terminology, the destruction of regularity enables the ideal culture outlined by Lenin to become real. Or, as Geoff Eley has put it,

the *aspiration* was in itself fundamentally important, because it decisively ordered the public and private environment by certain repressive principles of conformity and mobilized 'consent'. To neglect this overall context – not just the coercive state, but the *political culture* of Stalinism – is to discard the baby of analysis with the bathwater of the [totalitarian] model.[56]

Thus our amplified version of Tucker's political-cultural description portrays the induction under Stalin of the entire society into a movement whose chief characteristic (contrary to some versions of totalitarian theory) was its direction rather than its structure. It argues that induction was achieved, not only at massive cost, but *through* massive cost, to society. Atomization and disorganization left individuals open to the assertion of the total claim, to co-option into a social movement whose operating principles were rationalized by science and displayed as myth. Putting it another way, the dichotomy of real and ideal was transcended through chaos. A cultural revolution in the full sense that Tucker sees prefigured in Leninism was achieved.

AGAINST IDEALISM

Since we have arrived at the political-cultural interpretation of Stalinism just presented by abstracting somewhat from Tucker's analysis, it is worth making clear where its appeal lies. Tucker, we have seen, essentially makes two arguments in favour of seeing Stalinism as a culture. One is an argument in terms of continuity or revival of culture, mediated through Stalin's personality. The other places emphasis on the idea of cultural revolution, and draws attention to the comprehensiveness of both the aims of that revolution and its implementation under Stalin. The two arguments are not entirely compatible, in that the second has implications of novelty that sit uncomfortably with the first. While this is a problem for Tucker, for the present analysis it is less significant because we have chosen to focus on the second argument. The weaknesses of the first have already been described. The strength of the second, more consistently interpretive, argument is its integrative power. By integrating the manifold ways in which and massive extent to which Stalinism penetrated society, the interpretation offers us what appears to be an enriched understanding of the phenomenon.

Michael Waller has argued that while Tsarist ideology may be termed a 'culture', because of a close connection between it and 'social memory', Soviet ideology, as a 'project ideology', is merely imposed on society and is unrelated to 'social memory': 'the *results* are susceptible to discussion in terms of culture. For the *programmes* we dispose of another term that allows us to preserve the distinction, and that term is ideology.' [57] Putting aside the fact that one of Tucker's two arguments does assert a connection between Stalinism and 'social memory', we can see that in light of the interpretation we have presented, Waller's labels 'ideology' and 'programme' seem misleadingly thin. They lack the descriptive richness of the idea of Stalinist political culture, into which can be incorporated the complex combination of organizational form and doctrine, scientific rationalization and artistic mythicization to which Tucker and others have alerted us.

But the 'richness' of a description is a measure not just of the breadth of its content. It is a measure also of our own response as analysts. Once this important point is acknowledged, we can separate out an important question. To be sure, the political-cultural interpretation of Stalinism as the realization of Lenin's cultural revolution is rich: it is thought-provoking, it integrates many phenomena, and it seems to bring us as observers more closely in touch with Stalinism in all its enormity. But is it true? Was the Leninist ideal realized: did an ideal culture become a real one? Clearly, in one sense, the ideal was realized: the 'total claim' was asserted against the whole of society, and the whole of society was mobilized by it. But is this the same as showing that the above description is a description of the *political culture* of the Soviet Union in the Stalin period? Was the meaning and effect of these comprehensive and radical exhortations really to absorb the members of society into a single movement? Is this description meaningful for the participants, or only for the political or historical analyst? To suppose that only the latter is necessary would mean that no further evidence is required. But if the former, then it is noticeable that the evidence we have looked at so far is skewed somewhat towards the agents of mobilization rather than its subjects. We have plenty of information about the nature of the total claim, its institutional setting, and its extension into the realm of the arts and sciences. We have information about its objective effect on society at large. But for its subjective effect – the question of the *meaning* of its assertion – we need to depend on a theory such as Arendt's, that chaos and atomization in society led to incorporation of the mass of the population. There is no real evidence about the response of the masses. Despite the superiority of Arendt's theory of totalitarianism over others in its more realistic depiction of organizational chaos, in its analysis of the response of the population it is equally subject to a criticism that Daniel Bell has expressed thus: 'From such heights the terrain of politics, its ridges and gullies, become flattened and the weary foot-traveler finds few guides to concrete problems.'[58] We are, however, in a position to take the perspective of the foot traveller, thanks to a recent piece of political ethnography.[59] It is a perspective that entails considerable modification of the description we have been considering.

Vladimir Andrle provides an account which suggests the existence of islands of regularity and normality within the chaotic setting of Stalinism. Drawing on ethnographic studies carried out in the 1940s and 1970s in a factory in Chicago for his conceptual framework, and on official Soviet writings on factory organization as well as material such as remuneration claims submitted by workers for his evidence, Andrle argues that, despite the chaotic setting, local 'shopfloor culture' emerged in factories. It involved the subjective experience of work, 'local knowledge' and 'a sense of values around the self-consciousness of giving effort'. This culture was 'the informally organized response of workers to the managerial organization of "industrial culture"'.[60] Foremen played an important role as 'bearers of shopfloor culture', colluding with workers in signing false work claims.[61] The contradictory demands of 'industrial culture' (whose central feature was the organizational theory developed in the United States by F. W. Taylor in the early twentieth century) and 'taut planning', in other words the oscillating, confusing and potentially atomizing impact of Stalinist policy, were projected on to the workers from the managerial level. For this reason, shopfloor culture can also be seen as a response to the chaotic conditions of Stalinism itself.[62]

More such studies would no doubt be advantageous, but from this one alone we can draw an important conclusion: that however rich and compelling an interpretation such as the one we have termed 'Stalinist political culture', the question of its truth does arise. Hence the peril of idealism, of substituting what is meaningful for the analyst for what is meaningful for the subjects of analysis, is revealed. In particular, we discover from Andrle's work that Arendt's thesis of 'atomization' and Tucker's of a 'society in movement' are overstated. Their deficiency is not just that they overlook the existence of such islands of regularity. If Andrle's analysis is correct, the very imposition of exhortations provoked 'shopfloor culture' as a response. Far from atomizing, therefore, Stalinist policies at 'ground level' may have led to the emergence of a culture: not the inclusive culture of the Stalinist 'movement', but a form of counter-culture.

'Atomization' is a speculative diagnosis of the effects of imposing the 'total claim'. It is liable to inaccuracy because, in Bell's metaphor, of the great height from which it is made, and because of a failure to appreciate the possibility of a defensive reaction against it on the model of the organization of shopfloor culture against the managerial elite's demands, couched in terms of 'industrial culture'. This example raises again, in microcosm, the question of the utility of the concept of 'culture'. Andrle notes the inappropriateness of the managers' 'industrial culture', which required stable conditions to facilitate the analysis of tasks,[63] to the environment of 'taut planning'.[64] But if 'industrial culture' was an implausible set of demands drawn from an alien organizational theory[65] that was quite inappropriate to the circumstances, in what sense was it a culture? It is tempting to answer: in the same sense Tucker uses to justify his more general concept of 'communist political culture'; that it contained a cultural model or ideal.

However, we can say more than this. 'Industrial culture' was not only an ideal, but was one that was continually *asserted*, its assertion comprising a political process to which shopfloor culture was the response. But we should also notice that the managers were themselves a group subject to pressure from both sides: from recalcitrant workers and from impatient supervisors whose injunctions, under 'taut planning', were likely to be contradictory. It might therefore be suggested that industrial culture provides a basis for group self-identification whose extreme claim of rationality is a response to the extremity of the irrational pressures to which the group was subject.

This hypothesis triggers a similar one for the administrative elite as a whole. In the coercive environment of Stalinism many such situations must have arisen of power relations between groups giving rise to new bases for group identification and for boundary-setting between antagonists. Since it is implausible to see the entire coercive mechanism as flowing from one person throughout society, it must be acknowledged that something has to motivate the possessors of the means of coercion. Hence the role of exhortation in terms of the 'basic goal' of communism. It can further be suggested that the party and state *aktiv*, as the agents of mass mobilization, were themselves most in need of mobilization. This view is reinforced when we consider that they were the most exposed to 'deculturation', many of them having moved abruptly into the expanding party-state machine and rapidly up its hierarchy into vacancies created by Stalin's purges.[66]

The extravagance of the total claim, the radical extent of social upheaval, the heroic nature of political goals, the disorganization of the administrative mechanism, the direct communication offered by the Stalin cult, scientific rationalization and literary mythicization may all be seen, from this perspective, as interrelated aspects of an *elite* culture. This culture is a real culture, not an ideal, in the sense of providing a basis for self-understanding and group cohesion – a way of life. To be sure, an element of speculation is involved in this proposal, raising the possibility that, like Arendt's speculations about atomization on the mass level, it will be contradicted by detailed evidence. But, as already noticed, accounts such as those of Arendt, Rigby, Tucker, Gill and Clark provide evidence which addresses this elite level. The claim is therefore less vulnerable to evidential contradiction than Tucker's inferences from the argument that Stalinism marks the incorporation of the whole of society into a Leninist 'movement'. It allows us to retain the advantage of the integrative power of Tucker's account without succumbing to its idealist excess.

POLITICAL CULTURE AND IDEOLOGY AFTER STALIN

The advantages of the interpretive use of political culture we have been developing may be pointed up by looking at some interpretive accounts of post-Stalinist Soviet politics, and by contrasting these with the political culture research of comparative communism, already discussed in Chapter 3. In that research, a distinction has been drawn between 'official political culture' and 'dominant political culture'. Official political culture is not simply the political culture of officials: 'the status of the concept, "official political culture" is different from political culture in the normal sense of subjective orientation to politics . . . . In principle, . . . it is easier to identify . . . since it represents the official standards for a political culture which may, up to a point, be located in authoritative texts'. As such, it overlaps with official ideology, though it includes features, such as the leadership cult, which are not plausibly regarded as part of Marxist–Leninist thought.[67] Despite this qualification, the concept clearly has affinities rather with Waller's 'ideology' or 'programme' than with Tucker's 'communist political culture' – although it contains a 'model', it is one that resolutely remains in the 'authoritative texts'. Indeed, the concept was suggested by the findings, discussed in Chapter 2, of the failure of official attempts at resocialization; the values failing to be inculcated being 'official', and different ones surviving among the population. It might be argued that such a concept, providing a thin description of Soviet ideology, is more appropriate to the post-Stalin period, where, certainly, the full panoply of interrelated assertions of the total claim was absent. But it should be noticed that the implication of such a usage is that the question of the meaning for the administrative elite of their exhortational activities became an insignificant one; it is a usage that, unlike Tucker's, is consistent with an assumption of complete cynicism on the part of officials.

That assumption did indeed probably approach closer to truth as the 'heroic' phase of communism receded into the past, to be replaced by the more mundane task of 'consolidation'.[68] But this does not mean that the area of 'elite political culture' is lacking in interest or content. Investigating it requires the techniques exemplified in this chapter – and is also subject to their deficiencies.

The organizational confusion noticed by Arendt and Rigby has been described also by Michael Urban in terms of a 'double bind', where para-doxical injunctions such as 'obey the law, and fulfil the plan' reinforced the power of the state in that the threat of physical force was associated with an inability to avoid becoming subject to it. For Urban, this process is not just an ideological one, but is facilitated organizationally by the phenomenon of overlapping or dual control and the confusion of authority relations represented by the *nomenklatura* system.[69] Rachel Walker has developed this analysis by examining the 'deep structure' or 'internal logic' of a set of ideological texts, namely reports by the General Secretary of the Communist Party to a number of Party Congresses. The paradoxical injunction inherent in this deep structure is the insistence on loyalty to the principles of Marxism–Leninism as well as on their 'creative development': 'To defend the "purity" of Marxism–Leninism is to risk being labelled a "pendant" [*sic!*] or a "dogmatist". To develop creatively it is to risk being labelled a "revisionist" or some sort of "deviationist". To be seen doing neither is to risk the accusation of not being Marxist–Leninist at all.'[70] Urban has also written of a generalized 'ideology of administration' which, while emphasizing 'rationality', 'efficiency' and 'effectiveness' nevertheless supports certain class or power relations, since these notions are not 'defensible in the face of abstract or reasonable standards'.[71] Rigby has applied his perspective of the 'mono-organizational society' to the post-Stalin period, continuing to emphasize what he calls, in a modification of Weberian terminology, 'goal-rational legitimation'.[72]

Although having different emphases, these accounts are coherent with the one we developed from Tucker's description in that they stress the *assertion* of what in the Brezhnev era was less than a total claim, but was still a very comprehensive one. They also share the deficiency of Tucker's idealism in that they provide no evidence of the impact of this claim: Rigby frankly notes that his approach 'differs sharply from the frequently encountered view of political legitimacy which more or less equates it with positive popular acceptance or support'.[73] A critique of Rigby by Christel Lane fixes upon this admission, charging that since 'The goal of a communist society is too vague, abstract and distant to provide an impetus for action for the mass of Soviet citizens',[74] Rigby's 'goal-rational legitimation' becomes a purely formal or legal matter.[75]

In depicting the Soviet Union as a 'mono-organizational society', Rigby assumes the total absorption of society, exposing his argument to Lane's criticism. But while some advantage might be claimed for characterizing the Brezhnevite Soviet Union as a single vast bureaucracy, as a preliminary means of distinguishing it from Western societies, this metaphor should not be reified. To Soviet citizens, there was no doubt who was a bureaucrat and who was not. Thus we may suppose that Rigby's analysis is most appropriately directed at real, not just metaphorical, bureaucrats: that is, at the political elite. It was, moreover, against bureaucrats in this conventionally narrow sense, and not against ordinary people, that accusations of 'revisionism' or 'dogmatism' or the prohibition of 'metacommunication' were directed. As with Tucker's political-cultural interpretation of Stalinism, therefore, these analyses of post-Stalinist political culture should not be given unlimited scope.

Just as for the Stalin period we needed to supplement the cultural description derived from Tucker with a speculation as to the significance for society's members, at different levels, of the claims asserted – their *response* – so in this case must these potentially idealist arguments be supplemented. In the idea of 'bureaucratic culture' we can find at least the beginnings of such supplementation. 'Bureaucratic culture' has been given the narrow and somewhat Almondian definition of 'the pattern of orientation towards the political system and towards political action on the part of public officials'.[76] In Soviet usage, Ronald Hill reports, the concept acquired a somewhat pejorative meaning as a culture 'lacking in sophistication and sensitivity'[77] whose 'level' needed to be 'raised'.[78] But the approach to bureaucratic culture that best meets our needs is that of George Yaney (in fact an analysis of Tsarist bureaucracy). For Yaney, bureaucracy is itself not a 'system', a fact which is revealed by the lack of complete co-ordination of its parts. Instead, it is a 'state of mind': 'people in a bureaucratic culture are dependent on system as a basis for conceiving of their interests and rights'.[79] In this view, the components of the 'ideology of administration' do not only conceal the power of senior bureaucrats, they provide the cohesion of the bureaucracy as an organization and a culture. But Yaney's position has the advantage that it can account for conflict as well as agreement, and hence can contribute to an explanation of the persistent criticism of bureaucracy that Hill takes to be something separate from (and indicative of the resilience of) bureaucratic culture. For Yaney, monitoring of one organization by another 'can dramatize the contradiction between legality and purposeful operation', and conflict is 'a necessary element for binding the members together around a common habit of appearing to be people who act rationally within a systemic framework'.[80] Criticism, in this view, strengthens bureaucracy, since it reinforces the meanings that underpin it. Or, the practice of monitoring by the party and repeated attacks on bureaucracy (a feature of the Brezhnev period, not just of Gorbachev's 'reconstruction')[81] is itself part of bureaucratic culture. It is no great leap from this perspective to seeing criticism of ideological 'deviation' as serving a similar purpose of group reinforcement.

Although a complex period of history and numerous approaches to it have been considered in this chapter, its central concern has been with the utility of the denomination 'culture' or 'political culture' for the purposes of historical interpretation. We have approached that question by looking in detail at one example of such a usage. The example has offered a particularly rich field for theoretical discussion, though its construction in the first place required that we substantially modify and supplement the analysis of its main progenitor, Robert Tucker. The confusing mixture of approaches in his analysis of Stalinism illustrates a deficiency that we are becoming familiar with in political culture research. In the examination of Tucker's writings, we have been led to see both the temptations and the dangers presented, for the interpretive use of political culture, by idealism. This danger, we will see, originates in 'thick description' itself, and in Geertz's own ethnography there is a failure to maintain a clear distinction between using cultural description as an interpretive aid and positing its existence among and use by the ethnographic subjects. In Tucker's analysis, the danger has been of conflating a description of an ideal or model of culture, or the assertion of certain claims, with a *real* culture, or the *acceptance* of these claims. The danger arises most acutely because of the somewhat self-referential nature of the ideal: it aspires to its own totality, so that it is tempting to see its total imposition or comprehensive assertion as, *ipso facto*, its realization. While demonstrating as fully as possible the ability of cultural description – thick description – to broaden our understanding of Soviet, and particularly Stalinist, politics, this chapter has nevertheless drastically qualified that description, eliminating its idealist tendency by relating it to 'ground level' ethnographic findings. To do this, it has been argued, is not to reduce 'communist political culture' to a mere programme (to 'official political culture'), since relating culture to concrete social processes enables us to assess more precisely the function of the claims and goals, particularly in connection with the cohesiveness and identity of various sections of the elite.

The nature of the argument by which these relationships have been suggested is in essence phenomenological. What it means to say so is one of the themes of the next chapter. Chapter 6 will also address from a more philosophical perspective the confrontation between phenomenology and thick description and the importance of insisting on the study of concrete social processes.

6 Political Culture and Interpretation

The use of political culture that was considered in the previous chapter differed from those considered in earlier chapters both in its methodology and its purpose.[1] Both method and purpose were interpretive. Contrary to what Tucker at times suggests, interpretivism does not exclude explanation; but it does exclude the particular type of explanation that has been criticized under the heading of 'comparative political culture research'. What sort of explanation, then, is provided by the interpretive use of political culture? Answering this question is the main purpose of this chapter. We will approach the answer in a series of steps, some suggested by analyses already considered and some introduced for the first time. As in the previous chapter, not all of the writings we will consider explicitly use the concept of political culture. However, within interpretivism it is artificial to draw firm boundaries between culture and concepts such as ideology. In the first stage of the argument of this chapter, a range of anthropological sources will be used to illustrate what may be termed a broad 'movement of thought', by which is meant a very general rearticulation of concepts and explanations. The movement may in a preliminary manner be characterized as one from an emphasis on culture to an emphasis on interests and social structure. The relationship of this movement to the arguments of preceding chapters is already apparent, and will be made clearer in the following pages. In the second stage of the argument we will look at the philosophical foundations of 'thick description', with the aim of exposing both its idealist tendency and its phenomenological potential. Then we will turn to a more thorough discussion of phenomenological social theory itself, and the related ideas of social constructionism and ethnomethodology. The phenomenological potential of interpretive political culture, we will argue, offers a means of transcending the dichotomy of culture and interests, and in more particular terms offers a resolution of some of the problems in political culture research that we have already discussed.

CULTURE AS A RESOURCE

Robert Tucker's concept of political culture, we observed, was distin-

99

guished from the one which had been current in political science by drawing, as he saw it, more fully on the anthropological concept of culture. Among other things, Tucker saw anthropology as licensing a definition of political culture which included patterns of behaviour as well as attitudes. Archie Brown has questioned Tucker's reading of anthropology in this respect, and demonstrated its partiality, in a survey of recent definitions of a more 'subjective' or psychological character.[2] But conducting this debate in terms of *definitions* distracts attention from the broader and more important question of *uses*. Both because it has been taken to inform an interpretive use of political culture – Tucker's – and because it will raise important general questions, the anthropological use of 'culture' needs to be investigated further.

Historically, as illustrated by the definitions surveyed by A. L. Kroeber and Clyde Kluckhohn in 1952 (162 of them), anthropology had tended towards a holistic definition of culture, of which E. B. Tylor's (1871) definition of 'culture, or civilization' as 'that complex whole which includes knowledge, belief, art, law, morals, custom, and any other capabilities acquired by man as a member of society'[3] is the often-cited archetype. It might be argued that such holism was provoked by the confrontation with what seemed the *comprehensively* alien to which the fieldwork journey led. But in recent decades, anthropology has been subject to considerable change. For one thing, it has undergone a degree of what might be termed 'deromanticization'. Numerous tokens of this can be found, such as Derek Freeman's denunciation of Margaret Mead's ethnographic study of Samoa,[4] the publication of Bronislaw Malinowski's diaries, in which he expressed his frank doubts about the 'participant observer' methodology that he introduced in his pioneering ethnography of the Polynesian islands,[5] and various ironic descriptions by anthropologists of fieldwork as a 'cult' and a 'fetish'.[6]

More is in play than simply a change of mood, however; or rather that change is itself the symptom of a deeper one. From the 1950s onwards, the phenomenon of urbanization began to impinge on anthropology in two distinct ways: as the traditional communities they had hitherto studied began to be disrupted by urbanization, anthropologists turned to the study of migration to towns; and, additionally, the application of anthropological methods to the study of urban life itself – urban anthropology – began to be developed.

In the face of these trends, a holistic conception of culture has proved difficult to maintain. Urbanization, in both senses, involves rapid social change, the formation of new social roles and increasing differentiation, exposure to a vast range of new influences – phenomena that must come as a particular shock not only to the anthropological subject, but also to the anthropologist him- or herself. In a review of anthropological approaches to culture, Roger Keesing has expressed this impact as follows: 'standing amid the swirling tides of change and individual diversity, we can no longer say comfortably that "a culture" is the heritage people in a particular society share'. He rejects the holistic view distilled by Kroeber and Kluckhohn as being too broad and diffuse.[7] On urban anthropology, Richard Basham and David DeGroot write:

> Urban research quickly alters the meaning of the concept of 'culture' for the urban anthropologist . . . . One reason for the apparent disutility of the traditional culture concept among highly urbanized populations is the tremendous variety of discrete social roles which characterize all cities and the fact that the complexity of role juxtaposition make [*sic*] it extremely unlikely that significantly large segments of the community will occupy the same roles and have the same understandings of their positions to give even the idea of a modal cultural pattern consistent utility.[8]

Concurrently, anthropologists – notably of the 'Manchester School', who, typically of British social anthropologists,[9] gave less prominence to the notion of 'culture' and instead preferred to speak of 'ethnicity' or 'identity' – paid increasing attention to the realm of the political, specifically to the relationship between tribe and class among migrants to towns. J. C. Mitchell and A. L. Epstein, for instance, have both studied the persistence of tribalism in the urban settings of the Zambian copperbelt. Mitchell distinguishes between the structure of tribes and the category, with only the latter, he asserts, surviving into the urban setting.[10] Epstein writes of the 'military ethos' of the Bemba tribe surviving in terms of individual pride and ethnic ranking between groups – a persistence explained by the continued utility of the former values and identity, and the more general importance to Africans of a martial reputation as a psychic response to colonization.[11] Another anthropologist of the Manchester school, Max Gluckman, in a more general survey, writes: 'the moment an African crosses his tribal boundary to go to the town, he is "detribalized", out of the political control of the tribe', a view he justifies as follows:

> in the rural areas membership of a tribe involves participation in a working political system, and sharing of domestic life with kinsfolk; and . . . this continued participation is based on present economic and social demands, not merely on conservatism. On the other hand tribalism

in towns is a different phenomenon entirely. It is primarily here a means of classifying the multitude of Africans of heterogeneous origin who live together in towns, and this classification is the basis on which a number of new African groupings . . . are formed to meet the demands of urban life.[12]

The line of thought suggested by Basham and DeGroot, and Keesing – that urban life characteristically leads to the multiplication of social roles – has been taken to its most extreme conclusion by Abner Cohen. His case study describes the differential use of tribal categories by the Hausa and Western Ibo in Ibadan, Nigeria, and accounts for it by reference to differences in the socio-economic positions that members of each tribe assumed upon migration to the city. He concludes that the preservation or loss of autonomy by ethnic groups in urban settings is a function of the coincidence or non-coincidence of ethnic cleavages with power or structural cleavages in society.[13] Culture, in this analysis, is disaggregated and relativized: cultures are defined by interest groups. Accordingly, anthropology must shift its attention: 'the study of the informally organized interest group is the key to the development of an anthropology of complex society'.[14]

An almost opposite situation has been described by Anthony Cohen in his analysis of the 'symbolic construction of community', which emphasizes the creativity with which identities and boundaries can be marked. A boundary, he argues, can be a physical frontier, but is in many cases purely symbolic. Indeed, he argues that the erosion of the structural bases of the boundary reinforces the symbolic ones.[15] This situation arises when, as in the so-called American 'melting pot', modern Western society imposes its new structures on the identities of traditional society. Cohen argues that, in such cases, new 'alien' cultural forms may be used for traditional purposes. For instance, among the Naskapi of Labrador, 'while Father Pieter feeds his flock with the body . . . of Christ, and gives thanks for the conversion of the pagan, the Naskapi chew on the wafer and commune with the Caribou Spirit. In doing so they contemplate the essence of Naskapi culture and reaffirm the community's boundaries.'[16] He gives several further examples of the reinforcement of identity in this way: Third World 'cargo cults', African 'Négritude' (the use of alien art forms to express African content) and African Socialism (the use of tribalism to justify the modern concept of the one-party state).[17]

While Abner Cohen argues that traditional forms express new identities (roles in the urban social structure), Anthony Cohen's argument is that new forms can express traditional identities. The difference is partly accounted for by the fact that Anthony is describing communities which are coming to terms with incursions, of one sort or another, of modern Western society upon them, while Abner is describing the reactions of *migrants* from traditional communities *to* modern Western society. In both cases, symbols are used in the ongoing assertion of identity within an entire structural setting, whether a new setting or an old one. In neither case are the criteria of distinctness used directly emergent from the structural setting; they are instead resources brought to that setting from elsewhere. In the former case, they are ethnic or tribal categories which are the inheritance of an earlier process of opposition and competition in which they emerged and served as markers between traditional groups. In the latter, they are borrowed from alien sources and creatively reinterpreted.

In the study of ethnicity, too, analyses that emphasize the structural setting, and hence construe ethnicity as a resource to be used in the struggle for power, have gained prominence in the last two decades. In a seminal article, Nathan Glazer and Daniel Moynihan, reflecting on the persistence of ethnic identification in modern American society – the inappropriateness, in other words, of the 'melting pot' metaphor by which the supposed assimilation of immigrants was expressed – attribute it to the use of ethnicity in the pursuit of group interests.[18]

It would be absurd, of course, to represent the above short summary as an account of the recent development of the discipline of anthropology in its entirety. But in these examples a distinct and not altogether unrepresentative movement of thought can nevertheless be traced. It is a movement away from regarding culture as an all-encompassing context, in which people are unavoidably and to some extent unwittingly embedded, towards regarding it as a 'repertoire' or 'resource' – a range of meanings, symbols and identities that are in some sense available for use, and may be voluntarily selected from, on the basis of the requirements of new situations. This movement not only suggests a degree of alienation of culture from society, but also, as Abner Cohen's example makes most explicit, places at the centre of the explanatory effort these situational requirements, or what might generally be referred to as interests. It is a movement, we will say, from 'culture-determination' to 'interest-determination'.

Glazer and Moynihan make the point that 'one reason that ethnicity has become so effective a means of advancing interests is that it involves more than interests'. This point might seem only to indicate that the 'instruments' of ethnicity happen to be particularly persuasive ones, but the authors further claim that ethnicity facilitates organization into groups: 'It is as a group that its struggle becomes not merely negative, but positive also, not merely against the norms of some other group, but in favour of the already existing norms of its own.' [19] Here we meet an important point of resistance to the movement towards interest-determination: the hint that group formation is not wholly a product of the objective situation. A further suggestion as to the source of the excess of content of ethnicity over interests is suggested by Epstein's discussion of 'collective identity', of which a 'sense of history' is a major component.[20] Anthony Cohen's emphasis on boundary-setting forsakes culture-determination in showing that culture is not a phenomenon that persists by itself; but his focus on creativity does not by any means entail the irrelevance of culture as a basis for group cohesion. Even Abner Cohen's most extreme statements take the form of recommending an extension of anthropological attention to interest groups rather than the handing over of this area of research to political scientists, which would suggest that some distinctive perspective is to be obtained from the anthropologist. But what is the nature of this perspective?

Anthropology, in abandoning its original holistic view of culture, has found itself in a disciplinary crisis of confidence, and has sought help from political science in the form of the latter's analyses of structurally or situationally-determined interests. Was the original opening to anthropology by interpretive political science mistimed and misplaced? To pursue this question further, we turn to the anthropologist of choice of interpretive political culture research, Clifford Geertz.

GEERTZ ON CULTURE AND IDEOLOGY

Among Geertz's writings, of particular influence upon interpretive political culture research has been his idea of 'thick description'. For the purposes of answering the questions just posed, and the broader question posed in this chapter, it is worth delving further than has usually been done in political culture research into the philosophical sources of this idea.

Geertz's elaboration of thick description is itself influenced by Weber's *verstehende Soziologie* and by Wittgenstein's argument about the publicity of meaning, but draws specifically on the work of Gilbert Ryle, whose coinage the term is. Thick description is illustrated by Geertz with the example of a wink. While a wink may be described in terms of certain bodily movements – 'thin' description – an adequate description would involve specifying whether the movements were voluntary, what their intention was, what social conventions and cues governed their interpretation by the audience and so on. Only such thick description would successfully identify what was going on.[21] In other words, behaviour, while it can be described in terms of its 'objective' manifestations, cannot *usefully* be so described. Geertz's assumption is that the point of describing behaviour is to understand it. Hence the point of anthropology is to understand, in this manner, the whole range of behaviour that is typical of a society: 'Finding our feet, an unnerving business which never more than distantly succeeds, is what ethnographic research consists of as a personal experience; trying to formulate the basis on which one imagines, always excessively, one has found them is what anthropological writing consists of as a scientific endeavor.'[22]

The latter stage – the stage of 'formulation' – is where the concept of culture is invoked. Culture, in this view, is therefore merely the extension and elaboration of the normal process of coming to terms with puzzling phenomena: it is 'not a power, something to which social events, behaviors, institutions, or processes can be causally attributed; it is a context, something within which they can be intelligibly – that is, thickly – described'.[23]

Thick description, in this account, is primarily a *method*. Elsewhere, in the course of his well-known account of the Balinese cockfight, Geertz elaborates further on this method, assimilating the cockfight to a text: cultural analysis, he says, is 'in general parallel with penetrating a literary text . . . one is faced with a problem not in social mechanics but in social semantics'. But apart from the justification already offered for thick description, that it assists the ethnographer in self-orientation, a further justification is offered here for regarding the cockfight as a text, namely the role that, Geertz argues, it plays in the self-understanding of the Balinese: 'Its function, if you want to call it that, is interpretative: it is a Balinese reading of Balinese experience, a story they tell themselves about themselves . . . . Attending cockfights and participating in them is, for the Balinese, a kind of sentimental education.'[24]

Thus, it appears, the reason why cultural description enables the ethnographer to find his or her feet is that it is in some form part of the way that the ethnographic subjects view the situation. What is apparent right away is the possibility of idealism: the projection by the ethnographer of the cultural interpretation on to the subjects: the conflation of what makes the situation intelligible for the ethnographer with what makes it intelligible to the participants. Just this error, Jonathan Lieberson asserts, has been committed by Geertz in this case:

it is one thing to claim that devotees of the cockfight attribute deep significance to it because it serves as an opportunity to express and dramatize their individual status conflicts and rivalries; it is another to describe the cockfight as a 'commentary' by the Balinese on the social order and organization that makes these conflicts possible.

There is, he asserts, 'a lack of clear and cogent evidence for [Geertz's] conjecture about the "native point of view" of the cockfight'.[25]

Already, then, we can observe a pattern with which Tucker's political-cultural description has made us familiar: an idealist failure to provide adequate evidence about the perspective of the subjects of cultural analysis. This is likely to occur when it is the ability of the analyst to come to understand the situation that is regarded as the primary aim, which is just what Geertz's account of thick description asserts. With this aim, the possibility arises that culture will turn out to be what Roy Wagner has termed a 'mediation': 'a way of describing others as we would describe ourselves'.[26] The threat of idealism is therefore endemic to thick description. This does not mean, however, that the sin need always be committed. Geertz's failure to provide evidence about the subjects' own view of the situation, as well perhaps as his overly specific claim about what kind of view we would find if such evidence were available, allows the charge of idealism to be made; but his commitment to an explanation of the interpretive method in terms of observable phenomena at least offers the possibility of being redeemed, which would vitiate the charge, in just the same way that ground-level ethnographic findings enables the idealism of the Tuckerite thick description of Stalinism to be overcome.

Let us recall that the appeal of that description lay in its integrative power; its apparent richness compared with competing concepts, particularly 'ideology'. But the fact that the Stalinist 'total claim' ramified through so many realms of meaning – politics proper, popular culture, the arts and sciences – threatens to seduce the analyst into confusing the comprehensive assertion of the claim with its realization. Ground-level ethnography enables this temptation to be resisted. However, this did not force us back to the 'thin' description of a body of purely formal claims, perhaps cynically espoused, floating above an indifferent society. We argued that the integrative description of Stalinist political culture applies pre-eminently to the administrative apparatus. Thus, 'ideology' would still remain an inadequate descriptive term for the meanings contained in Stalinist political culture – unless, that is, we choose to interpret that term in a somewhat broader fashion. Such is, indeed, the purpose of another of Geertz's essays that has been widely quoted outside anthropology, namely the appropriately titled 'Ideology as a Cultural System'.

In this essay Geertz is concerned to rescue ideology from the simplifications that he alleges it has been subject to in treatments of it since

Mannheim. What he calls the 'interest' theory follows most directly from Mannheim's critique of ideology: taking what Geertz calls 'pathological' instances of ideology such as German Fascism as its paradigms, it makes the well-known assertion that ideology is merely a screen for interests. The somewhat more sophisticated 'strain' theory attributes various social functions to ideology. Geertz groups these under four headings: the 'cathartic' function, whereby ideology serves as a vent for social frustration; the 'morale' function, whereby it provides moral support in the face of chronic difficulties; the 'solidarity' function, whereby it helps to knit a social group together; and the 'advocatory' function, whereby it presses an agenda upon the wider public consciousness.[27] Discarding the interest theory on mere empirical grounds, Geertz takes issue with the strain theory not in terms of the social stimuli to which it points, but for its failure to describe the formulation of ideology and to examine how ideology can come to have these various expressive functions. His argument is that ideology is invented by political actors, especially in the context of unfamiliar conditions, as a means of elaborating, often in a non-literal or metaphorical manner, a route through the unfamiliar territory. 'It is a confluence of socio-psychological strain and an absence of cultural resources by means of which to make sense of the strain, each exacerbating the other, that sets the stage for the rise of systematic . . . ideologies.'[28] But this new theory is not so much a replacement of the 'strain theory' as a supplementation of it. The new element is an emphasis on the construction of ideology in particular political conditions.

Geertz's account is somewhat skewed by his explanatory target in this essay, which is the development of radical ideologies in the 'new states' of the post-colonial period. Like the theorists he is criticizing, he risks construing one form of ideology among many as paradigmatic. The unfortunate effect of this for our present, more general, purposes is to overemphasize cases of ideological innovation. However, once we diagnose the cause of the imbalance, we are in a position to bypass it, and to attend to the general implications of Geertz's essay.

These implications can be seen, for example, in an analysis of political thought of the Jeffersonian Republicans in late-eighteenth and early-nineteenth century America. Lance Banning's study of *The Jeffersonian Persuasion* contains the following definition:

By 'ideology' I mean the more or less coherent body of assumptions, values, and ideas that bound Republicans together as it shaped their common understanding of society and politics and lent a common meaning to events. I use the word in reference to a constellation of ideas – and not a formal 'theory' – which made it possible for members of the party to perceive a pattern in the happenings around them, to define a group identity in terms related to that pattern, and to sketch a course of action that would make the pattern change.[29]

Explicitly drawing on Geertz, Banning here presents a use of the term 'ideology' that relates it to group identity in much the same way that we saw culture being related to group identity in the previous section.[30] Thus while our anthropological examples led us to an emphasis on identity and boundary, and on the dynamic nature of culture and the role of invention and reinterpretation, Geertz's conception of ideology as a cultural system does the same for the former term. There is, perhaps, some ground for arguing that ideology should be distinguished as more formalized and elaborate than culture. But Geertz's argument helps us to look beyond content and instead to notice the dynamic nature and etiology of ideology, as well as culture. It invites us not to represent ideology or political culture as some already existing set of values, whether held by the elite or the mass of the population, but to investigate in detail the circumstances of their creation and modification.

We have now reached the point at which it is necessary to investigate the philosophical basis of the use of 'culture' and associated concepts that we have been tracing in several disciplinary settings. This will enable us to spell out the nature of the explanation offered by such an interpretation, and to distinguish it more clearly from the form of explanation in which, as Chapters 1 to 3 argued, political culture has normally been embedded. That philosophical basis lies in phenomenological social theory.

PHENOMENOLOGY AND SOCIAL CONSTRUCTION

The original problem of phenomenology was the explanation of the process by which the immediate elements of perceptual experience (colours, shapes, boundaries) are understood as distinct objects, distances and movements. It is therefore a philosophy of the attribution of meaning and form to experience, considered as a natural human response to experience.[31] The extension of this perspective to the analysis of the social world was first undertaken by Alfred Schutz. Peter Berger and Thomas Luckmann's elaboration of Schutz's position provides a convenient entry to the subject of phenomenological social theory.

Their account begins by reasserting the fundamental phenomenological claim that, within some extremely broad constraints imposed by physiology, 'man constructs his own nature'. The manner in which this occurs begins with 'habitualization': 'Any action that is repeated frequently becomes cast into a pattern, which can then be reproduced with an economy of effort and which, *ipso facto*, is apprehended by its performer *as* that pattern . . . . [H]abitualization makes it unnecessary for each situation to be defined anew, step by step.' Habitualization can in principle occur in the case of a solitary individual. The next step in the theory is to introduce a second individual. The result is 'typification', whereby each perceives the habitual nature of the other's action as representing a type or role. Moreover, each assumes the other to be engaging in the same kind of thinking, resulting in reciprocal self-typification. When a collectivity of actors is envisaged, the set of typifications comprises an 'institution'. All of this results from the need for economy of effort, from the advantage to be gained by taking things for granted.[32]

The origin of this view in the theory of perception is made apparent by Schutz:

> From the outset [the object of perception] is an object within a horizon of familiarity and pre-acquaintanceship which is, as such, just taken for granted until further notice . . . . The unquestioned pre-experiences are, however, also from the outset, at hand as *typical*, that is, as carrying open horizons of anticipated similar experiences.

Schutz arrives at a similar account of typification and self-typification. 'In defining the role of the Other,' he writes, 'I am assuming a role myself. In typifying the Other's behaviour I am typifying my own, which is interconnected with his, transforming myself into a passenger, consumer, taxpayer, reader, bystander, etc.'[33]

The second phase of phenomenological explanation is an account of the *inheritance* of meaning; in other words of the separation of meaning from its original sources. The development of this second phase in Schutz's account begins with the model of face-to-face interactions. In order to communicate, two individuals have to overcome their differences in biography and perception of the surroundings. They do this through two 'idealizations': the 'idealization of the interchangeability of standpoints' and the 'idealization of the congruency of the system of relevances'. Together these comprise the 'general thesis of reciprocal perspectives'. This thesis 'leads to the apprehension of objects and their aspects actually known by me and potentially known by you as everyone's knowledge, [which is] conceived to be objective and anonymous'.[34] Thus, for Schutz, the 'detachment' of meaning from specific social situations is what facilitates social interaction. Berger and Luckmann arrive at a similar conclusion by drawing attention to the role of memory, speaking of the 'sedimentation' of experiences, whereby they 'congeal in recollection as recognizable and memorable entities'. When this occurs intersubjectively, the experiences are ready to be 'objectivated' in a sign system, such as language, and thus become 'readily transmittable'.[35] Human beings come into a world of existing meanings, consisting of types, roles, 'formulae' (Berger and Luckmann's term) and the 'stock of knowledge' (Schutz's term). Or, as Geertz has put it somewhat similarly, revealing his debt to phenomenology, any particular individual finds 'significant symbols'

> already current in the community when he is born, and they remain, with some additions, subtractions, and partial alterations he may or may not have had a hand in, in circulation after he dies. While he lives he uses them, sometimes deliberately and with care, most often spontaneously and with ease, but always with the same end in view: to put a construction upon the events through which he lives, to orient himself within 'the ongoing course of experienced things'. [John Dewey's phrase][36]

The relationship of phenomenology to thick description, which is hinted at by Geertz's invocation of the Balinese view of the cockfight as justification for his own account of it, has been brought out in a discussion by Schutz of Weber's *verstehende Soziologie*. Schutz criticizes the abstractly methodological manner in which *Verstehen*, the notion that social science takes the form of 'understanding', has been conceived by social scientists, arguing that it is 'primarily not a method used by the social scientist, but the particular experiential form by which common-sense thinking takes cognizance of the social world'. *Verstehen* as a method is only the implication, therefore, of the fact that the objects of social science are conscious; are beings who, when they are studied, have already engaged in the task of interpretation. Social actors operate with 'constructs' with which they interpret social reality; thus the social scientist creates 'constructs of the second degree' in the process of observation and explanation.[37]

Phenomenology thus contributes to the methodology of *Verstehen* or thick description an explanatory component: an explanation of the origins of social meaning, and hence an explanation of the utility of the interpretive method. Essentially, because 'culture', in the form of an assemblage of emergent typifications, is a creation of social actors themselves, it becomes of use to the investigator in reaching an understanding of their behaviour.

What we have called the two 'phases' of phenomenological explanation are distinguishable only in the abstract. The situation of two people forming 'typifications' in the complete absence of existing meanings never occurs: it is an abstraction, like the 'social contract' of liberal theory. But just as that latter notion structures our understanding of the real social arrangements supposedly justified by the imaginary contract, so the idea of the construction of meaning is embedded in the Schutzian concept of 'stock of knowledge at hand'. In conceiving of that knowledge as objective, social actors push into the background the fact of its constructed nature, but it is important for the analyst to keep that background condition firmly in sight. Failing to do so leads to an implausible claim of culture-determination. For instance, Berger and Luckmann assert that the origin of meanings can become unimportant, and that 'the tradition might invent quite a different origin without thereby threatening what has been objectivated'.[38] The suggestion that 'tradition' itself, not social actors, creates meaning is a claim of culture-determination. It is also meaningless.

Thus, although phenomenology allows and accounts for 'inherited' meaning, that is for the fact that social actors conceive of meaning as objective, it makes the fundamental claim that any such conception of objectivity is necessarily provisional. In fact, the activity of construction of meaning is continuous. Evidence for this has been provided by the sociological school of ethnomethodology, which has gone so far as to argue that no commonly accepted 'culture' or set of background conventions exists, and instead that one has to be continually constructed in individual social encounters. Demonstration of this claim was the purpose of Harold Garfinkel's 'disruption' experiments, in which he and his students would violate established conventions of social interaction in order to test the effects. Contrary to the claim that social life is predicated on pre-existing common understandings, Garfinkel found that interaction is resilient to such disruptions; that, in response to them, various negotiations and circumnavigations usually occur.[39] Disruption experiments are, from the point of view of phenomenology, necessarily imperfect attempts to replicate the formation of 'typifications': they demonstrate the provisional nature of existing meaning.

It is, of course, an often-noticed characteristic of ethnomethodology that its studies are almost a parody of detail and small scale – one famous example concerns the sequence of contributions to the first five seconds of telephone conversations.[40] From this kind of basis it is notoriously difficult to regain the level of analysis that political culture is concerned with. Indeed the claim that there is no need to do so is part of the programme of ethnomethodology – hence its disparagement by mainstream sociology.

But for our purpose, studies at this intimate level do serve to show how fundamental is the application of the phenomenological idea of construction.

Another of the central figures in ethnomethodology, Harvey Sacks, was the pioneer of a subfield of sociology that has become known as 'conversational analysis'. Sacks's own interest in the detailed examination of conversations was in establishing rules for 'turn-taking'; but the methods he introduced, such as the detailed transcription, codification and study of tape-recorded conversations, have been used also in less technical investigations, for instance in the investigation of the social construction of memory. Social psychological interest in the phenomenological idea of 'construction', invoking the methods of conversational analysis, has led to the proposal of the theory that memory is not an attribute or activity of individual minds, but the product of a collective effort at reconstruction. David Middleton and Derek Edwards have illustrated this theory with several examples, including the analysis of a conversation in which the details of a film were reconstructed by students in a process of negotiation and adjustment. They conclude, 'Collective versions of past events are available as grounds for justifying current and future action; and because they are so "useful" it is quite ordinary to find them being reconstructed and contested.' [41]

Phenomenology offers a clearer perspective on the deficiencies of culture-determination by showing how meanings are in principle anchored to the detailed and concrete processes of their creation; that their 'objectivity' is a provisional assumption that may break down in conditions of disruption, exposing to view their constructed nature. Culture-determination overstates the resilience of that assumption of objectivity, and hence the stability of meanings. It is no coincidence that culture-determination within anthropology has been brought into question by processes and events that may also be seen as 'disruptions', on a somewhat larger scale than those created by Garfinkel and his students. In a social setting disrupted, for instance, by urbanization, social meanings do not simply press froward under their own steam, as they might mistakenly have been taken to do in the earlier stable setting. Social actors can instead be seen grasping for meanings as they seek to understand and reorient themselves within the new situation.

Does phenomenology, then, simply endorse the movement from culture-determination to interest-determination? Grounds for thinking so might be implied simply by its critique of the former. It might further be argued that meanings, once 'objectivated', are available for use as a resource and that, in disrupted settings, it is interests that account for the uses that are made of them, as ethnographic findings such as Abner Cohen's would suggest. But to draw this conclusion would be to underestimate the radical extent of the claims of phenomenological social theory. Phenomenology does more than challenge the 'givenness' of values, history and memory – though these are radical enough claims. In its analysis of typification it asserts also the constructed nature of social roles, hence of the entire social structure, and hence of the interests that flow from it. Interests, from the phenomenological perspective, are no more primordial and no less constructed than culture. While culture is the medium of understanding the social environment, interests are the medium of acting within it, but this does not mean that either can be specified in advance of the other.

Of course, that is a somewhat abstract claim. The phenomenological denial of the 'givenness' of any part of the social environment gives way, for the purpose of any particular sociological investigation, to a more limited assertion that some part of that environment is the product of social construction. In order for such an investigation to take place, the assumption must be made of a range of 'givens' that are external to the investigation. If, for instance, we are investigating the contribution of a set of party polemics to the construction of a group identity, we would not be directly concerned with the more fundamental question of the source of the detailed factual recollections that would be a part of such polemics. This phenomenological issue would be set aside. What the founder of phenomenology, Edmund Husserl, called the 'natural attitude', the common-sense perception of givens by which we orient ourselves in the world, cannot in other words be suspended *tout court* – in phenomenological terms it cannot be 'bracketed' in its entirety, at any rate for the purposes of sociological investigation. For those purposes, what is in essence a fiction of solid ground must be established, from which an investigation exposing the plasticity of some set of meanings may be launched. But that any particular investigation will in this way rely on a set of 'givens' does not invalidate the phenomenological insight that all such givens are provisional. Therefore, while any particular piece of phenomenological investigation may appear to make assumptions consistent with culture- or interest-determination, the perspective of phenomenology continues to make a fundamental challenge to the notion that interests and social structure exist independently of meanings, or vice versa.

PHENOMENOLOGY AND POLITICAL CULTURE

Despite its apparent abstractness, phenomenological social theory has some very concrete implications both for the research discussed in this chapter and for political culture research. It makes the positive contribution of answering the question posed in this and the preceding chapter; namely, to what sort of explanation does an interpretive use of political culture contribute? It also reinforces our earlier critique of political culture research, in ways that will shortly be explained.

We have seen that Clifford Geertz's reliance on phenomenology is considerable. To be sure, his own account of the methodology of thick description distracts attention from that influence. It emphasizes the role of the ethnographer in the elaboration of a cultural 'context', and thus makes it seem that culture is an abstraction from the observable events. But Geertz also, in the application of the method, relates it, though as it happens not with much evidence, to the interpretive practices of the participants themselves. His so doing strongly recalls Schutz's argument that interpretive sociology – in particular Weberian *verstehende* methodology – is only the methodological implication of the fact that its subjects have already engaged in the task of interpretation; their social life is facilitated by 'constructs' or 'typifications', making the sociologist's task one of developing 'constructs of the second degree'.

Geertz's account of the cockfight, we are now in a position to see, inadequately brings to bear the resources of phenomenological explanation. This is not only for the reason already mentioned, Geertz's lack of attention to the 'native point of view', but for a reason well expressed by William Roseberry. Roseberry has argued that in order to justify a claim about the function of the cockfight, Geertz would have to elucidate not just its 'reference' to status conflicts, but its exact relationship to status conflict, that is, its involvement in the process of status formation: 'The cockfight has gone through a process of creation that cannot be separated from Balinese history . . . . A text is written; it is not writing. To see culture as an ensemble of texts or an art form is to remove it from the process of its creation.' [42] Geertz's interpretive analysis of the cockfight as a text, in other words, treats it objectively, for all Geertz's commitment to thick description. Thick description in the full, phenomenological sense would involve showing how the meanings that it exposes are constructed and negotiated.

Thus one important feature of research that fully brings to bear the resources of phenomenological explanation is its strongly empirical nature. This is what enables the phenomenological potential of political culture research to counter the idealist tendency, whose deficiency consists chiefly in its inattention to concrete evidence for its rich, integrative and thought-provoking – and hence seductive – thick descriptions. We can now make some clarifications of the argument presented in Chapter 5. The idea of atomization is itself a phenomenological one: it is a hypothetical limiting case, where irregularity reaches such a level that meaning, and in particular social cohesion, is destroyed, exposing individuals to absorption and integration on the grand scale of Stalinist construction. This hypothesis does what Geertz demands of thick description – it helps us to find our feet when confronting the social upheaval cataclysm of Stalinism. But the hypothesis is, nevertheless, refuted by the counter-example of shopfloor culture – not a hypothesis but a finding, and one that is entirely consistent with the analysis of culture exposed in our anthropological survey. Our discussion of Stalinism also argued that 'Stalinist political culture' – the 'total claim' of incorporation into the heroic construction of an industrial state, reinforced by the arts and sciences – was a real culture, not just an ideal, for its own agents, who were most exposed to it by the recurrent and profound irregularity of their position. The culture provided, it was argued, a basis for their own continuance and functioning as a social group. In this argument the overlap between political culture and ideology may be observed, as indeed it can in the more specific case of the managerial organization of 'industrial culture' as an expression of regularity against the highly irregular setting of 'taut planning'.

But what also needs to be stressed is the way in which phenomenology, despite its implications for empirical research, casts doubt on the kind of empirical research that has been characteristic of non-interpretive uses of political culture. The following passage from Schutz, while hardly pellucid, repays examination:

> What we call the world of objective meaning is . . . abstracted in the social sphere from the constituting processes of a meaning-endowing consciousness, be this one's own or another's. This results in the anonymous character of the meaning-content predicated of it and also its invariance with respect to every consciousness which has given it meaning through its own intentionality. In contrast to this, when we speak of subjective meaning in the social world, we are referring to the constituting processes in the consciousness of the person who produced that which is objectively meaningful . . . . The world of subjective meaning is therefore never anonymous . . . .[43]

Here, Schutz is drawing attention to one of his central themes, the twin claims that the social world is perceived as 'objective' – his version of the 'natural attitude' – and that its objective meaning is, nevertheless, the product of an ongoing, if normally unrecognized, activity of construction and reconstruction. We can readily observe that political culture research in the behavioural idiom, whether comparative or sociological, also makes a distinction between 'subjective' and 'objective'. What is important, however, is that the two distinctions are not parallel. Political culture in the behavioural idiom has been defined, from Almond onwards, as 'subjective', but the meaning of this has been 'psychological'. This is not Schutz's meaning. From the phenomenological perspective, these 'subjective' data – values, recollections of history and the like – have been wrongly construed in political culture research *as if* they were objective. The use of the attitude survey, the ultimate instance of the assumption of anonymity, is the prime indication of this. For phenomenology, 'subjectivity' implies awareness of the continuous processes by which objects and actions are endowed with meaning. Phenomenology insists that, while the subjective is construed as objective by social actors, facilitating social interaction, this construal is provisional. Social actors take the objective as 'given' (that is what the term 'objective' means in phenomenology), but for analysts to do so exposes them to a range of potential errors.

These errors are just the ones we exposed in Chapters 1 to 4. The idea of cultural lag, which lies at the root of many of them, is an example of the analytical objectification of meaning. Again, it needs to be distinguished from the claim made in the second phase of phenomenological explanation that meaning may become detached from its original sources. The difference lies in the provisional nature of the latter claim, which in the notion of cultural lag is completely obscured. Two major problems result. Lacking an aetiology of meaning, the cultural lag hypothesis lapses into equivocation in cases such as those discussed in Chapter 2, where political culture presents itself as both an aspect of modernization and a context for it. Failing to note that the objectification of meaning is provisional, the hypothesis is unable to deal with what in Chapter 3 we termed the 'multivalence of history': the occurrence of contention over the value to be given to historical recollections, as well as their content. That in communist Eastern Europe 'constructions' of historical experience – indeed of memory itself – were serving purposes of group identification, in particular against history-denying Soviet rule, is clear. The idea of 'Central Europe' is a good example of what is an apparently factually incontestable field – geography – being invaded by constructs of a transparently political nature. A phenomenology of geography could no doubt present many more examples.

The issues raised by the movement in anthropology from culture-determination to interest-determination, as well as both the idea of Stalinist political culture as an elite culture and the claims of the critical sociologists that the 'civic culture' may best be seen as a source of cohesion for the political elite and a means of preserving its dominance, also merit a phenomenological response. The essence of this response is the phenomenological denial of the duality of culture and interests. However, the implications of this denial need to be brought out in much more detail. We have already hinted that a phenomenological perspective on political culture suggests the role of political culture in the formation of group identity, which is a more 'political' use of phenomenology than can be found in Schutz's writings. This line of thought needs to be pursued further. Moreover, mention of 'elite culture' brings into play an important question that also merits further discussion: how are the apparently more discretionary and self-conscious 'inventions' and 'mystifications' in which political and intellectual elites engage to be fully incorporated into a phenomenological analysis? Pointing to the porousness of the boundary between political culture and ideology is far from a complete answer. These questions suggest that we have as yet only begun to expose the phenomenological potential of political culture research. The project is continued in Chapter 7.

This chapter has argued that the nature of the explanation offered by the interpretive use of political culture is phenomenological. Phenomenological social theory is a very abstract set of claims, but its attention is focused very concretely on matters such as common-sense knowledge and identity. It demands a posture of doubt as to the fixed or given nature of any of the social phenomena it may be used to study. In particular, it precludes the comparative politics conception of political culture as a set of attitudes and values that may be specified in abstraction of their own social context. At the concrete level, phenomenological social theory is characterized by an insistence on detailed investigation of the process of the construction of meaning – something that furthermore distinguishes it from an idealist and purely hermeneutic focus on culture as an orienting device for the investigator. As we have seen, some writings on culture in general have made use of such methods and assumptions, but it is clear that for the most part political culture research has not. In this regard it has failed to exploit the most useful potential of the concept of political culture.

7 Political Culture and National Identity

There are several reasons why it is appropriate at this point to shift attention to the topic of national identity. The most important of these is that doing so provides a test of the usefulness of the phenomenological perspective developed in the preceding chapter – indeed, as will become apparent, a particularly severe test. The nature of the test will be to see in what way a phenomenological perspective contributes to the theory of nationalism, which has recently been an arena of lively debate. Before that, however, some other reasons for turning to the investigation of national identity may be mentioned. The most obvious of these is that, since *The Civic Culture*, national identity has been seen as a central component of political culture. The unreflective way in which it was invoked by Almond and Verba has also been characteristic of later research. For instance, Brian Girvin proposes that political culture be split into three levels: the 'macro-level', consisting of a 'core' of national identity and rarely questioned 'absolute presuppositions'; the 'meso-level', consisting of long-term but nevertheless contested political 'rules of the game' (such as 'Thatcherism'); and the 'micro-level', at which 'normal political activity', such as elections, occurs.[1] The theory which he develops from this basis relates the three levels, but it is noteworthy that national identity is explained only by reference to the supposed necessity of a 'sense of belonging'. More than this, we might suspect, needs to be said about the 'core' of political culture.

A further reason for turning to national identity concerns what was termed in Chapter 4 the 'indexicality' of some descriptions of political culture. Examples of indexical descriptions abounded in Chapter 3, which argued for the contestability and multivalence of historical symbolism. National identity, it is easy to see, is an indexical component of political culture *par excellence*. We will see that it is also a contestable one. Thus by examining it we can advance a phenomenological understanding of the issues raised in those earlier chapters, exposing both the significance and the source of indexical descriptions of political culture. We will begin by discussing the possibility of a phenomenological approach to national identity and the problems it would face. Then theoretical debates in the field of nationality and nationalism will briefly be surveyed. Finally, we will turn to two case studies, selected not for their typicality, but because in the specific nature of their atypicality they serve as pointed illustrations of the utility of existing approaches and of the one we are developing.

OUTLINE OF A PHENOMENOLOGICAL APPROACH TO NATIONAL IDENTITY

The applicability of the approach developed in the preceding chapter to the study of national identity is not immediately obvious. Indeed, just to reach the point at which the specific problems presented by this application become apparent requires further theoretical elaboration. We begin by considering the relationship between culture and identity, already touched on in Chapter 6.

We noticed, in that chapter, that the holistic definition of culture was in part a response by the anthropologist to his or her confrontation with the comprehensively alien. Putting aside the question of definition, this fact suggests that in anthropology, the first use of the concept of culture has been to assert a certain range or degree of difference between societies. Hence our tendency in ordinary speech to use the word 'culture' to refer to societies themselves, rather than to one of their attributes. Claude Lévi-Strauss has expressed this as follows:

> What is called a 'culture' is a fragment of humanity which, from the point of view of the research at hand and of the scale on which the latter is carried out, presents significant discontinuities in relation to the rest of humanity . . . . This is true as a limit; however, anthropologists usually reserve the term 'culture' to designate a *group* of discontinuities which is significant on several of these levels at the same time.[2]

But if the concept of 'culture' is a 'response' of the anthropologist; if its application is relative to 'the research at hand'; if (in Geertz's phrase) its purpose is to help ethnographers 'find their feet', we are left with only indirect guidance as to the true nature of culture: its nature, that is, 'on the ground'. This is a very general way of characterizing the problem of idealism that is faced by interpretive anthropology, and, we have seen, by the interpretive use of political culture too. In Chapters 5 and 6 we tried to surmount it by advocating the study of concrete social processes. Our question here is, are discontinuities that are apparent to the observer significant also for the observed, and if so, in what way?

The phenomenological perspective begins not with the interpretive effort of the ethnographer but by supposing that that effort is necessitated by the interpretive practices of the participants themselves. From this perspective, the establishment of identity and boundary becomes a salient issue; it is a matter not of discontinuities perceived from outside, but of boundaries created from within. The idea of 'typification', which, as we saw, lies at the heart of phenomenological social theory, is closely related to that of identity. Social roles are, indeed, identities. Whether identities are individual or collective is, again, a matter that is determined not by the observer but by the situation on the ground. 'Bystander', to use one of Schutz's examples, is a momentary and individual identity or role; 'shopfloor worker', to use our example from Chapter 5, is an enduring and collective one. More than the breadth of our ethnographic focus determines these distinctions.

A culture, for instance 'shopfloor culture', consists of values, knowledge and skills. These attributes, since they provide criteria of distinctness between one group and another, for instance between workers and managers, may also constitute expressions or markers of identity. At the point where a significant difference occurs in one of these dimensions, a boundary between one group and another may be indicated. Whether a boundary is established at such a point is an empirical question. Identity therefore involves not only the presence of such distinctions but their use as markers; hence it involves the explicit self-consciousness of a group as a group. Identity in this sense is the core, or carrier, or symbol, of the culture. Because of its explicitness, identity may be seen as the 'cutting edge' of a culture: the 'edge' in that identity expresses the boundary, and defines inclusion and exclusion; a 'cutting edge' in that the identity is not a mere formality, but structures conflict with groups beyond the boundary.

Group identity in its simplest form establishes a 'we/they' boundary. In some situations, no more specific content is required; for instance, in the isolated and primitive communities studied by early anthropologists. But in most cases the 'we' and the 'they' are explicitly named. The idea that identity involves an act of naming is important for the analysis of national identity. For it opens up the possibility, not immediately apparent in the simpler phenomenological example of shopfloor culture, that different acts of naming may be made in competition. Although, in that example, the identity follows fairly directly from the criteria of differentness of the culture, this, we shall argue, is not always the case, and a disjunction between the two is made possible by the assertion of identity being a conscious act.

A first attempt at extending the phenomenological perspective to national identity would be to argue, by analogy with 'shopfloor culture', that national identity emerges from and in turn contributes to a process of opposition between nations, and that just as the discontinuities encapsulated in the idea of shopfloor culture are drawn upon as criteria of boundary, so the differences we refer to with the term 'political culture' provide a basis for the assertion of national identity. There are several related reasons why this analogy might seem a little too neat. The first concerns scale. The size of nations means that the development of group self-consciousness in them is not the straightforward matter it may be among workers on a shopfloor. A nation, as Benedict Anderson has put it, is an 'imagined community'.[3] Put another way, nationality is not for the most part a social role, constantly being used and reinforced as one moves through social life; it is for most of the time a background condition. Even when nations are at war, the confrontation between them is for much of the population an imaginary affair, represented in the media. This is true even in a 'total war', such as the Second World War, when civilian populations are at risk and hence are in some sense participating; the technology that puts them at risk, in this case aerial bombing, also makes more anonymous the 'opposition process'.

Secondly, nations are not only large, they are also highly internally differentiated. The significance of this banal fact is that the 'imagining' of the national community is not a spontaneous act of the whole population; it is to some extent initiated and controlled by certain sectors of the population, specifically the intellectual and political elite. The sense, by all accounts quite real, that the British population in the Second World War was ready to fight 'on the beaches and in the towns' was instilled by Winston Churchill, with the help of the BBC; it did not simply emerge from the experience of war.

Thirdly, the role of the act of naming which we have argued is necessary to the formation of group identity is potentially more complex in the case of nations. As a conscious and voluntary act, it is contestable. In other words, there may be political struggle over the very name to give a population, or more generally over its allegiance, the meaning of national symbols, and the facts of national history.

As the first step towards overcoming these barriers to a phenomenological approach to national identity, it is worth pointing out that the differences between this case and our paradigm case are, though considerable, differences of degree. Shopfloor workers may be able to see themselves as a community in a direct manner, but in many cases, even conceivably in the Stalinist case, and certainly in more familiar Western ones where trade unions have some independence, an imaginary component is present too. What is imagined is the existence of similar groups, in similar situations, having similar relationships with the authorities. What may follow from this is 'collective action', such as striking, in which the collectivity is itself imagined. Secondly, it is likely that even at this local level, some people will take on the role of leaders in the opposition process, and some of followers, leading to some degree of internal differentiation. The leaders, we might expect, would try to represent the history and scope of the opposition process in such a way as best to meet their goals. Finally, even in this example it is not hard to visualize competing acts of naming; 'shopfloor workers' *versus* 'builders of communism', or 'employees', for instance.

Thus in developing a phenomenological approach to national identity, we encounter difficulties whose resolution is important for our whole enterprise, not just at this level. They can, however, be resolved, as the arguments and examples below will show. We will see that the case of national identity does indeed require greater attention to elites and greater scope for invention, but that approaches that press these emphases too far have deficiencies which only a phenomenological approach can repair. We will need to examine debates in the theory of nationalism and specific cases in order to establish this claim.

THE THEORY OF NATIONALISM

As Eric Hobsbawm, one of its major contributors, has pointed out, the last two decades have seen a burgeoning of theoretical debate on the subject of nationalism and national identity.[4] To do full justice to this debate would require more space than is available here; nevertheless it is necessary to form an idea of its outlines for the purpose of framing our discussion. Broadly speaking, the debate has concerned the question of the novelty of nations. The view that they are of ancient lineage has been challenged by a number of provocative syntheses claiming in various ways that nations are constructs of comparatively recent origin. That view, which has become a new orthodoxy, has, however, itself been challenged. The debate recalls the 'movement of thought' from the holistic view of culture to its being viewed as a resource, which we recorded in the preceding chapter.

Although several versions of the 'mobilizationist' position, as it has been called, have been put forward, we will concentrate on the most forceful, that of Ernest Gellner. Gellner's argument is that industrialization and modernization require the creation of national educational and communications systems as 'breathing chambers' for industrial man.[5] Only a state can preserve such a system. That nations apparently become distinguishable in terms of underlying ethnicity results from the fact that in the conditions of widespread, homogeneous high culture, the only bases remaining for legitimacy are 'units of culture' (tantamount to ethnic groups); but since these were historically much more numerous, diverse and interpenetrating than nation states, an act of selection and invention had to be undertaken. Its agents were a nationalist intellectual and political elite. Moreover, 'The cultural shreds and patches used by nationalism are often arbitrary historical inventions. Any old shred and patch would have served as well.' Nations and hence states were the result: thus it is 'nationalism which engenders nations, not the other way round'. Gellner writes, 'The basic deception and self-deception of nationalism is this: nationalism is, essentially, the general imposition of a high culture on society, where previously low culture had taken up the lives of the majority, and in some cases the totality, of the population.'[6]

Thus, in the mobilizationist view, nations are novel; they are arbitrarily 'invented' by intellectual and political elites; these 'inventions' are imposed on the mass of society; and the whole process is an effect, indeed a functional requirement, of modernization and industrialization. There are a number of points at which these claims have been challenged, but we should notice first that the claims of arbitrariness and of imposition present, if they are true, the most serious obstacles to a phenomenological approach to national identity. The first denies the emergence of meaning, and hence culture and identity, from ongoing social life, while the latter portrays the mass of the population as passive recipients of the invented meanings. In combination, these claims deny what is necessary to the phenomenological analysis, that nationality can ever be a social role. However, we will see that they are too strongly stated, and that some scope for that necessary condition remains.

The role of invention has also been stressed in a much-cited study of symbolic and historiographical representations of the national past in the cases of Scotland, Wales and England.[7] This study provides many striking examples of invention, such as the Ossian myth, a forged national epic, in Scotland and the myth of Madoc (supposed discoverer of America in the twelfth century) in Wales, as well as the invention of the Scottish kilt by a Lancastrian mill owner in the eighteenth century. However, invention need not necessarily be arbitrary, as is suggested by Hobsbawm's concluding observation that 'the most successful examples of manipulation are those which exploit practices which clearly meet a felt – not necessarily a clearly understood – need among particular bodies of people'.[8]

On the basis of a comprehensive survey of nationality and nationalism, Anthony Smith argues that 'in most cases, the mythologies elaborated by nationalists have not been fabrications, but recombinations of traditional, perhaps unanalyzed, motifs and myths taken from epics, chronicles, documents of the period, and material facts'. They are thus 'inventions' only in a limited sense of the word. Smith makes a distinction between 'full' and 'drained' (or 'empty') national histories, the former providing a bounteous range of myths and symbols from the history of an ethnic group, the latter requiring a process of disentanglement and recombination in order to simulate a national history for an ethnic group which does not have one. 'In the first case, it is more a case of selective memory "rediscovering" the past; in the second, a more conjectural "reconstruction" of the past from such motifs and myths as can be unearthed.' It is true, Smith notes, that an elite sector of society is responsible for these activities. However, he makes a point that has the same implication for the elite that Hobsbawm's does for the masses: 'Such novel recombinations are pre-eminently the work of intellectuals in search of their "roots".' [9]

The implication is that inventions or recombinations are not and cannot be entirely arbitrary, either for the perpetrators or for the recipients. So far as the elite nationalists are concerned, it is true that they might indeed be somewhat estranged from the mass of the population, and uniquely able to engage in relevant intellectual activities such as historical research. But to suppose, as Gellner, does that their formulations are always arbitrary is to posit an extreme form of estrangement. A higher level of education offers the possibility of a degree of detachment from history necessary for the conscious invention of national myths, but to suppose that this is always or even usually the case is to commit a rationalist fallacy. It is to suppose that the elite is estranged also from its own history. We will shortly consider a case which exposes the fallaciousness of this claim. So far as the 'receiving' masses are concerned, if some inventions are more successful than others at meeting 'felt needs', it is necessary to ask what is the source of these needs. Again, we will argue that it is concrete historical processes.

Without pre-empting the discussion to follow, we can see the basis for a phenomenological analysis. We saw that such an analysis encounters difficulties if national identity is regarded as the natural product of 'national experience', essentially because in concrete terms there is no such thing as national experience. The historical experience of the nation, like the nation itself, is imagined. But if instead of arguing analogically as if the nation were just a large version of a social group, or indeed an individual in its own right, we continue to pursue the investigation of concrete social processes, we will observe ample scope for national identity to be seen as a response. We turn now by way of illustration of this claim to two case studies.

POLAND: THE NATION AS RESPONSE

The Polish case is distinctive in that the nation has an ancient lineage while at the same time its existence as a state has not been continuous – it was decisively interrupted for most of the period from 1795 to 1918, the most active period of nationalism in Europe. This is one source of its interest for our purposes, since it allows us to investigate the degree to which the re-emergent Polish state of 1918 was the result of preservation or invention, and in what manner. The case is interesting too, we will see, because of the relatively high level of contestation that occurred over what we have been calling the act of naming; over what we may call 'nominal national identity'. We begin with a brief survey of Polish history, drawing on the work of Norman Davies.[10]

　　The first important factor in Poland's development is its location – both geographically and geopolitically. So far as the first is concerned, its lack of defensible boundaries (except to the south, where it is bounded by the Carpathian mountains) has been a contributor to its political vulnerability. The same problem has afflicted Russia: however the results in terms of political organization have been radically different, the necessity of military mobilization contributing to the latter's extreme centralization, whereas decentralization and even anarchy were characteristic of independent Polish politics. The nobility had a great deal of autonomy: it elected the king and individual members of the Sejm (parliament), and retained the right to bring proceedings to a halt, effectively a veto power. This circumstance contributed to the paralysis of the state in the face of increasing external threats in the eighteenth century. Geopolitically, Poland's location between Muscovy, subsequently Russia, whose growth in size was slow but apparently inexorable, and Prussia, subsequently Germany, which grew from an enclave of the Teutonic Knights to become a continental power, combined with its internal organization to render it increasingly vulnerable.

　　In the period 1569–1795, the Polish-Lithuanian Republic was one of the Great Powers of Europe, extending at its maximum size (in 1634–35) to a line well to the east of Kiev, and northwards almost to the Gulf of Finland, later to become the location of St Petersburg. However between 1772 and 1795 Poland was partitioned between Russia, Prussia and, to the south, Austria. Following the defeat of Prussia in the Napoleonic Wars, the Duchy of Warsaw was created in 1807, but this 'rump Polish state' was 'an expression more of the balance of power than of the wishes of the people' (II, pp. 296f.). Its precariousness was quickly confirmed after Napoleon's retreat from Russia when, in 1813, the Duchy was occupied by Russian forces. The Congress of Vienna in 1815 created a new Kingdom of Poland, also centred on Warsaw. This 'Congress Kingdom' was as stable as the Vienna settlement – that is, instability was not long in coming. The Russian Tsar had the title of King of Poland, with considerable executive powers; however the constitution provided, 'on paper', 'many of the marks of a genuine constitutional monarchy' (II, p. 309). A constitutional monarchy with a Russian Tsar as monarch was not a felicitous combination, and clashes of interests developed, coming to a head in the abortive November Rising of 1830. This ill-planned rebellion led, through the intransigence of Tsar Nicholas I, to a Russo-Polish war in which the Russians were eventually victorious. The Kingdom persisted in formal terms until 1874, but its annexation by Russia had largely been achieved *de facto* in 1832.

The end of the First World War on the Eastern Front saw the emergence of a new independent Poland, the Second Republic, on frontiers considerably to the east of the present ones, marking the recapture for Poland of much territory that had been under Russian control since the Partitions. The Polish-Soviet War of 1919–20 and the resulting Treaty of Riga confirmed these possessions. A further partition, the seventh in Davies's count (II, p. 433),[11] occurred under the secret protocols of the Nazi-Soviet Pact and the ensuing invasions and occupation. The post-war settlement, initiated at Yalta, shifted Poland to the west, at the expense of Germany; and, moreover, the occupying forces brought about a huge movement of population – of Poles in the Ukraine and Byelorussia into the new Poland, and of Germans in Pomerania and Silesia to Germany. Under communist party rule, the familiar experience of domination by Russia was relived, exacerbated by the absence of a substantial domestic source of support for communism in the activities of a wartime communist resistance movement.[12] Postwar history up to 1989 was marked by cycles in which national self-assertion, coupled with economic or political crisis, led to 'palace revolutions' which appeared, misleadingly, to address fundamental national grievances.[13]

The 'historical experience' of Poles and hence the content of national identity might therefore appear to be easily specified: memories of the status and extent of the Polish-Lithuanian Republic; resentment of its dismemberment and of the perpetrators of that act; further resentment of the Russians fuelled by subsequent hostilities; consciousness of the lengthy struggle of Poles for lost nationhood; and Roman Catholicism. A closer look reveals various complexities. The Republic involved an act of self-deception – that administrative paralysis comprised a form of freedom – which the Russian Tsar (who claimed in the period of growing Russian hegemony to be the 'protector' of Polish freedoms against encroachment by central authority) was able to exploit. The partition period saw widespread 'loyalism' (that is, loyalty to the partitioning authorities):

predictably enough, opposition was a minority activity. The Catholic Church played a particularly ambiguous role. Its symbolic representation of nationhood could only be enhanced by the fact that the main oppressing powers were, respectively, Lutheran and Russian Orthodox. However, the Catholic Church is an organization as well as a symbol, and moreover a supranational one with its own political interests. The Catholicism of the Hapsburg rulers of Austria-Hungary impinged on these interests. The November Rising, one of the most salient symbols of nationhood, was condemned by Pope Gregory XVI, and a favourable Papal response to the January Rising of 1863 was somewhat tardy. But at a lower level, and among Polish Catholic intellectuals, the role of the clergy in the preservation of national identity was more positive (II, pp. 213–216).

Thus it is clear that a substantial element of myth contributes to Polish national identity. This element is perhaps unusually large because of the fact that, for much of its history, '"Poland", as an abstraction, could be remembered from the past, or aspired to for the future, but only imagined in the present'; 'Poland was . . . an Idea' (II, pp. 8f.). Davies notes that the idea replaced the real nation 'on the eve of the birth of Nationalism and Liberalism' (I, p. 525), thus facilitating the preservation of national identity in the particularly potent form of nationalism, as well as enabling Poland to serve as a symbol of the new principle of self-determination throughout Europe. As a result, 'the modern Polish nation is the end-product of modern Polish Nationalism', that is, of the overtly political, even if minority, struggle for statehood in the nineteenth century (II, p. 13).

According to Davies, the definition of Polishness has varied substantially. In Poland-Lithuania, its application was geographically wide but socially narrow. Nationality was equivalent to citizenship, and thus referred to many peoples – such as Ruthenes and Lithuanians – who were not ethnically Polish; but at the same time 'citizenship' denoted political participation, and thus was confined to the nobility. During the nineteenth century, he argues, the idea of Polishness became more widely disseminated, as a result both of social change (such as the emancipation of serfs in the Great Reforms of Tsar Alexander II) and of the publicity attending uprisings. At the same time, it became narrower geographically, as outlying groups, particularly the Ruthenes, who became Ukrainians and Byelorussians, began to assert their own identity. Despite changes in the composition of the population, Davies argues that 'the net result is clear': 'The multinational, multilingual, multistratified society of the old Republic, ruled by its noble Polish *národ*, or nation, has been transformed over five or six generations into a far more homogeneous society where the *lud*, the common people of workers or peasants, have risen to a position of apparent supremacy' (II, p. 179).

In view of these changes in social structure and in the scope of nationality, the suggestion that a sense of Polish identity could be explained by simple inheritance – the socialization process – is implausible. Davies's account of the preservation of the Polish 'idea' during the partition period puts decisive emphasis on the role of the cultural intelligentsia and the small minority of insurrectionists, noting the absence of an 'organic social process' which is Polish (II, pp. 178f. and n. 1, p. 652), and the wide differences between the three partitioned areas in terms of laws, institutions and way of life. To this extent, it would appear that the bearers of Polish identity continued to be a minority elite stratum of the population. On the other hand, Davies's account of the emergence of Polish nationalism in the Prussian, subsequently German, partition, points to a different social locus of identity. Two policies towards the Polish territories initiated by Bismarck had counterproductive effects: that of 'colonization', designed to encourage Germans to settle in the east, and the *Kulturkampf*, which involved (as we will soon see in more detail) an attack on the Polish language, and other attempts at cultural 'Germanization'. Where the state, in conformity with Prussian tradition, while being authoritarian nevertheless operated within a framework of legality, scope was offered for Polish nationalism to reassert itself: but it was the vigour of the attacks made on it, and particularly their penetration to low levels of society, that provoked the widespread emergence of national identity (II, pp. 124–132).

The nineteenth-century extension of Polish nationality to the mass of the population is, as the mobilizationist school in the theory of nationalism has made clear, a widespread phenomenon, not confined to Poland. It is indeed, as Gellner suggests, part of a more general political development of the political incorporation of the masses, marked in many countries by the spread of mass education and the broadening of the franchise. Davies's assertion of the 'supremacy' of the Polish people is a claim about changes in social structure and the political importance of the masses – essentially about the beginnings in Poland of mass society – and not one about the degree to which a Polish identity was actually possessed by the majority of the population. Evidence for the response of the mass of the population to the assertion of Polish identity is in short supply. A distinction needs to be made, this example suggests, between the new political principle that the masses possessed citizenship and hence politically significant national attributes, and the claim that they experienced Polish identity. The former is a normative claim, and involves the transition from naming a *territory* to naming a *population* Polish; the latter is an empirical claim for which we lack evidence. The age of nationalism to which Davies refers is so precisely because of the establishment of the former principle, extending *nominal* national identity to the masses. But that principle, whose assertion was in general terms a once-and-for-all event, comprising part of the development of mass politics, merely opened up a new field for political contestation, in which people, not land, were the target, and rival assertions of nominal national identity were the substance of the contest. The empirical claim was swept up into the normative struggle, and not just as a question of which assertion of nominal national identity was empirically correct, but also, as the *Kulturkampf* graphically illustrates, as a question of which assertion was going to be *made* correct.

The *Kulturkampf* was an attempt by Germany to invalidate the 'Polish question' by eliminating the phenomenon of Polishness, and thereby simultaneously to justify, on the basis of the new principle of popular national identity, the boundaries of the German Empire. To be sure, these policies had wider ramifications in the rest of the German Empire also, involving an attack on the Catholic Church. But, as a monograph by Lech Trzeciakowski makes clear, in Poland Catholicism and Polishness merged into a single target, as for instance the much greater percentage loss of Catholic clergy there reveals.[14] A series of legislative acts in the 1870s progressively weakened the authority of the Catholic Church by eliminating its educational role. In the Polish partition, senior Polish bishops were replaced by Germans and local clergy removed. German was propagated as a compulsory language of instruction from 1872, Polish being made a supplementary language. Local government and the courts were Germanized in 1873–76, leading to considerable inconveniences for all concerned, and place names were changed. Bismarck, Trzeciakowski reports, wanted to spread knowledge of German as a means of access to pro-German propaganda. But the effect was the reverse: these policies made contact with German a source of difficulties for the population, reciprocally reinforcing Polish national identity: 'For many it was to constitute a moment of passage from an objective to a subjective national consciousness, consisting of a participation in the fight against germanization.'[15]

Trzeciakowski's account of this response concentrates on the sector for which more evidence is available – the political elite – but does not ignore the mass response. Evidence for the latter includes the signing of petitions and attendance at rallies. He attributes the largest role in the diffusion of nationalistic ideology to the Polish-language press; many journalists were themselves active politically. Other contributions were made by economic, educational and cultural societies, by political theatre, and by election campaigns, whose purpose was indeed *primarily* mobilizational, since Polish deputies, even when their election was unhampered by the authorities, had little influence in the Prussian and imperial legislatures.[16] Trzeciakowski's conclusion is that the *Kulturkampf*, while its influence varied across the regions of Poland, was an experience for the whole population. It originated as an elite-level contest over the assertion of nominal national identity, but the comprehensive penetration of that assertion provoked a 'continuous everyday struggle to retain national distinctness, a struggle that took in the widest mass of Polish society'.[17]

What Davies's hints about the *Kulturkampf* and Trzeciakowski's fuller examination suggests is that the implication of active subject and passive object carried by terms such as 'incorporation' and 'imposition' is erroneous. It is certainly true that we have more evidence concerning the elite activists, mainly because much of their activity consisted in writing; and it is also true that intellectual and political elites are better equipped, through their education and indeed through their possession of leisure time, to engage in the activity of reconstructing or inventing national identity. But the claim that the mass of the population is a passive object is nevertheless false. In the *Kulturkampf*, an assertion of nominal national identity by the political authorities provoked a counter-identity on the part of the population, seeking a means by which to analyze and react to the concrete and day-to-day disruption that the *Kulturkampf* brought about. Once made objects of the claim of nominal national identity, and thereby admitted into political significance, the masses at once become subjects, experiencing their own *phenomenological* national identity.

The admission that intellectual elites are better equipped for reconstruction and invention of national identity, and that the identity they elaborate provides the content sought in the popular response to German oppression, does not, furthermore, justify the Gellnerite claim of the 'arbitrariness' of their activities. We argued in the abstract that this claim isolates the national activists from their own history. In the concrete Polish case we can see what this means. That case illustrates quite clearly that increased education might simply bring increased exposure to discrimination and a more dramatic and painful confrontation with an asserted nominal national identity. No less than the masses, and perhaps a good deal more, the Polish elite has ample stimulus in its own experience to construct a national identity – to 'search for its roots'.

Distinctions between elites and masses, therefore, although they exist, should not be drawn too strongly. It is true that, among the Polish elite, nationalism was an active principle well before the *Kulturkampf*, whereas for the mass of the population it seems that the latter provided the decisive moment. It is also true that, in its contributions to written debate about national identity and the threat of Germanization, particularly in newspapers but in other forums as well, the elite is in a position to make a more elaborate construction of national identity than ordinary people can in their response to an event such as the loss of their local priest or an incomprehensible encounter with a state official. It is the elite who are in a position to make connections between the *Kulturkampf* and the earlier indignities and injustices of Polish history, and thus to give reaction to it a national character. But, we are suggesting, in both cases the formation of national identity needs to be seen as a response to social conditions. The conditions are such as to make nationality a social role, creating the possibility for the community first 'imagined' by the elite to be joined by the whole population. Polish response to the *Kulturkampf* is a good example of the typification and *reciprocal* typification of phenomenological social theory; and phenomenology in particular enables the Gellnerite supposition of free-floating intellectuals arbitrarily inventing national identity to be avoided.

GERMANY: THE NATION AS INVENTION

The case of Germany merits consideration if only as a counterpoint to our discussion of the *Kulturkampf*. Of more relevance to our argument, however, is that it provides an extreme example of the creativity involved in elaborating nominal national identity. Despite this it also illustrates the utility of a phenomenological explanation of the etiology of this identity.

The German nation was first, but only minimally, embodied in the Holy Roman Empire, a 'transnational, rather metaphysical' structure 'without its own statehood, organization or power'.[18] The Empire was a structure, therefore, not only isolated from the mass of the population, but also and more unusually lacking any basis in its historical existence upon which a national idea, or nominal national identity, could be built. Its final abolition in 1806 by Napoleon was a mere formality. The wars against Napoleon which led to the amalgamation of the 314 large and small states and principalities comprising the Holy Roman Empire into the 39 components of the German Confederation at the Congress of Vienna were regarded as 'wars of liberation', but the Germany that resulted remained a 'multinational complex': the area was organized 'not as a German nation-state but as a region where European interests were balanced out'.[19] The specification of boundary, crucial to nominal national identity, remained vague: the Confederation included various foreign monarchs (such as the king of England, a Hanoverian), and excluded large parts of Prussian and Austrian territory.

The proclamation of the German Empire in 1871 marked the culmination of the growth of Prussian domination over Germany and the exclusion of Austria (militarily defeated by Prussia in 1866). Germany was thus a good example of a nation with an 'empty history': it lacked any history as a nation state; it was a multinational empire, making the construction of national identity from mythic sources especially problematic; and no particular specification of boundary was suggested by its history. Indeed, debate over a 'greater' or 'lesser' Germany (including or excluding Austria) was an overt and salient feature of the growth of German nationalism in the period up to 1871.

German nationalism could not fail, in this setting, to be an invention. In the eighteenth century, Hagen Schulze reports, it was the development of a language of German high culture that provided the only basis of national sentiment; hence 'The German nation . . . was to be found solely in the heads of its educated members.' Defeat at Napoleon's hands in 1806 led to the assertion of the new principle: 'the people and their language were discovered as the only and final legitimising basis for the nation'. This assertion of nominal national identity was, Schulze explicitly states, the product of a confrontation with 'aggressive French nationalism'.[20]

In the case of a nation with a 'drained' history, Smith writes, the construction of national identity must be creative, and hence romantic.[21] German nationalism has indeed been seen as a 'romantic nationalism'; as perhaps the first.[22] Its symbolism has included Goethe, the city of Weimar, Gothic architecture, the Germanic legend of tribal leader Armenius and his ancient struggle against the Roman Empire. These are romantic notions in the everyday sense of the word, as well as being instances of the nineteenth-century European mood known as Romanticism. An important component was provided by the speculative linguistic theories of Fichte, which posited the superiority of the German 'mother tongue' over the 'derived' French language, and inferred boundaries from the linguistically-based idea of the *Kulturnation*.

Although the linguistic definition of boundary helps to explain policies such as the *Kulturkampf* in the Polish partition, the existence throughout Central and Eastern Europe of a large German-speaking diaspora made the expansionist implications of that definition geopolitically impractical for most of German history. Together with the feebleness of the Holy Roman Empire and the Confederation as symbols of the national past, the infeasibility of the romantic conception of nominal national identity has been seen by Harold James as provoking an alternative 'doctrine of nationality', a doctrine 'that justified the existence of the nation primarily by reference to the inexorable laws of economic development',[23] a doctrine that was in time challenged from the romantic perspective in diverse ways, for instance by Wagner and Nietszche.

The Weimar Republic, which so conspicuously failed to meet the economic criterion of national progress (being the victim first of hyperinflation and then in the late 1920s of the Great Depression), also failed to create a new 'national iconography'.[24] Its successor, National Socialism, was a synthesis of many of the components of nominal national identity already mentioned. It rejected the modernistic aesthetic culture of Weimar, reviving not only some of the symbols of German romantic nationalism but also, and fatefully, its definition of boundary.[25] At the same time it was constructive, in the specifically German sense of using economic advance to create community. Architectural gigantism, as in the Soviet Union, was a symbol of this economic effort. 'There is no better way to educate a people to self-consciousness than grandiose communal tasks which show each individual that such a people is at least equal to all other nations', Hitler said in an address in 1939, revealing both his concern with defining national identity and, most interestingly, under-confidence in the German people's possession of it.[26]

Although, as Schulze, in a bibliographical essay, makes clear, research into the social basis of the rise of German nationalism, in other words into the transformation of nominal national identity into genuine popular national identity, is at only a preliminary stage, German historiography has in recent years investigated in much greater detail the elite debates of which the foundation of the German Empire in 1871 was the culmination.[27] These investigations have served to counter earlier assumptions of the inevitability of that outcome, stressing the diversity of the conceptions of German nationality that the debates featured. Significant moments, such as the debate in the Frankfurt Paulskirche Assembly following the revolution of 1848 over whether the Confederation should be succeeded by a greater or lesser Germany (in which the initial presumption in favour of the former was transformed into an unrealized decision for the latter) expose for analysis processes which in the case of most nations are less public and for which minutes are not usually taken: processes of the construction of national identity. It is indeed worth suggesting that the records of such occasions be examined with the rigour of conversational analysis (although minutes of political meetings are, of course, less susceptible to such detailed analysis than tape-recorded conversations) in order to expose how fundamental was the process of construction. In any case, awareness of the fluidity of the definition of Germany certainly aids in understanding the vigour of the attack which the *Kulturkampf* subsequently made on the Polish minority.

IMPLICATIONS FOR POLITICAL CULTURE

It has been an important contribution of the recent debates in the theory of nationalism to deny that nations can be explained simply on the basis of inheritance, or that national identity can be explained simply in terms of socialization. These factors undoubtedly play a role, but it has been salutary to have historical attention directed to those mainly nineteenth-century periods in which nationalism and nations were in many cases created. Profound social changes occurred in the nineteenth century, and to suppose that nations served simply as the unmodified receptacles for these changes is implausible, and is contradicted by evidence unearthed by recent research. In neither the Polish nor the German cases were the receptacles 'given'; they were created and struggled over.

This new view itself begins to shed more darkness than light, however, when an excessive emphasis is placed on invention, particularly on its arbitrariness and on the ease of its imposition. Our examples have served to show that construction of national identity is not an *act*, but a *process*. The process is no doubt made up of a series of individual acts, such as the forgery of a fragment of 'ancient' national literature, the making of a speech in the Paulskirche Assembly, or the passing in the German Reichstag of an item of *Kulturkampf* legislation. Nevertheless, to see construction as a process is more fully to recognize social reality; to see its participants as trying to project a path through a changing and conflict-ridden political landscape, and to see the constructs themselves as new entries into that landscape that have to be comprehended and negotiated by participants lower down the social hierarchy. It is, therefore, to adopt a phenomenological perspective on national identity.

This conclusion has more general implications for our understanding of political culture. The study of national identity presents obstacles to a phenomenological approach, but they may be overcome, indicating the usefulness of that approach in the otherwise problematic study of the indexical aspects of political culture. We have seen that, while a mass/elite distinction needs to be taken into account in the study of national identity, it should not be overstated, and both levels should be approached with the phenomenological orientation towards political and social process, and the abandonment of assumptions about what is given or 'primordial'. The same is true in the study of political culture more generally. The behavioural definition of political culture as mass attitudes towards politics and political symbols might, for instance, be regarded as a means of investigation of the success of claims of nominal national identity. Alternatively, those who, applying to political culture research the 'movement of thought' we traced in Chapter 6, construe culture as a resource, make the opposite emphasis, on the discretionary activities of the political elite. David Laitin, for instance, writes: 'a good theory of culture must also point to the fact that people are instrumental about which aspect of their cultural repertoire is of primary significance and that shared symbols constitute a political resource that can be effectively exploited by political entrepreneurs'.[28] The last phrase, particularly, recalls Gellner's idea of elites arbitrarily gathering 'shreds and patches' to create national identity. What we learn from studying the case of national identity more carefully is that neither of these approaches is adequate, and that not only does attention to mass and elite levels have to be combined, it also has to take the phenomenological form that we have outlined.

Although deriving from a quite abstract discussion of issues in anthropology and social theory, the phenomenological analysis throws considerable light on the more down-to-earth questions that political culture research has raised. We have seen examples of political contestation over the meaning of historical symbols, of the formulation of elite cultures as ways of life depending on elaborate rationalizations, and of cultures emerging in response to these. This complex range of phenomena, all of which comprise the context that an interpretive use of political culture refers to, cannot adequately be taken into account if either of the two restrictions on the scope of political culture just mentioned (restricting it to a mass or elite focus) are in effect. To take account of them requires placing emphasis on the invention of meaning, on the dependency of this process on political circumstances, and on its contribution to the evolution of new political circumstances. The study of national identity provides the most effective demonstration of the necessity of doing so.

8 New Trends in Political Culture Research

This final chapter, like the preceding one, aims to develop and refine further the phenomenological analysis of political culture. Here, however, we are concerned not to extend the analysis beyond the scope of existing political culture research, but to show how it can be used in the evaluation of recent and novel examples of that research. In part, the argument to follow will illustrate the use of the phenomenological analysis as a critical tool, as we investigate developments in the political-scientific use of political culture, particularly the impact of anthropological structuralism and its derivative, the 'grid/group' typology of Mary Douglas. In the latter half of the chapter, however, a more positive argument is made. We will examine the use of political culture in American historiography, a setting in which the concept has in recent years undergone a rapid rise in popularity. The best of these uses, we will argue, illustrate not only the utility but also the detailed form of a phenomenological analysis of political culture.

STRUCTURALISM

The methodological and interpretive principles of structuralism that were borrowed by political scientists from anthropologist Claude Lévi-Strauss were first borrowed by him from linguistics, particularly the structural linguistics of Ferdinand de Saussure. Some of the key features later to be found in political cultural structuralism can be seen in this original version. Of crucial significance is Saussure's claim that the relationship between sign and signified is arbitrary. This somewhat oracular utterance encapsulates much of the structuralist programme, because it entails that meaning is to be sought not in the 'reference' of sign to reality, but in relations between signs, that is, in linguistic structure. In Saussure's linguistics, units of sound or 'phonemes', rather than words or other supposedly meaningful units, provide the basic data, and the general rules by which they are combined provide the analytic framework.[1] Among these rules, the most important is 'binary opposition', the dictum that 'Concepts are purely differential, and are defined not by their positive content but negatively by their relations with other terms of the system.'[2]

Lévi-Strauss's borrowing from structural linguistics was essentially ana-
logical, as is exemplified by his structuralist theory of myths. He coined the
term 'mytheme' to refer to the 'constituent units' of myths, and his goal,
analogously, was to expose the universal relations by which mythemes are
connected. The analysis attempts to show that myths consist of repetitions
of the same sequences – just as a musical score, if it were read line by line
as a book, would contain repetitions (with variations for each instrument) of
the same themes. As with the musical score, the myth ought not to be read
sequentially, and its full meaning is brought out only when the 'harmony'
between the repeated themes is exposed by structural analysis.[3] This was
not, however, the only application: the structural linguistic paradigm came
to be applied by Lévi-Strauss to more general phenomena too, such as
kinship systems, the layout of cities, and other manifestations of social
organization.

Lévi-Strauss's structuralism has in turn been adopted by political scientists. If Lévi-Strauss's theory of myth is an extension of Saussure's
linguistic structuralism, the concept of 'narrative' used by political culture
researchers is a further extension, although as just noticed, grounds for
it are already suggested by Lévi-Strauss's own wide applications of
structuralist analysis. Like myths, narratives are said to 'act out' the
culture and in particular to enact, through binary oppositions, relations
and transformations, the contradictions inherent in it. Like myths, they
need to be read in a structuralist manner in order for their meaning to be
exposed; their meaning lies in their structure, in the relations between their
universal elements, not in what might appear in a non-structuralist reading
to be their particular content. The concept of 'narrative' is of very broad
application. Myths become merely a subset of narratives; anything can be
termed a narrative and interpreted structurally that can be represented as
a story. Oral narratives, that is, stories told to one another by members of
a community, have, for instance, been the subject of structuralist analysis
by Eloise Buker.[4] A wider range of material has been examined in this
manner by Richard Merelman, including accounts of historical events
in high-school textbooks, the content of corporate house journals and
magazine advertisements, and the plots of TV sitcoms.[5] The concept of
narrative has even been extended to the record of a series of legislative
enactments in the Brezhnevite Soviet Union.[6]

Part of the legacy of structuralism in political culture research, then,
has been a readiness to consider a much wider range of phenomena as
data. But neither this attribute nor the location of structuralist political
culture research within the broad category of interpretivism exhaust that
legacy. Its crucial component is the claim that meaning is expressed

through structure, or what is sometimes called 'deep structure', a term which further emphasizes the structuralist notion that meaning is never immediately apparent, but can only be exposed through analysis. This view has considerable ramifications. It means that structuralist analyses explicitly and self-consciously abstract the meaning of 'narratives' from what may be understood by the participants. It therefore does as a matter of programme what thick description is sometimes in danger of doing accidentally.

This characteristic of structuralism has been criticized, by Sebastiano Timpanaro, as 'objective idealism'.[7] This contradictory-sounding label is not altogether inapt. Not only is emphasis in structural interpretation squarely placed on the interpretive achievement of the researcher in exposing the structure of narratives clearly an example of what we have termed idealism. But in contrast to Geertz's agnosticism about what form that achievement should take, structuralism is insistent that it should expose the universal pattern of relations, transformations and, fundamentally, binary oppositions. This is not yet perhaps an 'objective' idealism, but it is certainly a universalistic or formalistic one, and it threatens to become objective when structuralists argue that there is something in the structure of the human mind that gives rise to the alleged structure of its products.[8]

When the same critic writes,

> the anthropologist . . . invites [the linguist] not to furnish historical or empirical merchandise but rather *a priori* models, inventories by means of which all cultures can appear as the result of various random correlations of a few invariant elements[9]

he goes too far, since structuralism certainly does not posit random combinations of elements, but instead combinations that 'express' contradictions. His identification of the *a priori* nature of structuralism, hence its idealism, is, however, accurate. With reference to the actual form of the structure held to be present, Ernest Gellner has alleged that 'some of these "binary oppositions" do not genuinely explain or generate anything', and that structuralist analyses are 'open to the suspicion that they are just the pursuit of pretty and fanciful patterns, in a language which is suggestive but which, like the various Hegelian and Freudian languages, is over-adaptable and hopelessly loose'.[10]

However, lest our own critique of structuralism seem excessively *a priori*, it is time to examine in detail one of its exemplars. Because it not only illustrates in its findings the structuralist use of political culture but is also concerned to draw a contrast in theoretical terms between structuralism and earlier modes of political culture research, we will turn to Merelman's contribution. So far as the theoretical discussion is concerned, it is unsurprising that Merelman somewhat caricatures what he calls the 'political culture approach', but rather than correct this error, we may notice that the caricature is itself instructive. Merelman first notes that descriptions of American political culture are far from being mutually coherent. This fact alone does not vitiate cultural description, he says: it may be that American political culture consists of 'a perhaps fuzzy, yet nevertheless real pattern of attitudinal correlations'. Such a claim, however, would already go beyond what attitude survey data reveal, since a 'pattern' can only be identified by the analyst. The structural approach, as we have seen, is characterized by the assumption of a pattern, and not just any pattern. 'Cultural form', Merelman says, is provided by opposition, an assumption that is at variance with the 'expectation of consensus' in existing analyses of American political culture. The 'cultural process', moreover, consists in the repetition of narratives which depict opposition and hence 'act out', 'display' and 'exercise' the culture. A crucial difference between structural and pre-structural analyses occurs in their treatment of individuals. Political culture research has aggregated individual attitudes, whereas in fact people 'have at best partial, distorted views of society's inner workings'. Culture has what is explicitly called an *a priori* quality; it imposes itself on individuals whether they like it or not, in the form of 'collective representations'. Not only are individuals represented as recipients of cultural processes; the question of what effect on individuals they have is put to one side: 'the structural approach does not depend for its account of culture and politics on audience reaction. Its first question is the nature of collective representations themselves; only later does it concern itself with the effects of such representations.' Eclectic use of data is justified by the structuralist argument that the deep structure of collective representations has its existence as deep structure only through 'metaphor', by which structuralists mean its repetition in diverse settings. Here, again, the analyst's priority is emphasized, since the links between these settings are not necessarily apparent to the participants, just as in Lévi-Strauss's analogy each musician is ignorant of the entire score.

There is a peculiar difficulty in objecting to the idealism of the structuralist approach, in that the approach is explicit in admitting it. Nevertheless, we can notice that structuralism contrasts rather starkly with a phenomenological approach to political culture. To be sure, the latter, as we have outlined it, pays considerable attention to processes of opposition and to the reciprocal typification that they facilitate. But it directly counters the idealist claim that meaning is not to be sought in the understanding of the participants but in the structure-making and metaphor-recognition of the analyst. It makes precisely the opposite claim, that meaning is constituted through concrete social processes – and this does not entail, as Merelman's caricature of non-structuralist political culture research would imply, that it may be fully described by administering attitude surveys. But given structuralism's disarming frankness about its lack of interest in the 'native's point of view', how are we to criticize it? Merelman's findings provide the means.

The essential problem of idealism is of the validation of its claims. If all data other than the interpretation offered by the analyst are declared irrelevant, how can that interpretation be compared to a rival one? Merelman interprets the deep structure of American political culture in terms of 'mythologized individualism': its narratives 'all depict a deep structure which poses group repression in an unjust society against individual freedom in a just, naturally sound society'.[11] This structure is derived from a cursory reading of American history, with its tales of 'American heroes who have successfully negotiated the deep structural passage from group-based constraint to individual freedom', people like Andrew Jackson, Abraham Lincoln and Franklin Roosevelt. Merelman then claims to find this representation recurring in his sample of sitcoms, magazines, textbooks and company newsletters, providing a 'statistical' test of his 'hypothesis'. These scientific-sounding words are, however, rather out of place, given the nature of the 'demonstration' – a scanty collection of generalities about advertising, house journals and sitcoms that do not even forcefully state the hypothesis, let alone demonstrate it.[12]

The problem, obviously, is not that the idea of individualism cannot be found in media representations, but that many other values or even 'oppositions' no doubt can be too. The most cursory thought about the sitcoms currently most popular in the United States ('Roseanne' and 'Cheers') suggests that the values of family and community are at least as important as that of individualism. This is not to deny the significance of individualism, only to deny that Merelman's methods effectively demonstrate its presence or say anything new about it. If all that structuralism has to offer is another statement of the idea of the 'American dream' we may indeed wonder what all the fuss was about. Yet Merelman cannot in principle offer more because all evidence about what this representation means to people has been deemed irrelevant. Structuralism offers collective representations but eschews investigation of whether anything is represented *to* anybody. Describing them in terms of 'binary oppositions', especially when, with Gellner, we notice how easy such redescription is, is in itself not at all compelling, except to a convert.

Merelman begins by accepting that a choice needs to be made between what he terms 'idealist' and 'materialist' assumptions, the latter asserting the 'economic and ecological' basis of culture, the former its irreducibility. This dichotomy is denied by phenomenology (which Merelman erroneously places in the 'idealist' camp). Meanings are socially constructed, it argues, and the appearance of their 'objectivity' or 'givenness' is merely a common-sense agreement that provisionally enables social life to proceed. They are constructed, moreover, in social processes, particularly in the process of opposition. Opposition, in this view, is a concrete social process from which meanings emerge, not an abstraction in which they are elaborated by the analyst. We have seen in this section how such abstraction deprives structuralist political cultural description of evidential support. In the last section of this chapter we will look at some examples of the kind of description sanctioned by the phenomenological approach.

THE GRID AND THE GROUP

Of all recent entries into political culture research, the most ambitious has been the so-called 'culture theory' derived by Aaron Wildavsky and others from the work of anthropologist Mary Douglas.[13] In a number of ways this theory resembles the structuralist approach to political culture; indeed it may be seen as a derivative of it.[14] Of greatest importance among these similarities is the formalistic or universalistic quality of the theory, which, in like manner, is in danger of seeming at best irrelevant and at worst misleading when it is applied to concrete cases.

The theory, which has been developed by Wildavsky in several articles and more fully set out in a recent book co-authored by him, Michael Thompson and Richard Ellis,[15] draws its initial impetus from an argument that sits comfortably with the phenomenological approach to political culture that we have advanced in preceding chapters. This is Wildavsky's argument that, while 'the politics of interests is the mainstay of political science', the construal of interests as unanalyzable 'givens' by economics and its derivative, rational choice theory, is unwarranted. Interests should instead, he argues, be defined as 'preferences' that emerge out of social relations and people's participation in politics: '[people's] continuing reinforcement, modification, and rejection of existing power relations teaches them what to prefer'. Wildavsky defines 'cultures' as groups possessing a distinct set of preferences, requiring others against which to define themselves, again suggesting the phenomenological analysis, though without using that word.[16] In *Cultural Theory*, this view is considerably expanded. Not only are interests denied the status of 'givens', but so are 'myths of nature' (that is, views of the bountifulness or otherwise of nature), views of human nature, and perceptions of needs and resources (chs. 1, 2). Thus a culture is a coherent set of biases and patterns of behaviour which is typified and perpetuated by what amounts to a distinct rationality.

Somewhat provocatively, the authors describe their analysis as 'functional'. This has the unfortunate result of forcing them to defend their account against the well-known objections to functional explanation that it incorporates 'illegitimate teleology' and makes an implicit assumption of homeostasis (chs. 10, 11). The defence consists in the claim that such objections are valid only against functionalism as applied to whole societies, when it unwarrantably obscures the existence of conflict and change. In the new theory, culture is explicitly separated from societies or countries, each country being seen as having only a particular *combination* of cultures.[17] When applied to 'ways of life' or cultures within societies, attention is, on the contrary, directed to conflict and change, in the form of the process of rivalry between the cultures. 'Functionalism', then, is supposed to refer only to the logical interconnections between preferences, interests, views of nature, views of human nature and conceptions of needs and resources, and to the contribution each of these makes to the perpetuation of a distinct way of life. We will see, however, that in the particular form taken by the claim that cultures require each other for self-definition, a hint of societal functionalism is present, to damaging effect.

That claim of reciprocal dependence in its own right is, of course, consistent with a phenomenological analysis, and indeed 'phenomenological' would be a more accurate label than 'functional' for the analysis as presented thus far. This is, however, only the first phase of the argument made by Thompson, Ellis and Wildavsky. Its second and more distinctive phase is the claim that there is only a limited number of 'viable' ways of life: five, to be exact.

The basis for this claim lies in Douglas's theory of the 'grid' and the 'group'. Douglas posits two 'dimensions of social control': the degree of prescriptivity or grid dimension, which specifies whether prescriptions and constraints are numerous, and the degree of collectivity or group dimension, which specifies whether group boundaries are weak or strong. From these two dimensions is derived a four-place matrix of cultures or ways of life, each defining itself in contrast with its opposite along each dimension. The four cultures are termed (in the most recent version) 'egalitarian', 'hierarchical', 'individualistic' and 'fatalistic'. The fifth viable culture is the antithesis of all these, in a sense a 'special case': the way of life of the 'hermit'.

The implications of the proposed limitation in number of viable cultures are considerable. As Thompson, Ellis and Wildavsky put it:

> Anyone who sets out to draw parallels between one culture and another (or, loftier still, to formulate a universal generalization about human behavior) is liable to have those whose stock-in-trade is the deep-seated peculiarities of a society or organization immediately step in with the anthropologist's veto: 'Not in my tribe.' Our aim is to override this veto by showing that although nations and neighborhoods, tribes and races, have their distinctive sets of values, beliefs, and habits, their basic convictions about life are reducible to only a few cultural biases. By limiting the number of viable ways of life, we contend, one can rescue the study of culture from the practitioners of 'spiteful ethnography', who conceive of culture solely as a means to invalidate social science theories. (pp. 4f.)

A number of arguments are marshalled in support of the proposed typology. Its fecundity is illustrated, the authors assert, by a 'wide and impressive body of applications' (p. 14). This support is rendered doubtful, however, when some of these 'applications' are examined. The work of Arthur Asa Berger is a case in point. His collections *Political Culture and Public Opinion* and *Agitpop: Political Culture and Communication Theory* gather accounts (in the first case by other writers, in the second by himself) of popular culture as diverse as the description of the creation of the Washington Vietnam Veterans Memorial and semiotic analysis of its function, an analysis of graffiti by homeless youth, and dissections of a music video and the Arnold Schwarzenegger film *The Terminator*.[18] Whatever the merits of the individual analyses (and some of them are certainly thought-provoking), only the most cursory editorial justification is offered for placing them under headings derived from Wildavsky's categories. The categories offer little to the analyses. In this respect, the typology, like the structuralist idea of binary opposition, appears to be not merely available, but promiscuously so, to an extent that threatens to discredit it.

The same point can be made about the more general justification offered by the authors for their four-place typology (ignoring, as the authors frequently do, the special case of the hermit's way of life), that it comprehends and better accounts for numerous existing typologies. A theory that claims to comprehend not merely several of the many typologies presented by existing political culture research (chs. 12–14), but also such broad typologies as Marx's distinction of feudal and capitalist society (p. 155) and Weber's distinction of 'traditional', 'legal-rational' and 'charismatic' types of authority (pp. 162–164), must either be one of the most striking achievements in the history of thought or be subject to the suspicion of banality. Perhaps the expansion of the explanatory scope of a theory may reach a point of diminishing returns.

However, these arguments do not address the central justification proposed for the typology, which is of a distinctively formal nature. That is, the very form of the typology is held to be its main strength. The authors make much of the 'asymmetric' nature of other typologies, and the fact that some of them are not derived from the interaction of dimensions. In a field where, as was observed in the Introduction, typologies have proliferated, sometimes to no discernible benefit, some consideration of the criteria of a good typology is certainly in order. But the insistence on 'symmetry' and 'dimensionality' is unjustified. Thompson, Ellis and Wildavsky make a distinction between explanation and labelling, arguing that only when the types derive from the interaction of dimensions is the former, that is, a causal account, achieved: 'A single dimension is insufficient to compel anything. It is the organizational imperatives created by the interaction of the grid and group dimensions that compel people to behave in ways that maintain their way of life' (p. 262). But if the dimensions themselves are mere labels, how does their interaction transcend description? If the distinction between high and low levels of prescriptivity on the 'grid' dimension is not in itself explanatory, why does it become so when combined with the perpendicular 'group' dimension? Why, for that matter, may not a third dimension, or more, be added? The addition of the category of 'hermit' may indeed be seen as introducing a third dimension. But this upsets the 'symmetry' of the Wildavsky typology, by which the authors assert its superiority over others. In general, it appears that an aesthetic judgement of the typology's formal elegance is substituted for a scientific judgement of its usefulness.

The claim that cultures require opposites against which to define themselves, which as its stands is phenomenologically valid, becomes dubious when the number of cultures is restricted, and moreover leads to an important contradiction in the theory. The authors note the dynamic nature of their theory; they allow for 'migration' from one culture to another, prompted by 'surprises', that is the discovery that 'the world as it is' does not in crucial respects 'fit' the cultural model (p. 69). They give the analogy of a flock of starlings, each bird having to move constantly in order to keep the flock intact (p. 84),[19] but the implication of this claim is that all four cultures need to be present if any of them are to be. Thus a claim to societal functionalism is implicit. Not only does this undermine the authors' defence of their variant of functionalism, it makes the application of the typology to concrete cases highly problematic. The capacity of the grid/group typology to absorb all existing characterizations and typologies of political culture is touted as one of its strengths, but in order for it to do so, the claim of mutual dependence of the four cultures has to be abandoned. This is true not only for small-scale accounts, such as Edward Banfield's study of an Italian peasant community (pp. 223–227), redescribed by Thompson, Ellis and Wildavsky in terms of 'fatalism'. It is also true for countries as a whole, in keeping with Wildavsky's claim that countries are typified by a certain distribution of cultures. Lucian Pye's account of two political cultures in China (pp. 228f.), and Almond and Verba's of the three components of the civic culture in the United States (pp. 247–258)[20] provide examples of studies that, viewed through the lens of the grid/group typology, reveal incomplete sets of cultures. These findings, if they are to be so reinterpreted, indicate that the claim that each culture needs its opposites in order to exist must be false. But that claim derives from the fundamental structuralist basis of the theory – it cannot easily be discarded. A tension thus appears between the phenomenologically plausible claim of reciprocal cultural definition and the formalistic and basically structuralist insistence that only four cultures are viable.

That the four cultures really are fundamental to the theory may be demonstrated by looking at how Thompson, Ellis and Wildavsky treat a typology of American political culture that superficially bears a strong resemblance to theirs, namely Daniel Elazar's. As we saw in Chapter 4, Elazar argues that American political culture is a synthesis of three subcultures: 'individualistic', 'moralistic' and 'traditionalistic', whose central concepts, respectively, are the marketplace, the commonwealth, and hierarchy. He describes the geographical distribution of these subcultures, the result, he says, of migrations of their original bearers.[21] Thompson, Ellis and Wildavsky criticize this analysis on two counts (the number of applications it has generated not appearing to provide immunity). One is that the categories are wrongly specified, some being translatable into Thompson, Ellis and Wildavsky's, others requiring disaggregation (the 'moralistic' culture of Massachusetts, for instance, is found to contain both 'hierarchical' and 'egalitarian' elements – p. 240). The other is the formalistic argument that Elazar's types are differentiated not in terms of underlying dimensions, but in terms of their concrete manifestations: that is, their geographical distribution (pp. 240f.). They are thus instances of mere 'labelling'. The redescription of Elazar's categories in terms of the four cultures is supposed not merely to provide a more differentiated and accurate description, but also an *explanation*, which follows from the 'compulsion' inherent in the interaction of the two dimensions. Elazar's historical and hence contingent explanation of the presence of the three subcultures is superseded by an ahistorical and formal claim that four cultures must necessarily exist.

Thus the theory has some self-destructive contradictions. It is dynamic without being historical. It is phenomenological without being concrete. It posits a universal condition that is patently not met in specific cases. This does not mean, however, that it is without application. A revealing assertion by Wildavsky is that the limit of four cultures is generous by the standard of the usual political dichotomy of left and right.[22] This suggests that the greatest utility of the grid/group typology might lie in the analysis of policy preferences and groupings in electoral politics. It is not only more discriminating than the left/right dichotomy, but in its phenomenological or 'functional' aspect makes more explicit than that dichotomy the linkages between different policy preferences and between preferences and lifestyles. But as a tool of policy analysis, the grid/group typology becomes itself mired in cultural specificity. Its grand ambitions then have to be exchanged for the less impressive though still significant purpose of analyzing electoral politics, in particular of demonstrating the interconnection of social, economic and environmental political issues.[23]

Even here, however, the formalism and resulting abstractness of the theory may prove its undoing. Wildavsky has derided the insistence that cultures be attached to whole societies as 'nominalism',[24] with the implication that just because a society has a name does not mean that it has a culture. While not endorsing the view that cultures do necessarily attach to societies and not to subgroups, the phenomenological argument counters that dismissal. If the attribution of a national, tribal or more generally 'cultural' label were merely an act of the observer, 'nominalism' – reserving the denotation 'culture' for such named groups – would be arbitrary. When, however, the act of naming is seen primarily as an act of the group itself or of its elite, one with potential significance for the political demands that are pressed on the basis of identity, and one which might reflect the group's or its elite's own (phenomenological) response to its history in relation to other groups, 'nominalism' assumes great descriptive utility. What is more generally implied is that the concrete processes of group formation and reciprocal definition may tell us much more than the abstract framework of grid and group. The phenomenological perspective invites such concrete investigation: that is why it is in fundamental conflict with formalism, structuralism and idealism.

THE HISTORIANS

Political culture research intersects with historiography in a number of ways. Within comparative political science, even when political culture is characterized mainly through survey data, historical findings are frequently alluded to by way of consolidation of the descriptions gleaned from surveys, or indeed by way of accounting for the results they demonstrate. In the comparative use within communist studies, we saw, the relative scarcity of survey data led to a much more central use of historical data in accounts such as Stephen White's of Russian political culture. Even in this case, however, no claim was made to novel historical insight; White explicitly says of his use of historical findings that it 'reflects the scholarly consensus'. These cases represent the use of historical findings for the purposes of comparative political culture research, and as is typical of cross-disciplinary borrowings, the borrowers pay little attention to the conflicts within or purposes of the donor discipline.

Although, like White, Robert Tucker (and for that matter Alfred Meyer, whose usage is similar to Tucker's) makes the claim that Soviet political culture is in large measure a continuation of Tsarist Russian political culture, his purpose in making this claim is somewhat different. The difference is an instance of a banal but nevertheless valid distinction that may be made between historiography and political science: Tucker is concerned less to explain the present than to describe the past. To be sure, his account of 'Stalinist political culture' involves explanatory claims, contrary to his theoretical supposition that political culture may be useful 'without explaining anything', and in part these are indeed claims, similar to White's, of cultural continuity. But Tucker's account involves more than this, as we saw in Chapter 5; it also concerns itself with the novel aspects of Stalinist politics, such as its impact on the arts and sciences, and is amply aware of the novelty of the scope of the Stalinist imposition on society. Somewhat modifying and expanding Tucker's analysis to present it in its most distinctive light, we saw that it is an attempt at the thick description of Stalinist politics; we saw that 'political culture' is held to be an apt term not only because of the presence of cultural lag, but also because the Stalinist attempt at culture-building in all its comprehensiveness and radicalism can be supposed to have a meaning for its agents and victims – to be a culture in its own right. It is true that such thick description is vulnerable to idealist excess; the description that is meaningful for the analyst might not reflect what is meaningful for the participants. The thick description we elaborated in Chapter 5, moreover, was guilty of this excess. Nevertheless, the attempt is what distinguishes Tucker's approach from White's, making it not simply a use of historical findings in political culture research, but a use of political culture in the production of historical findings.

The potential offered by the concept of political culture for historians has been most fully taken up in American historiography. Within the study of American political history by American historians we can trace in microcosm many of the issues that we have been pursuing at a more general level throughout this book. This is one reason why it is convenient to end with a survey of American historiography's use of political culture. The more important reason, however, is that in the most sophisticated uses one can see grounds for reborrowing by political scientists of the concept originally borrowed from them. And the grounds for saying that certain uses are the most sophisticated, we will see, recall the phenomenological analysis of political culture that we have been advancing.

It would be naive to say that historians, or indeed any researchers, approach their subject matter free of hypotheses or theoretical frameworks, not to mention political preferences, that in some manner delimit or constrain their investigations. Nevertheless it is obviously true that a researcher investigating the past with the tool of political culture is much less constrained than one investigating it with a view to justifying this or that theory of comparative politics. One very important result of this difference is in the degree of openness each displays to the possibility that political culture might change. This possibility, we have seen, although it is acknowledged in the comparative politics use of political culture, is somewhat played down, as it needs to be if the main instrument of comparative explanation – cultural lag – is to be effective. Historians investigating the political cultures of the past labour under no such constraint. Something similar can be said about the possibility of variations in political culture across space. Again, political scientists frequently make prefatory remarks about 'subcultures', but equally frequently fail to follow these up, revealing the nature of these remarks as hedging clauses. This is not so say that historians are uninterested either in cultural continuity or in similarities across cultures. But it does make clear why historians who contradict such claims feel no apparent embarrassment in doing so under the rubric of political culture, and hence why historiographical uses, even if we restrict ourselves to the American context, show such wide variety.

In what, then, does this variety consist? We will approach this question by describing a series of characteristics of American historiography's use of political culture. These are not shared characteristics; we will progressively narrow the field by converging on the characteristics of the most sophisticated uses, by which is meant not only the most theoretically self-conscious uses, but also those that derive the greatest explanatory advantage from the concept. In the first place, we may observe that the comparative politics notion that political cultures are relative to nations is far from absent in the historiographical use. Perhaps, indeed, the majority of historiographical uses make reference to or imply an 'American political culture'. This is not, however, done for comparative purposes, in the sense of using this object to explain the divergence of the American outcome from other outcomes to a common stimulus or situation. Such descriptions are what we may term 'inclusive', then, without necessarily being comparative.

Inclusive descriptions of political culture often have a purely prefatory character: they are used to refer to the area of study without making a substantial contribution to the research method or indeed the elucidation of findings. This is also true, of course, of many uses within political science, uses that were characterized in the Introduction as casual. The area of study to which reference is thereby made is American values, ideology and political thought, without any specific commitment being made to the investigation of these on the mass or any other level or by any specific method. Many examples could be given, but an interesting example of the inclusive use is Richard Hofstadter's, because in addition to this casual use he also makes a more substantive one. In his *Idea of a Party System*, a study of the growth of a tolerance for political parties within an originally highly unfavourable context (illustrating, we may note in passing, the ready acceptance by the historian of change in political culture), Hofstadter says in his preface that his subject is a 'development in American political culture'. This inclusive phrasing is shortly followed, however, by the statement of his thesis, which is that the 'political culture of the Albany regency' is the source of this development.[25] This thesis is amplified in the text in a description of the Albany regency's political history and practices, and the 'New York philosophy' that emerged along with them.[26] Thus a casual inclusive reference to political culture is combined with an investigation of the local and particular, change issuing from the latter being seen as the source of a 'development' of the former.

Localism, then, is a characteristic found in some historiographical uses of political culture, sometimes, indeed, in combination with inclusiveness. Many examples of such localism could be cited. In some cases, its purpose is to throw light on the more general environment, as, for instance, in the work of Ronald Formisano, perhaps the leading exponent of this 'case study' method. Formisano's description of Massachusetts' political culture is explicitly aimed at describing at this detailed level changes that he takes to be general – changes in the same area broached by Hofstadter, that of the development of party politics.[27] A more extreme example is John Brooke's examination of political culture in Worcester County, Massachusetts. No claim is made of the representativeness of this county for the purposes of Brooke's account; indeed, he states that it is the site of a 'dramatic and *unique* concentration of political insurgencies' for much of the period of his study.[28] Nevertheless, his theme – oscillations between the dominance of alternative liberal and republican visions of American politics – is of great generality. His book, for all its narrowness of scope, is thus a contribution to the debate between liberal and republican interpretations of American political history, a debate that in our terms is certainly inclusive. Another example of extreme narrowness of investigative scope is Robert Kelley's study of the history of flood control efforts in the Sacramento Valley, California. Here we have not only a small region but also a debate highly constrained as to its subject. Kelley nevertheless insists that the politics of flood control illustrates larger themes in American political culture.[29]

Attention is sometimes focused on a locality for the latter's intrinsic interest, although in such cases more general implications are usually implicit. Philip VanderMeer's study of Indiana's political culture, and Robert Weir's of South Carolina, are examples of this approach.[30] Weir's account, in particular, cannot help but have general implications, precisely because of the distinctiveness of the political culture of South Carolina. This state preserved a political environment that was hostile to parties far longer than any other state, but the peculiarity of its politics led not to its marginalization but instead to its leading role in the secession of the South.

If the inclusive characterization of political culture merely orients the reader as to the area of investigation – values, political thought, ideology and so forth – what is the purpose of political cultural localism? In some cases, it is just the same. For Formisano, for example, political culture consists of 'all those parts of a culture which are political', especially the taken-for-granted components.[31] It is, he has written elsewhere, 'an inclusive term referring to the "givens" and implicit values of a polity seen as a whole'.[32] With such a view, political culture may be studied as easily in microcosm as macrocosm, so long as the microcosm is sufficiently representative. But this case study method is not the only possible ground for examining political culture at the local level. In fact, two other grounds present themselves, though they are not always explicitly stated in the examples we are considering. One of these is that at the local level it is more likely that a distinct way of life of which the political culture is a part will be observable. The other is that the very self-consciousness of the inhabitants of the locality as a separate group may be politically significant. Both of these grounds recall the arguments we have been making in other chapters.

Several examples of the use by American historians of political culture as a means of describing a local way of life have recently appeared. The prediction made in 1964 that the most fruitful direction for historical research would be towards 'retrospective cultural anthropology' appears, as Kelley has observed, to have been fulfilled.[33] It is true, in the light of our examination of anthropology in Chapter 6, that this suggestion looks like another instance of the simplifying effect of cross-disciplinary borrowing; however, if historians, being already attuned to the possibility of change, have avoided the disorienting effects that change in the form of urbanization has had on the holistic definition of culture within anthropology, that is so much the better for them. The claims made by historians when they point to a 'way of life' are in any case less grand than those made by the early anthropologists. This is mainly because, like Thompson, Ellis and Wildavsky, whose theory also needed to be defended against criticisms that had been made of anthropological holism, they make no assumption that a way of life need be coextensive with a society. In the very narrowness of their focus the historians avoid the charge levelled at anthropological holism that the notion of a way of life precludes the possibility of conflict or change.

Hofstadter's description of the political life of the Albany regency might be seen as a tentative move in this direction, but its scope remains quite narrow in that only the political aspects of the lives of certain political activists are considered. A fuller illustration of the historian's idea of a way of life is provided by Kenneth Greenberg's study of the impact of slavery on the political culture of the antebellum South.[34] Greenberg argues that the master-slave relationship was 'paralleled' by political relations among Southern whites and between the South and the North. Greenberg's account is a thick description of Southern politics, but he averts idealist excess by providing ample evidence that matters were perceived in these terms by the participants. He argues, for instance, that the oratorical and honour-seeking style of the Southern statesman reflected the relationship he aspired to have with his slaves – that of unbridgeable social distance combined with trust and respect. Similarly, the longer survival, in South Carolina especially, of the principle of virtual as opposed to actual representation both justified and was sustained by the claim of harmony of interest between master and slaves.[35] Underlying all of this was what another historian has called 'The Fear' – fear of the ultimate uprising of the slaves. The fear of enslavement was, Greenberg suggests, an overt and powerful motor of the Southern politician's striving for political independence from party and from the North. Apart from drawing these metaphorical connections Greenberg pays much attention to more direct effects of social structure, such as the impact of the lower level of urbanization on the plausibility of the claim of Southern unity. Thus, 'slavery in the antebellum South was intimately connected to a distinct set of political values and practices. Ultimately, these values and practices – this political culture of slavery – helped shape the form and content of conflict with the North.'[36]

In a similar vein is the description of Southern political culture provided by Anne Norton.[37] Norton differs in paying less attention to slavery and more to the agrarian lifestyle in general. Its effects, she holds, were to perpetuate the notion of republican virtue through the fact of greater mutual independence and, in the annual rhythm of agriculture, to facilitate periods of leisure, much misunderstood by the North, in which politics could be practised. Norton, like several of the authors we have mentioned, is concerned to relate her account to the debate between liberal and republican interpretations of American political thought, and specifically argues that the deficiency of each has been its claim to inclusiveness. Louis Hartz's liberal tradition thesis dismissed the political thought of the South as a mere 'deviation', while in turn the republican revision has substituted a new cultural monolith.[38] Along with Greenberg, Norton argues that the South's way of life enabled classical republican values and political style to persist there far longer than they did in the North.[39] Here we may see how the use of political culture to describe a way of life can contradict more inclusive uses of the term.

The American South is, of course, a rather large locality; large enough for objections to be made to its being said to have a single political culture or way of life. Both Greenberg and Weir pay particular attention to South Carolina, because that state represented the most extreme manifestation of Southern culture, but it follows that the picture is less clear elsewhere. How may inclusiveness at this level be justified? Part of the answer lies in the fact that, for all its internal diversity, the South did come to define itself in opposition to the North – in short, the Civil War took place. Here we begin to converge on a final characteristic of the historiographical use of political culture, that of reciprocality. What is emphasized by uses with this characteristic is the idea that cultures are defined through the process of opposition. Norton, for instance, writes of 'a network of meaning [created] through the articulation of difference'.[40] Thus the fact that the plantation economy was far from universal in the antebellum South, that rivalry between 'upcountry' yeoman farmers and 'lowland' planters was widespread, that in some states urbanization and its concomitant socioeconomic differentiation proceeded much further than it did in South Carolina, that in general there was at least one 'other South', does not necessarily tell against the idea of Southern political culture. For all its diversity, the South was sufficiently different from the North to come to define itself in terms of these differences. Thus, for these historians, it is not simply that the South is, in Josiah Joyce's terminology, a 'province', 'part of a national domain, which is, geographically and socially, sufficiently unified to have a true consciousness of its own unity, to feel a pride in its own ideas and customs, and to possess a sense of its distinction from other parts of the country'.[41] They do not simply regard southern distinctness as a natural fact, but in part as a function of opposition. To be sure, opposition cannot get started without some original criteria of distinctness, but these were clearly present in the South, notwithstanding its internal diversity. There is, in other words, a dynamic relationship between the process of opposition and the criteria of distinctness adopted and promoted by the opposing groups. What John Shelton Reed has called the South's 'sense of grievance' and 'siege mentality' needs to be taken into account in the description of its political culture.[42]

Within American historiography several studies which emphasize reciprocality have appeared in recent years. It is an emphasis which need not be restricted to the rivalry between North and South. Weir, for instance, in an essay on South Carolinian political culture in the revolutionary era, suggests that the revolution itself may be partly explained in terms of the development of a 'contraculture' in the colonies as a reaction to the 'metropolitan culture' of Britain, the latter having been manifested not just in the assertion of political hegemony but in the style and tone adopted by British governors and emissaries. He draws an analogy from social psychology: 'Abrupt juxtaposition of the metropolitan culture and provincial subcultures dramatized the differences between them, and the experience appears to have been as painful for many local leaders as adolescence is for some twentieth-century youths.'[43] In nineteenth-century American politics, a second major rivalry, cutting across that between North and South, was that between the two major parties in a succession of 'party systems': the Federalists and the Jeffersonian Republicans, the Whigs and the Jacksonian Democrats, and the Republicans and the Democrats. The study of the 'second party system' of Whigs and Democrats has been the beneficiary of two of the most fully developed historiographical applications of the concept of political culture, by Daniel Walker Howe and Jean Baker.[44]

Howe's and Baker's accounts are distinguished both by a concern to trace the whole complex of extrapolitical values and way of life found

among leaders and adherents to these respective parties and by a sensitivity
to the formative effects of the opposition process. As it happens, they also
demonstrate the fullest familiarity with theoretical debates on political
culture, though this has not prevented them from extending the use of the
concept in fruitful ways. Howe's method is to investigate Whig political
culture by concentrating on the activities of its leaders, but his is far
from a conventional account of elite-level politics. He emphasizes the
connections between the Whigs' policies of strong government, tariff and
internal improvement and their broader culture of 'aggressive didacticism',
'Victorian values', anti-masonry and pro-temperance.[45] Their preoccupation
with social control was intimately linked, Howe asserts, with their concern
for self-control. Baker discusses the inculcation of the 'partisan culture'
of the Northern democrats in family, school and party itself. She also
concentrates on specific individuals: 'the life history', she says, 'becomes
the historian's completed questionnaire'.[46] The Democrats opposed central
authority and stood for the sovereignty of the states and the people.
Their disposition was to support the humble against the arrogant and the
entrenched. Despite being the source of the newer understanding of party
that derived from Van Buren's circle, the Democrats continued to think
of themselves as a 'movement', expressed by their use of the term 'the
Democracy'. Their rallies had a militaristic quality, and the now familiar
militaristic language of politics as a 'battle' requiring 'enlistment' and
'mobilization' originated in Democratic electioneering.[47]

It is noteworthy that Howe's and Baker's studies reveal a good deal of
similarity between the two sides. For instance, both adopted pessimistic
republican rhetoric while somewhat contradictorily expressing an optimistic view of time as progress. Both began with a sceptical view of
political parties as expressions of faction that undermined the common
good. Yet bitter and prolonged conflict between them occurred. Howe and
Baker enable us to see that this was not simply a product of confusion,
as Hartz's placing of both sides within the 'liberal tradition' implies.[48]
Fundamental differences in lifestyle were involved, and on that basis the
conflict itself served to reinforce party identity. The similarity of their
rhetoric – the Whigs in republican fashion criticized Jackson as 'King
Andrew' for his Bank veto while the Democrats in turn made a republican
critique of corruption in Whig relations with financial interests – belies
profound differences in the uses to which it was being put, which included
reinforcement of party identities. The development of a more positive
attitude towards party politics and the use of republican rhetoric were both
aspects of 'American political culture', but they also took place within a
context defined by the opposition of two distinct political cultures.

The reconciliation of, on the one hand, the inclusive description of American political culture and, on the other, the emphasis on local ways of life and on the reciprocal relations between cultures may be best approached through the work of historian Robert Kelley.[49] Kelley takes his approach, which he terms 'cultural political history', to combine the best features of the 'new political history' or ethnohistory and the more traditional form of intellectual history practiced pre-eminently by Hofstadter. The latter concentrated on political elites, but the former, with its emphasis on quantification and on local political contexts, is guilty of the opposite bias, eschewing links to national politics.[50] The analysis that Kelley's cultural history provides contains all of the features that we have been discussing hereto. His conception of American political culture is that it features a continuing rivalry between what he calls the 'host culture' and the 'outgroups'. A link is thereby effected between the familiar structure of party conflict in the successive party systems and the newly discovered environment of ethnic politics at the local level. The core of the host culture consists of descendants of the English, based in New England and politically active through the Federalist party and its successors the Whigs and the Republicans. The outgroups consist of successive waves of immigrants, bringing with them ethnic hostility to the English and finding a welcoming home among the Jeffersonian Republicans and their successors. Thus American political culture is made up of an ongoing bipolar conflict that in turn can be analyzed as the aggregate manifestation of a series of ethnic rivalries.

Kelley's claim to have blended traditional and newer historical understandings may be somewhat overconfident. Baker, indeed, distances her approach from that of the new political history, arguing that the latter obscures the existence of what she calls 'partisan', as opposed to ethnic, cultures; and Howe similarly points out that ethnohistory is an incomplete guide to the culture of the Whigs. Historical ethnic rivalries may stimulate the construction of a political rivalry, but they do not necessarily exhaust it. Kelley, to a large extent, seems to adopt a view of ethnicity as primordial, whereas we have seen that it, like other criteria of identity, needs to be seen as a product of social construction, in the same way that Baker and Howe view the political cultures of Democrats and Whigs. On the other hand, his extension of the label of ethnic group to poor white Southerners indicates a more fluid use of the term, tantamount in this case simply to 'culture'. With this understanding, no distinction would be possible, for instance, between the 'ethnic' sources of Whig politics and those outlined by Howe. The false assumption that rigidly distinct aetiologies can be provided for ethnicity and culture appears to underlie

Formisano's criticism of Kelley's 'fusion' of the two, a criticism that ignores Kelley's own nods in the direction of this assumption. Formisano is more on target when he alleges that '[Kelley's] understanding of how community context creates variations in social group or subcultural alignments is minimal if not absent'.[51] This judgement, however, suggests only the incompleteness of Kelley's ambitious synopsis, not its erroneousness. It provides a framework into which later and more detailed accounts of partisan ways of life and the construction of partisan identities such as Howe's and Baker's may, without too much strain, be inserted.

This synthesis is usefully brought to bear in Kelley's account of the politics of flood control in the Sacramento Valley. The problem faced by residents, landowners and politicians in the valley was the propensity of the Sacramento River to flood over a wide area at quite frequent intervals. The problem was exacerbated by the growth of the hydraulic gold-mining industry, which produced vast quantities of mine tailings that clogged the river system, making flooding more likely and more damaging. This 'objective' problem might appear to call for an 'objective' solution, but it is the thrust of Kelley's argument that quite different world-views were brought to it by the Democrats and the Whig-Republicans, making different 'solutions' look natural and obvious. The Whig-Republicans had a deep trust in experts, and favoured large-scale government intervention, even though the solutions proposed by experts were consistently inadequate. The Democrats, on the other hand, distrusted experts and intervention, regarding the problem as one best solved on the local level, a view that resulted in a destructive and futile competition to build ever-higher levees. Through what in retrospect can be seen as a fifty-year process of trial and error, the correct solution was finally reached, but the open-minded empiricism suggested by that phrase was absent from most of the debates of the period. In highly concrete terms, Kelley demonstrates not only the persistence over generations of 'distinctive policy potentials', but shows how they relate to the broader values and ways of life of the opposing sides. Not only that, but in describing the direct effects which the activities of each side had on the other, in the tangible form of ruptured dams and levees and flooded farms, Kelley provides us with an example of literal, down-to-earth construction of opposing identities.

Kelley's explanation of his use of the concept of political culture provides a helpful guide to the relationship between the conceptions of political culture that we have been discussing. Political culture, he says, is not simply the story of everyday politics. He continues:

A useful analogy could be the difference between reporting the flow of play in a particular sporting event and describing the larger framework that sets up its overall nature: the rules of the game; the contrasting ideas about it, even its purpose in the larger scheme of things, believed in by the opposing coaches; the kinds of people the two teams tend to recruit, their values, and their consequent style of play; who their traditional 'enemy' is, toward whom they orient themselves; and their sense of identity, of cohesion.[52]

Inclusive descriptions of American political culture are concerned with the rules of the game. For Louis Hartz, these rules were extremely rigid: anyone who did not stay within the bounds of the 'liberal tradition' was doomed to marginality. Following the republican revision, we have been able to see that the repertoire of criticism was somewhat larger, but the availability of a certain critical language is still one of the rules. The teams playing within these rules in turn have their own distinctive values and practices, partially constituted by their leaders, which are reinforced by the competition between them. Where this analogy is a little misleading, however, is in implying that the rules always exist prior to the competition. In sport, that is true. Even in politics, it may seem obvious that a competition such as the one over flood control in California follows guidelines established nationally. But these broader guidelines are themselves established in a series of identity-defining competitions, of which the most important for the case we are considering is the mid-nineteenth century 'Bank war'. In phenomenological terms, Kelley 'brackets' this fact for the purposes of his local investigation, that is, he takes the opposing cultures as given at the national level. But in showing how the two cultures of Whig-Republicans and Democrats are not only enacted but also reinforced by their conflict over flood control, his account also indicates why this bracketing is necessarily provisional.

There is no reason in principle why political scientists may not also emphasize reciprocality, providing findings that exploit the phenomenological potential of political culture research. But it happens that they have not done so. Elazar's account of American political subcultures, we have seen, is historical but nevertheless lacks a true grasp of historical process. Its history is only that of migration, offering some explanation of the distribution of subcultures, but scarcely addressing the question of their origin. Analyses of American subcultures influenced by Almond and Verba's approach fail in a similar way, since the only aetiology of political culture admitted by this approach is cultural lag.[53] One might suggest that the empirical bounty offered by the attitude survey has encouraged behavioural political scientists to imagine they have the fullest conception of political culture, and has distracted them from the more fertile modes of inquiry to which historians have perforce been led.

On the other hand, juxtaposing the historians' use of political culture, especially the most developed examples, with recent interpretive political scientific uses influenced by structuralism makes clear the deficiencies of the latter. The deficiencies of both structuralism and its derivative, Wildavsky's 'culture theory', result from their extreme idealism, which may be termed formalistic idealism. This involves what amounts to disdain for historical contingency, an error, of course, to which historians are for the most part professionally immune. Historical research takes many forms, and some of its forms would certainly be vulnerable to the opposite criticism, that the detail of the historical narrative obscures or even prohibits general conclusions. Such is not the case in the examples we have considered, however. Their use of political culture is such as to admit a large range of data in its description, but not to the exclusion of what in the best cases is a strong theoretical framework. That framework, we have seen, incorporates many of the implications of the phenomenological analysis of political culture. Like that analysis, it denies the necessity of choosing between interests and culture as explanations, instead using political culture to transcend that dichotomy. Even in its points of deficiency, such as Kelley's partial assumption of the primordial and unanalyzable nature of ethnic ties, it illustrates the utility of the phenomenological analysis. And in keeping with the argument of Chapter 7, it places emphasis on the construction of identity and meaning through the process of opposition. Perhaps, in that last regard, it does tell us something about the structure of the human mind, but it does so much more richly and convincingly than the loose generalities of structuralism. It provides what Schutz envisaged for phenomenological social theory, a means of connecting the analyst's thick description with the self-understandings of the participants, a connection that can only be enhanced by more and more detailed empirical investigation of concrete social and political processes.

Conclusion

As already observed, reports of the death of the concept of political culture have been not only exaggerated, but diametrically wrong: it is more widely used than ever, and has perhaps reached the stage of conceptual maturity, where debates over definition are no longer prominent, and it is routinely invoked as if there were no question as to its meaning or usefulness – and not only by academic analysts. One might perhaps argue that its routinization in the vocabulary of political scientists, commentators, journalists and even politicians marks the ultimate indignity, demonstrating only the concept's extreme vagueness and malleability – its having been 'stretched' to the point of fatigue. That argument would posit an inverse relationship between a concept's degree of acceptance and its scholarly interest. While this is not a particularly plausible general claim, it is worth considering in the present case. This Conclusion aims to account for the continued appeal of the concept of political culture and to summarize the arguments of preceding chapters in order to show to what extent and in what ways it is justified.

It was suggested in the Introduction that the issue of definition with which theorists of political culture have been much concerned is something of a red herring. The main organizing categories for the preceding argument have been categories of *use* of the concept of political culture, though we have also referred more vaguely to 'tendency' and 'potential'. These categories, it is apparent, fail to provide a neat typology of political culture research, if 'neat' is taken to mean mutually exclusive and single-dimensional. But they have fulfilled what the Introduction described as the main purpose of categorization, that is, providing a theoretical orientation to a complex body of material. Assigning labels and differentiating types is, however, only the first stage in analysis, despite the fact that in political culture theory it has sometimes been seen as sufficient. Of much greater interest and significance are the relationships between the categories and the theoretical and philosophical foundations and assumptions of each. It is these matters that the above argument has aimed to expose.

As anticipated in the Introduction, the multiplicity and incommens-urability of the scholarly activities that have been undertaken under the rubric of 'political culture' have meant that traversing the field of political culture research has involved many digressions and detours. Our theoretical concerns have indeed necessitated looking at writings in which the term 'political culture' does not figure at all, although the *concept* is often implied. Nevertheless, our journey across this jungle has been one journey, following one route. An overly precise stipulation as to how political culture research should be conducted, or what definition of political culture should be used, cannot be the outcome of such a journey. Many, indeed, are the attempts at this that have been made, only to be roundly ignored, simply because the field of study is too large to admit of such constraint. Despite this, the above argument does have certain implications, negative and positive, for the future conduct of political culture research.

It has a number of negative implications concerning the prospects for further development of comparative political culture research. The comparative use of political culture is the most widespread use, ostensibly providing a scientific means of investigating the common-sense perception that, across nations, people differ in ways relevant to political outcomes. We saw in Chapters 1 to 4 that this use encounters many problems. One is its interference with the sociological use of the term. The damaging effects of interference were illustrated by the case of Almond and Verba's *The Civic Culture*; however, the issues raised by that case are quite general, and are not to be resolved solely by assuming carelessness or excessive ambition on the part of Almond and Verba. The sociological use, in which political culture is investigated intranationally, exposes numerous possibilities that make the comparative use difficult to sustain. Construing political culture as a label for a field of study and not necessarily as a variable, political sociologists have drawn attention to cleavages within it and to their relationship to socioeconomic cleavages. The role of political culture in contributing to the internal cohesion of the elite, the possibility that it includes 'mystifications', and hence the function of 'the' national culture (and academic analyses of it) in reinforcing domination are thereby suggested. Modernization theory in its numerous variants presents another instance of the sociological use of political culture, in which it is related to stages of modernity. Here, too, conflict with the comparative use appears, in the form of an unresolved division between 'world' and national cultures, which arises in even the most sophisticated versions of this sociological use.

When such conflict arises, we have seen, the comparative use is invariably the weaker party, and political culture is thus gradually made a residual category. The residue is never completely eliminated, however. The continued presence of national differences prompts *ad hoc* references to events in national history and hence to 'cultural factors' that, however unscientific and hence embarrassing, seem to be unavoidable. The embarrassment here is really over the limitations of the comparative use, indeed of the comparative method in general. It cannot by definition deal with what we have termed indexicality; indexical components of political culture are not comparable. The problem does not end there: indexical components are also susceptible to contestation over their meaning, as we saw from our East European examples, casting fundamental doubt on the comparativist notion of cultural lag.

None of this means that the 'sensitivity to context' of which political culture research has been both a token and a result should be abandoned. Indeed it is rendered all the more necessary by the discovery that generalizations about the effect of context are dubious. The entry of each new common stimulus, whether it be a multinational corporation or Soviet-inspired communism, an investment programme by the World Bank or the arrival of an academic team of advisors on electoral systems, should be seen as a new experiment in political culture research. The recommendation that follows is that if political culture is to be used as an explanatory variable, comparisons must be much more specific than they have typically been. Perhaps, over time, a body of comparisons of the scale of Hofstede's will contribute to a more general characterization of national or regional political cultures, but this equally well might not occur, and should not be the goal of comparison. In some particular setting, some values might be malleable, and some not. Perhaps the values which communist regimes tried to change are resistant to change, or perhaps they are resistant only to those methods – maybe even *because* of those methods. It is not enough to disaggregate the components of political culture, though doing this already makes the prospect of a cumulative description of national political cultures recede. The further possibility that values, attitudes, identities and in general culture may be a response to a political setting, like the dissidents' now-receding elaboration of the idea of 'Central Europe', in other words the dynamic nature of political culture must also be acknowledged.

Our argument also provides a platform for criticism of interpretive political culture research, although here the issues are confused by the fact that interpretivism itself draws, not always consciously or without contradiction, from the phenomenological tradition that provides the critical platform. The target of criticism is what we have termed the idealist tendency of interpretivism. We have taken idealism to refer not to the general claim of the paramountcy of ideas, but to the claim, explicit or implicit, of the paramountcy of the *analyst's* ideas. Thick description, we have seen, places decisive emphasis on the interpretive achievement of the analyst. We need only recall Alfred Meyer's assertion, recorded in the Introduction, that culture is distinguished not by its contents but by a 'manner of ordering and viewing' them to see the influence of such an emphasis on the interpretive use of political culture. The error of idealism consists in mistaking the interpretive richness of a description for its truth. To be sure, investigating the ideas of the participants, such as those manifested in the arts and sciences in the Stalinist Soviet Union, is likely to contribute to greater insight on the part of the investigator, but there is always a danger of that insight being over-extended. This is what happens in the case of the hypothesis of atomization; it is an *a priori* hypothesis of great interpretive richness which we nevertheless find in at least one case to be untrue. Phenomenology provides a means of avoiding this danger by its strong emphasis on the concrete process of meaning-construction, though in a sense it also admits its own culpability by arguing that thick description is a second-order effect of this first-order process. Restoring the phenomenological basis of interpretivism enables us to return the cart, with Geertz as passenger, to its proper place behind the horse.

Exposing and elaborating upon the phenomenological potential of interpretivism does two things: it accounts for many of the problems that have arisen in the various uses of political culture and more generally for the vacuity of the debate between cultural and interest- or structure-based explanation; and it also refocuses political culture research on a new range of phenomena at a new empirical level.

The fundamental posture of phenomenological social theory, indeed of phenomenology in general, is the claim that the social environment through which people move is constituted and made meaningful by them. It denies the 'givenness' of any part of that environment. Although phenomenological justifications are implicit, and sometimes explicit, in some anthropological uses of the concept of culture, and hence, through Geertz's influence, in some political scientific and historiographical writings too, phenomenological social theory is not, in fact, a theory of culture. Indeed, the concept of culture is not much used by the classic phenomenological social theorists we have considered. The reason for this is that phenomenological perspective denies the 'givenness' and asserts the 'constructedness' of all social objects. Thus it denies the duality of culture and its various supposed ontological opposites, 'structure', 'power', 'interests' or 'objective circumstances'. Culture is not itself any more a 'phenomenological' notion than these others. In this way phenomenology transcends the question of the superiority of explanations with any of these 'objects' as their basis. It suggests that this debate is as meaningful as one in physics would be over whether electrons are best regarded as particles or waves.

What, then, does it mean to introduce the concept of culture to phenomenology, or to approach culture in a phenomenological manner? In a sense, it involves a restriction of the scope of phenomenology, or at least a specification of the level at which we are applying it. Only a subset of the typifications of which Schutz speaks could be awarded the denomination 'culture'. Phenomenological social theory, we saw from Schutz's examples of social roles – 'passenger, consumer, taxpayer, reader, bystander' – does not distinguish between evanescent and more stable roles, and between ones with and without political significance. Our analysis, in contrast, has made such a distinction, and has marked it with the denomination 'culture'.

The concept of 'interest group' represents interests as objectively given and not related to self-understanding or other aspects of meaningful context, and hence provides only a 'thin' description. The concept of culture offers the advantage of relating interests to identity. Just as a role is not necessarily a culture, neither, necessarily, is an interest group. In the language of political science, an interest group may be a fleeting and minimally coherent association of individuals, such as the opponents of a road-building proposal. The members might not know each other. But suppose that such an association broadens its interests, becomes more cohesive, its members establishing a common life together in a process of opposition, becoming perhaps an environmental or local autonomist movement. In that event it is clear that the label 'interest group' would be somewhat lacking in descriptive richness – in fact to apply it, as the group's opponents might, would have become an act of derogation. The group would instead be a culture.

Thus, while 'interest groups' are differentiated only by their interests, cultures are differentiated by a variety of phenomena, the distinctiveness of which gives rise to an identity, enabling a role to be constituted as an interest group. Thus the advantage of the denotation 'culture' is that, on the one hand, a social role that is described as a culture is one that, on the basis of its identity, can be seen as proceeding to assert itself in the political arena; and, on the other hand, an interest group that is described as a culture is thereby provided with a plausible and enriched aetiology, drawn not from some claim of objective interests individually perceived, but from the kinds of phenomenological perspective we have been discussing.

The restriction we have made in the scope of phenomenology therefore consists precisely in its application to political settings. Tucker, we saw, argued that Almond was wrong to separate political culture from culture in general; however, he himself erred in assuming that it was unproblematic to speak of an 'anthropological' meaning of culture. Looking at debates within anthropology, we observed that culture had already been somewhat politicized *before* being borrowed by political scientists, and was in danger indeed of being made merely an epiphenomenon of interests and structure. We deployed the phenomenological argument to show why the extreme position of reducing culture to interests needs to be avoided. But to deploy phenomenology in this manner is to apply it to political settings, and hence to provide what is already a phenomenological approach to *political* culture. Culture is not a set of givens of which political culture is a subset; it is a process, and 'political culture' refers to that process in its political aspects.

The phenomenological approach to political culture has a wide range of applications. It is not, as we have seen, irrelevant to the investigation of national identity; indeed it serves to resolve some problems in the recent debates in that field. In this connection we were led to investigate the phenomenological basis of 'invented' meaning, an investigation that provides us with a template for the analysis of the indexical components of political culture and of the functions of political culture exposed by critical sociologists, such as its contribution to the internal cohesion of elites and to the perpetuation of their dominance through cultural 'mystifications'. But although the phenomenological approach is applicable to a wide range of levels of investigation, its scale is necessarily intimate. It seeks, at its most thorough, the detailed empirical manifestation of the creation of meaning and identity. In this respect it is no less empirically demanding than the comparative use. Indeed, it is more so, since such is the fundamentality of its assertion that human circumstances are human constructs that in many cases the degree of detail that the analysis would ideally require is not available. Parliamentary debates and journalism may both contribute to the creation of national identity, as they did in Germany and Poland respectively; but in these records we lack the kind of detail that conversational analysis is able to provide: hesitations, ambiguities, ellipses and so forth. These are cleansed from most historical records, leaving only the finished edifice, not the half-used supplies, the plastered-over mistakes, and the spillages, that went into building it. Nevertheless, the phenomenological analysis at its most thoroughgoing at least provides a posture that sensitizes us to these matters, and alerts us to the source of the dynamism that we may locate in political culture. And in some cases, comprehensive application of this detailed methodology may yet be possible.

Thus the phenomenological approach to political culture explains many of the deficiencies of the uses we have considered, and sets political culture research on a new course. It also, finally, illustrates the particular utility of the concept. What is distinctive about the concept of political culture, as we noticed at the outset, is the enduring nature of its appeal in the face of a large body of criticism. This may partially be explained by the common-sense connotation of national difference it has been given in its comparative use. But perhaps the concept has some more fundamental appeal. Perhaps the juxtaposition of the two words 'political' and 'culture' has struck a deeper chord than even Almond envisaged when he introduced it to political science. If so, we may suggest that its resonance derives from a dissatisfaction both with an account of politics that ignores the issues of meanings and culture, and with an account of culture that ignores issues of politics and power. Each of these accounts, we perhaps implicitly recognize, fails to do justice to our experience of the social world. Hence the appeal of the juxtaposition, and hence the above argument, which has attempted to reveal the origins and ramifications of the seductive quality of political culture.

Notes

Introduction

1. David J. Elkins and Richard E. B. Simeon, 'A Cause in Search of its Effect, or What Does Political Culture Explain?', *Comparative Politics* 11, 1979, 127–145, p. 127.
2. For instance, advertisement for Basil Blackwell/Polity Press, *New York Review of Books* 31, 20 December 1984, p. 29.
3. Typologies of political culture research are to be found in John R. Gibbins, 'Introduction', in John R. Gibbins (ed.), *Contemporary Political Culture: Politics in a Postmodern Age* (London: Sage, 1989), Dennis Kavanagh, *Political Science and Political Behaviour* (London: George Allen & Unwin, 1983), and Glenda M. Patrick, 'Political Culture', in Giovanni Sartori (ed.), *Social Science Concepts: A Systemic Analysis* (Beverly Hills, CA and London: Sage, 1984).
4. Arthur Kallenburg, quoted in Michael Thompson, Richard Ellis and Aaron Wildavsky, *Cultural Theory* (Boulder, CO and Oxford: Westview, 1990), p. 14.
5. Robert Brown, quoted in Thompson, Ellis and Wildavsky, *Cultural Theory*, p. 261.
6. David Truman, quoted in Robert A. Dahl, 'The Behavioral Approach in Political Science: Epitaph for a Monument to a Successful Revolution', *American Political Science Review* 55, 1961, 763–772, p. 767.
7. Gabriel A. Almond, 'Introduction', in Gabriel A. Almond and James S. Coleman (eds), *The Politics of the Developing Areas* (Princeton, NJ: Princeton University Press, 1960), p. 4.
8. Bernard Crick, *The American Science of Politics: Its Origins and Conditions* (Berkeley: University of California Press, 1964), p. 234.
9. Gabriel A. Almond, 'Separate Tables: Schools and Sects in Political Science', in Gabriel A. Almond, *A Discipline Divided: Schools and Sects in Political Science* (Newbury Park, CA and London: Sage, 1990), pp. 27–29.
10. Anthony Giddens, *The Constitution of Society: Outline of the Theory of Structuration* (Cambridge: Polity Press, 1984), p. 333.
11. See Kavanagh, *Political Science and Political Behaviour*, pp. 3f.
12. F. M. Barnard, 'Culture and Political Development: Herder's Suggestive Insights', *American Political Science Review* 63, 1969, 379–397, p. 392; Archie Brown, 'Introduction', in Archie Brown (ed.), *Political Culture and Communist Studies* (London: Macmillan, 1984), p. 1.
13. Gabriel A. Almond, 'Comparative Political Systems', *Journal of Politics* 18, 1956, 391–409, p. 396.

14. Almond, 'Comparative Political Systems', p. 396.
15. Barnard, 'Culture and Political Development', p. 382. See also Raymond Williams, *Marxism and Literature* (Oxford: Oxford University Press, 1977), p. 17.
16. Barnard, 'Culture and Political Development', p. 390.
17. Almond, 'Separate Tables', p. 28.
18. See Clifford Geertz, 'Thick Description: Toward an Interpretive Theory of Culture', in Clifford Geertz, *The Interpretation of Cultures* (London: Hutchinson, 1975), and the discussion in Chapter 6 below.
19. Charles Taylor, 'Interpretation and the Sciences of Man', *Review of Metaphysics* 25, 1971, 3–51.
20. Stephen White, *Political Culture and Soviet Politics* (London: Macmillan, 1979), p. 1.
21. Alfred G. Meyer, 'Communist Revolutions and Cultural Change', *Studies in Comparative Communism* 5, 1972, 345–372, p. 349.
22. Stephen White, 'Political Culture in Communist States: Some Problems of Theory and Method' (Research Note), *Comparative Politics* 16, 1984, 351–365, p. 352.
23. Lucian W. Pye with Mary W. Pye, *Asian Power and Politics: The Cultural Dimension of Authority* (Cambridge, MA and London: Belknap Press of Harvard University Press, 1985), p. ix.
24. Richard H. Solomon, *Mao's Revolution and the Chinese Political Culture* (Berkeley: University of California Press, 1971), p. 521. Solomon's and Pye's writings fall within the 'psychocultural' category of approaches to political culture that Yung Wei has noticed the Chinese case has attracted. Yung Wei, 'A Methodological Critique of Current Studies on Chinese Political Culture', *Journal of Politics* 38, 1976, 114–140, p. 122. As White makes clear in a useful survey of Sovietological examples, psychoculturalism is a modern version of the earlier and much criticized 'national character' literature. White, *Political Culture and Soviet Politics*, pp. 6–14.
25. Robert D. Putnam, 'Studying Elite Political Culture: The Case of Ideology', *American Political Science Review* 65, 1981, 651–681.
26. See David Easton, *A Systems Analysis of Political Life* (New York: John Wiley and Sons, 1965). For a behavioural analysis of political culture that makes a non-casual use of Easton's concept, see Donald J. Devine, *The Political Culture of the United States: The Influence of Member Values on Regime Maintenance* (Boston: Little, Brown, 1972).
27. See Williams, *Marxism and Literature*, ch. 1, and the discussion in Chapter 5, below.
28. See Archie Brown, 'Soviet Political Culture Through Soviet Eyes', in Brown, *Political Culture and Communist Studies*.
29. For this debate, see Robert Tucker, 'Culture, Political Culture and Communist Studies', in Robert C. Tucker, *Political Culture and Leadership in Soviet Russia: From Lenin To Gorbachev* (Brighton: Wheatsheaf,

1987) and Archie Brown, 'Conclusions', in Brown, *Political Culture and Communist Studies*, pp. 149–155.

1: Political Culture and Democracy

1. Gabriel A. Almond and Sidney Verba, *The Civic Culture: Political Attitudes and Democracy in Five Nations* (Princeton, NJ: Princeton University Press, 1963; abridged edn Boston: Little, Brown, 1965, repr. Newbury Park, CA and London: Sage, 1989). In the present chapter, page references to this book will be made in parentheses in the text. References will be to the abridged edition, since it is the most widely available; it differs from the Princeton edition principally in omitting a description of the methodological apparatus of the study.
2. Brian M. Barry, *Sociologists, Economists and Democracy* (Chicago: University of Chicago Press, 1978), p. 51.
3. Barry, *Sociologists, Economists and Democracy*, pp. 49f.
4. Barry, *Sociologists, Economists and Democracy*, p. 94.
5. W. G. Runciman, 'Some Recent Contributions to the Theory of Democracy', *European Journal of Sociology* 6, 1965, 174–185, p. 183.
6. Gabriel A. Almond and Sidney Verba (eds), *The Civic Culture Revisited* (Boston: Little, Brown, 1980, repr. Newbury Park, CA and London: Sage, 1989)
7. Sidney Verba, 'Germany: The Remaking of Political Culture', in Lucian W. Pye and Sidney Verba (eds), *Political Culture and Political Development* (Princeton, NJ: Princeton University Press, 1965), p. 133.
8. Verba, 'Germany', pp. 147, 170.
9. David P. Conradt, 'Changing German Political Culture', in Almond and Verba, *The Civic Culture Revisited*, quotation from p. 263.
10. Geoffrey K. Roberts, '"Normal" or "Critical"?: Progress Reports on the Condition of West Germany's Political Culture', *European Journal of Political Research* 12, 1984, 423–431. For an interesting comparison with the former East Germany which also emphasizes the growth of 'alternative' political culture, see Christiane Lemke, 'New Issues in the Politics of the German Democratic Republic: A Question of Political Culture?', *Journal of Communist Studies* 2, 1986, 351–358. See also Henry Krisch, 'Changing Political Culture and Political Stability in the German Democratic Republic', *Studies in Comparative Communism* 19, 1986, 41–53.
11. Roberts, '"Normal" or "Critical"?', p. 428.
12. Walter A. Rosenbaum, *Political Culture* (London: Thomas Nelson & Sons, 1975).
13. Rosenbaum, *Political Culture*, pp. 37–55.
14. Ronald Inglehart, *Culture Shift in Advanced Industrial Society* (Princeton, NJ: Princeton University Press, 1990), ch. 1, also published

as Ronald Inglehart, 'The Renaissance of Political Culture', *American Political Science Review* 82, 1988, 1203–1230.

15. Inglehart, *Culture Shift*, p. 43.
16. Inglehart, *Culture Shift*, p. 46.
17. Carole Pateman, for instance, suggests that 'throughout *The Civic Culture* it is assumed that there are no problems in talking about *the* political culture or *the* civic culture of Britain and the United States'. Carole Pateman, 'The Civic Culture: A Philosophic Critique', in Almond and Verba, *The Civic Culture Revisited*, p. 76. Michael Mann also characterizes *The Civic Culture* as a 'consensus theory' of society, in Michael Mann, 'The Social Cohesion of American Liberal Democracy', *American Sociological Review* 35, 1970, 423–439. Bob Jessop writes of 'the temptation to talk of *the* political culture and its effects in any given society' and the necessity of instead specifying 'exactly what orientations . . . are related to which actions among which members of society'. R. D. Jessop, 'Civility and Traditionalism in English Political Culture', *British Journal of Political Science* 1, 1971, 1–24, p. 21. Jessop further asserts that it is an *assumption* of Almond and Verba's that consensus supports stability, and argues that the study fails to recognize 'the implications of inequalities in the distribution of power for the relevance of consensus in producing stability'. Bob Jessop, *Traditionalism, Conservatism and British Political Culture* (London: George Allen & Unwin, 1974), p. 53. This position is spelt out further in Bob Jessop, *Social Order, Reform and Revolution: A Power, Exchange and Institutionalization Perspective* (London: Macmillan, 1972), p. 78: 'The greater the structural differentiation and power hierarchization, the less the need for consensus and the more the need for institutional integration.'
18. Mann, 'Social Cohesion', p. 435.
19. For a survey of this debate, see Paul G. Lewis, 'Legitimation and Political Crises: East European Developments in the Post-Stalin Period', in Paul G. Lewis (ed.), *Eastern Europe: Political Crisis and Legitimation* (New York: St. Martin's Press, 1984).
20. Nicholas Abercrombie and Bryan S. Turner, 'The Dominant Ideology Thesis', *British Journal of Sociology* 29, 1978, 149–170, p. 159.
21. Jessop, *Traditionalism*, pp. 255f.
22. Jessop, *Traditionalism*, pp. 53, 60.
23. Barry, *Sociologists, Economists and Democracy*, pp. 51, 94.
24. Carole Pateman, 'The Civic Culture', p. 78.
25. Quentin Skinner, 'The Empirical Theorists of Democracy and Their Critics: A Plague on Both Their Houses', *Political Theory* 1, 1973, 287–306, pp. 298–304.
26. Carole Pateman, 'Criticizing Empirical Theorists of Democracy: A Comment on Skinner', *Political Theory* 2, 1974, 215–218, pp. 216f. Other writers who have seen *The Civic Culture* as a covert justification of the political status quo in Britain and the United States, apart from

Barry, include James A. Bill and Robert L. Hardgrave, Jr, *Comparative Politics: The Quest for Theory* (Lanham, MD: University Press of America, 1981), pp. 90f. Pateman's critique is found also in Carole Pateman, 'Political Culture, Political Structure and Political Change', *British Journal of Political Science* 1, 1971, 291–305.

2: Political Culture and Modernity

1. Gabriel A. Almond and James S. Coleman (eds), *The Politics of the Developing Areas* (Princeton, NJ: Princeton University Press, 1960); Lucian W. Pye and Sidney Verba (eds), *Political Culture and Political Development* (Princeton, NJ: Princeton University Press, 1965).
2. Contrary to Barry's assessment. Brian M. Barry, *Sociologists, Economists and Democracy* (Chicago: University of Chicago Press, 1978), p. 93. See Gabriel A. Almond and Sidney Verba, *The Civic Culture: Political Attitudes and Democracy in Five Nations* (Princeton, NJ: Princeton University Press, 1963; abridged edn Boston: Little, Brown, 1965, repr. Newbury Park, CA and London: Sage, 1989), pp. 267f.
3. Cyril E. Black, *Understanding Soviet Politics: The Perspective of Russian History* (Boulder, CO: Westview, 1986), p. 90.
4. Lucian Pye, 'Introduction: Political Culture and Political Development', in Pye and Verba, *Political Culture and Political Development*, p. 13.
5. Raymond Grew, 'More on Modernization', *Journal of Social History* 14, 1980, 179–187, p. 179.
6. Archie Brown, 'Introduction', in Archie Brown (ed.), *Political Culture and Communist Studies* (London: Macmillan, 1984), p. 1.
7. Gabriel A. Almond, 'The Intellectual History of the Civic Culture Concept', in Gabriel A. Almond and Sidney Verba (eds), *The Civic Culture Revisited* (Boston: Little, Brown, 1980, repr. Newbury Park, CA and London: Sage, 1989), pp. 6–10.
8. Cyril E. Black, 'Eastern Europe in the Context of Comparative Modernization', in Charles Gati (ed.), *The Politics of Modernization in Eastern Europe: Testing the Soviet Model* (New York: Praeger, 1974), p. 25.
9. Lucian W. Pye, 'Political Science and the Crisis of Authoritarianism', *American Political Science Review* 84, 1990, 3–19.
10. Pye, 'Political Science and the Crisis of Authoritarianism', pp. 11f.
11. Gabriel A. Almond, 'Introduction', in Almond and Coleman, *Politics of the Developing Areas*, pp. 22–25.
12. For a critique of such 'dichotomous schemes' see James A. Bill and Robert L. Hardgrave, Jr, *Comparative Politics: The Quest for Theory* (Lanham, MD: University Press of America, 1981), pp. 50–57.
13. Stephen Chilton, *Defining Political Development* (Boulder, CO and London: Lynne Reiner, 1988), pp. 68, 76.

14. Alex Inkeles and Raymond A. Bauer, *The Soviet Citizen: Daily Life in a Totalitarian Society* (Cambridge, MA: Harvard University Press; London: Oxford University Press, 1959), pp. 383, 391.

15. Margaret S. Archer, 'Theory, Culture and Post-Industrial Society', in Mike Featherstone (ed.), *Global Culture: Nationalism, Globalism and Modernity* (A *Theory, Culture and Society* special issue) (London and Newbury Park, CA: Sage, 1990), pp. 98–107.

16. Archer, 'Theory, Culture and Post-Industrial Society', pp. 98f.

17. Archer, 'Theory, Culture and Post-Industrial Society', p. 117.

18. John R. Gibbins, 'Contemporary Political Culture: An Introduction', in John R. Gibbins (ed.), *Contemporary Political Culture: Politics in a Postmodern Age* (London: Sage, 1989), p. 14.

19. Gibbins, 'Contemporary Political Culture', pp. 17f.

20. Bryan S. Turner, 'From Postindustrial Society to Postmodern Politics: The Political Sociology of Daniel Bell', in Gibbins, *Contemporary Political Culture*, p. 213.

21. Gibbins, 'Contemporary Political Culture', p. 15.

22. See particularly Ronald Inglehart, *The Silent Revolution: Changing Values and Political Styles Among Western Publics* (Princeton, NJ: Princeton University Press, 1977) and Ronald Inglehart, *Culture Shift in Advanced Industrial Society* (Princeton, NJ: Princeton University Press, 1990). The latter study, a continuation of the former, but drawing on a wider range of data, will provide the basis of our discussion. Page numbers will be cited parenthetically in the text of the present section.

3: Political Culture and Communism

1. In recent years this constraint has evaporated. For an example of conventional survey-based political culture research in the Russian case see Jeffrey W. Hahn, 'Continuity and Change in Russian Political Culture', *British Journal of Political Science* 21, 1991, 393–421. Hahn's main conclusion is that Russian political culture is 'not strikingly different from what is found in Western industrial countries', and thus that it 'would appear to be sufficiently hospitable to sustain democratic institutions' (pp. 420f.).

2. Harry Eckstein, 'A Culturalist Theory of Political Change', *American Political Science Review* 82, 1988, 789–804.

3. Samuel P. Huntington and Jorge Domínguez, 'Political Development', in Fred I. Greenstein and Nelson W. Polsby (eds), *Handbook of Political Science Volume 3: Macropolitical Theory* (Reading, MA: Addison-Wesley, 1975), p. 17.

4. Barbara Jancar, 'Political Culture and Political Change', *Studies in Comparative Communism* 17, 1984, 69–82, pp. 79–81.

5. Archie Brown, 'Introduction', in Archie Brown and Jack Gray (eds),

Political Culture and Political Change in Communist States (London: Macmillan, 1977), p. 5.

6. Brown, 'Introduction', p. 1 (for the definition); Archie Brown, 'Introduction', in Archie Brown (ed.), *Political Culture and Communist Studies* (London: Macmillan, 1984), pp. 153f. (for the argument).

7. Brown, 'Introduction', in Brown, *Political Culture and Communist Studies*, p. 3.

8. Richard R. Fagen, *The Transformation of Political Culture in Cuba* (Stanford: Stanford University Press, 1969), p. 6.

9. Fagen, *Transformation of Political Culture in Cuba*, pp. 152f. See also the discussion in Stephen Welch, 'Issues in the Study of Political Culture: The Example of Communist Party States', *British Journal of Political Science* 17, 1987, 479–500, p. 482.

10. Stephen White, *Political Culture and Soviet Politics* (London: Macmillan, 1979).

11. White, *Political Culture and Soviet Politics*, chs. 4, 5. See also Stephen White, 'Political Socialization in the USSR: A Study in Failure?', *Studies in Comparative Communism* 10, 1977, 328–342 and Stephen White, 'Propagating Communist Values in the USSR', *Problems of Communism* 34, 1985, 1–17.

12. Gabriel A. Almond, 'Communism and Political Culture Theory', *Comparative Politics* 15, 1983, 127–138, pp. 127f.

13. Huntington and Domínguez, 'Political Development', pp. 15f. (for the definition), 31.

14. Almond, 'Communism and Political Culture Theory', p. 127.

15. Archie Brown and Gordon Wightman, 'Czechoslovakia: Revival and Retreat', in Brown and Gray, *Political Culture and Political Change*, p. 178.

16. There are two main representatives. The Harvard Project on the Soviet Social System involved the application of questionnaires to a group of about three thousand of the up to half a million former Soviet citizens who for various reasons were not repatriated after the Second World War, and the conducting of long interviews with 764 of them. The research was carried out in 1950–51, and the results were published in several studies during the 1950s, notably in Alex Inkeles and Raymond A. Bauer, *The Soviet Citizen: Daily Life in a Totalitarian Society* (Cambridge, MA: Harvard University Press; London: Oxford University Press, 1959). The General Survey of the University of Illinois Soviet Interview Project was applied to emigrants, primarily Jewish, from the Soviet Union to the United States in the 1970s, the results being published in book form as James R. Millar (ed.), *Politics, Work, and Daily Life in the USSR: A Survey of Former Soviet Citizens* (Cambridge: Cambridge University Press, 1987). Surveys applied to much smaller samples of Jewish migrants to Israel provided material for studies by White and Zvi Gitelman: Stephen White, 'Continuity and Change in Soviet Political Culture: An Emigré Study', *Comparative*

Political Studies 11, 1978, 391–395; White, *Political Culture and Soviet Politics*, ch. 5; White, 'Political Socialization in the USSR'; Zvi Gitelman, 'Soviet Political Culture: Insights from Jewish Emigrés', *Soviet Studies* 29, 1977, 543–564.

17. Stephen White, 'Soviet Political Culture Reconsidered', in Brown, *Political Culture and Communist Studies*, p. 66.
18. White, *Political Culture and Soviet Politics*, pp. 24–39.
19. White, *Political Culture and Soviet Politics*, ch. 3, quotation from p. 58.
20. White, *Political Culture and Soviet Politics*, p. 65.
21. Jancar, 'Political Culture and Political Change', p. 73.
22. Mary McAuley, 'Political Culture and Communist Politics: One Step Forward, Two Steps Back', in Brown, *Political Culture and Communist Studies*, p. 18.
23. White, 'Soviet Political Culture Reconsidered', p. 90.
24. Archie Brown, 'Conclusions', in Brown, *Political Culture and Communist Studies*, pp. 188f.
25. Stephen R. Burant, 'The Influence of Russian Tradition on the Political Style of the Soviet Elite', *Political Science Quarterly* 102, 1987, 273–293, p. 284. See also Frederick Barghoorn, 'Stalinism and the Russian Cultural Heritage', *Review of Politics* 14, 1952, 178–203.
26. Seweryn Bialer, *The Soviet Paradox: External Expansion, Internal Decline* (London: I. B. Tauris, 1986), p. 6; see also Frederick C. Barghoorn and Thomas F. Remington, *Politics in the USSR* (3rd edn) (Boston: Little, Brown, 1986). Robert Tucker's argument, in 'Stalinism as Revolution from Above', in Robert C. Tucker, *Political Culture and Leadership in Soviet Russia: From Lenin To Gorbachev* (Brighton: Wheatsheaf, 1987), will be discussed at length in Chapter 5.
27. Archie Brown, 'Ideology and Political Culture', in Seweryn Bialer (ed.), *Politics, Society, and Nationality Inside Gorbachev's Russia* (Boulder, CO: Westview, 1989), p. 19.
28. White, *Political Culture and Soviet Politics*, pp. 189f.
29. Brown, 'Ideology and Political Culture', pp. 21 (for the quotation from Burlatsky), 26. What has happened to the 'cultural supports for the status quo'?
30. 'In the view of senior members of the Institute of Public Opinion expressed later in 1969' – Brown and Wightman, 'Czechoslovakia', n. 14, p. 192.
31. Brown and Wightman, 'Czechoslovakia', p. 173.
32. There is a certain irony in the symbolic role that Masaryk has come to play for the Czechs. He had earlier been involved (though how crucially is a matter of controversy) in the 'Battle of the Manuscripts', in which the forgery in the nineteenth century of a manuscript previously taken to be an ancient symbol of Czech nationhood was exposed. The liberal rationalist's fate was to become himself the subject of myth. See Stanley B. Winters (ed.), *T. G. Masaryk (1850–1937). Volume 1:*

Thinker and Politician (Basingstoke: Macmillan, 1989), p. 5 and Robert B. Pynsent (ed.), *T. G. Masaryk (1850–1937)*. *Volume 2: Thinker and Critic*, p. 155. On the creation of romantic national myths see Chapter 7 below.

33. H. Gordon Skilling, 'Czechoslovak Political Culture: Pluralism in an International Context', in Brown, *Political Culture and Communist Studies*, p. 121.
34. David W. Paul, 'Czechoslovakia's Political Culture Reconsidered', in Brown, *Political Culture and Communist Studies*, pp. 137–139.
35. Brown and Wightman, 'Czechoslovakia', pp. 170–172.
36. David W. Paul, *The Cultural Limits of Revolutionary Politics* (Boulder, CO: East European Quarterly, 1979; distributed by Columbia University Press, New York), p. 175.
37. Brown and Wightman, 'Czechoslovakia', p. 166.
38. Janina Frentzel-Zagorska, 'The Dominant Political Culture in Poland', *Politics* 20, 1985, 82–98; Stefan Nowak, 'Values and Attitudes of the Polish People', *Scientific American* 245, 1981, 23–31.
39. Frentzel-Zagorska, 'The Dominant Political Culture in Poland', pp. 82f.
40. Nowak, 'Values and Attitudes', p. 27.
41. Frentzel-Zagorska, 'The Dominant Political Culture in Poland', p. 95.
42. Brown, 'Conclusions', in Brown, *Political Culture and Communist Studies*, p. 188.
43. Kristian Gerner, *The Soviet Union and Central Europe in the Post-War Era: A Study in Precarious Security* (Aldershot: Gower, 1985), p. 31.
44. White, 'Soviet Political Culture Reconsidered', p. 83.
45. Václav Havel's phrase, quoted by H. Gordon Skilling, 'Sixty-eight in Historical Perspective', *International Journal* 33, 1978, 678–701, p. 700. The idea is implicit in many responses to the more recent events, and thus may serve as a token in the following discussion.
46. See Charles Gati, *The Bloc That Failed: Soviet-East European Relations in Transition* (Bloomington, IN: Indiana University Press, 1990), pp. 164–167.
47. Václav Havel, 'The Power of the Powerless', in Václav Havel et al., *The Power of the Powerless* (London: Hutchinson, 1985), pp. 42f.; Milan Kundera, *The Book of Laughter and Forgetting* (Harmondsworth: Penguin, 1983), pp. 219–221.
48. Havel, 'Power of the Powerless', pp. 35–38.
49. Cyril E. Black, 'Eastern Europe in the Context of Comparative Modernization', in Charles Gati (ed.), *The Politics of Modernization in Eastern Europe: Testing the Soviet Model* (New York: Praeger, 1974), p. 35.
50. Dennison Rusinow, 'Introduction', in Dennison Rusinow (ed.), *Yugoslavia: A Fractured Federalism* (Washington DC: Wilson Center Press, 1988), p. 4.
51. This explanation has been proposed by Mary McAuley in the guise of devil's advocate against Stephen White. Mary McAuley, 'Political Culture and Communist Politics: One Step Forward, Two Steps Back',

in Brown, *Political Culture and Communist Studies*, pp. 24f. It is in fact an exaggeration to say that Eastern Europe lacks experience of the operation of the market. But its experience is hardly such as to generate enthusiasm. Rivalries between the new states of Eastern Europe after the First World War led to the erection of tariff barriers, to a general weakening of the already underdeveloped economy of the region, and to its susceptibility to economic imperialism on the part of Nazi Germany. See Iván T. Berend and György Ránki, *Economic Development in East-Central Europe in the 19th and 20th Centuries* (New York: Columbia University Press, 1974), esp. chs 8, 9.

52. Karen Dawisha, *Eastern Europe, Gorbachev, and Reform: The Great Challenge* (2nd edn) (Cambridge: Cambridge University Press, 1990), pp. 40f.

53. Quoted in Dawisha, *Eastern Europe, Gorbachev, and Reform*, p. 43.

54. Black, 'Eastern Europe in the Context of Comparative Modernization', p. 35.

55. Joseph Rothschild, *Return to Diversity: A Political History of East Central Europe Since World War II* (New York and Oxford: Oxford University Press, 1989), p. 225. Both the 'return' and the 'diversity' of Rothschild's title are rendered questionable by the latter statement.

56. Havel, 'Power of the Powerless', pp. 49–57.

57. George Konrád, *Antipolitics: An Essay* (trans. Richard E. Allen) (New York and London: Harcourt Brace Jovanovich, 1984), p. 95.

58. Timothy Garton Ash, 'Does Central Europe Exist?', *New York Review of Books* 33, 9 October 1986, 45–52.

59. Dawisha, *Eastern Europe, Gorbachev, and Reform*, pp. 43f.

60. Gerner, *The Soviet Union and Central Europe*, p. 59.

61. Quoted in Dawisha, *Eastern Europe, Gorbachev, and Reform*, p. 69.

62. Paul, 'Czechoslovak Political Culture Reconsidered', p. 140.

4: Political Culture and Comparative Explanation

1. Almond, 'The Intellectual History of the Civic Culture Concept', in Gabriel A. Almond and Sidney Verba (eds), *The Civic Culture Revisited* (Boston: Little, Brown, 1980, repr. Newbury Park, CA and London: Sage, 1989), p. 29.

2. Brian M. Barry, *Sociologists, Economists and Democracy* (Chicago: University of Chicago Press, 1978), p. 49.

3. Mary McAuley, 'Political Culture and Communist Politics: One Step Forward, Two Steps Back', in Archie Brown (ed.), *Political Culture and Communist Studies* (London: Macmillan, 1984), p. 26.

4. Archie Brown, 'Conclusions', in Brown, *Political Culture and Communist Studies*, p. 187.

5. Arend Lijphart, 'Comparative Politics and Comparative Method', *American Political Science Review* 65, 1971, 682–693. See also the

synopsis in David Collier, 'The Comparative Method: Two Decades of Change', in Dankwart A. Rustow and Kenneth Paul Erickson (eds), *Comparative Political Dynamics: Global Research Perspectives* (New York: HarperCollins, 1991), pp. 8–11.

6. One of Lijphart's justifications of the comparative method was the limited quantity of research resources; the profession of political science has expanded considerably since he wrote, helping to overcome this problem.

7. Collier, 'The Comparative Method', pp. 15–19.

8. Collier, 'The Comparative Method', p. 13.

9. David J. Elkins and Richard E. B. Simeon, 'A Cause in Search of its Effect, or What Does Political Culture Explain?', *Comparative Politics* 11, 1979, 127–145.

10. Elkins and Simeon, 'A Cause in Search of its Effect', pp. 127f., 132, 137–139.

11. Elkins and Simeon, 'A Cause in Search of its Effect', pp. 129f.

12. Fransisco José Moreno, *Legitimacy and Stability in Latin America: A Study of Chilean Political Culture* (New York: New York University Press; London: University of London Press, 1969), p. 182.

13. Geert Hofstede, *Culture's Consequences: International Differences in Work-Related Values* (Beverly Hills, CA and London: Sage, 1980).

14. Hofstede, *Culture's Consequences*, p. 25.

15. 'Masculinity' is found to be 'negatively correlated with the percentage of women in professional and technical jobs'. Hofstede, *Culture's Consequences*, p. 262.

16. Hofstede, *Culture's Consequences*, p. 336.

17. In Easton's theory the universality of political systems derives from a functionalist perspective – its aim was to 'extricate from the total political reality those aspects that can be considered the fundamental processes or activities without which no political life in society could continue'. David Easton, *A Systems Analysis of Political Life* (New York: John Wiley and Sons, 1965), p. 13. Clearly, these functionalist assumptions are much more open to question than Hofstede's organizational categories – and this is before we begin to consider the role of attitudes or 'culture'.

18. Miller, 'Political Culture: Some Perennial Questions Reopened', in Brown, *Political Culture and Communist Studies*, p. 56.

19. Lucian W. Pye, 'Culture and Political Science: Problems in the Evaluation of the Concept of Political Culture', in Louis Schneider and Charles M. Bonjean (eds), *The Idea of Culture in the Social Sciences* (Cambridge: Cambridge University Press, 1973); see also McAuley's commentary in 'Political Culture and Communist Politics', pp. 20f.

20. Pye, 'Culture and Political Science', p. 73; also Pye, 'Introduction', in Lucian W. Pye and Sidney Verba (eds), *Political Culture and Political Development* (Princeton, NJ: Princeton University Press, 1965), p. 8.

21. Bradley M. Richardson, *The Political Culture of Japan* (Berkeley: University of California Press, 1974), p. 7.

22. Glenda M. Patrick, 'Political Culture', in Giovanni Sartori (ed.), *Social Science Concepts: A Systemic Analysis* (Beverly Hills, CA and London: Sage, 1984), p. 279.

23. Daniel J. Elazar, *American Federalism: A View from the States* (New York: Thomas W. Crowell, 1966), pp. 85–97.

24. Ira Sharkansky, 'The Utility of Elazar's Political Culture: A Research Note', in Daniel Elazar and Joseph Zikmund III (eds), *The Ecology of American Political Culture: Readings* (New York: Thomas W. Crowell, 1975), table 2, p. 254; pp. 255–259.

25. Compare Barry's similar criticism of *The Civic Culture*: Barry, *Sociologists, Economists and Democracy*, p. 89.

26. Judith N. Shklar, *Montesquieu* (Oxford: Oxford University Press, 1987), pp. 106, 125.

27. Miller, 'Political Culture', p. 42.

28. Gabriel A. Almond, 'Comparative Political Systems', *Journal of Politics* 18, 1956, 391–409, p. 396.

29. Moshe M. Czudnowski, 'A Salience Dimension of Politics for the Study of Political Culture', *American Political Science Review* 62, 1968, 878–888, pp. 881f.

30. Ann L. Craig and Wayne A. Cornelius, 'Political Culture in Mexico: Continuities and Revisionist Interpretations', in Almond and Verba, *Civic Culture Revisited*, pp. 331–333.

31. A later edition is Frederick C. Barghoorn and Thomas F. Remington, *Politics in the USSR* (3rd edn) (Boston: Little, Brown, 1986), p. 45.

32. Wayne DiFranceisco and Zvi Gitelman, 'Soviet Political Culture and "Covert Participation" in Policy Implementation', *American Political Science Review* 78, 1984, 603–621.

33. Richardson, *Political Culture of Japan*, p. 78.

34. Czudnowski, 'A Salience Dimension of Politics', p. 882. A somewhat similar suggestion has been made by Edward Lehman, who proposes that, instead of political culture being related causally to other variables, it be construed as a 'specifying variable'. Such a 'variable' '"specifies" the conditions under which more strategic correlations will exist in greater or lesser intensity'. Edward W. Lehman, 'On the Concept of Political Culture: A Theoretical Reassessment', *Social Forces* 50, 1972, 361–370, p. 368.

35. In addition to 'filter variable' and 'specifying variable', political culture has been described as an 'intervening variable' and a 'supervenient variable' – Dennis Kavanagh, *Political Science and Political Behaviour* (London: George Allen & Unwin, 1983), p. 72 and David W. Paul, *The Cultural Limits of Revolutionary Politics* (Boulder, CO: East European Quarterly; distributed by Columbia University Press, New York, 1979), p. 5, respectively. However, a variable can only be dependent or independent, or both; that is what the term 'variable'

means in this context. The last two usages reduce to dependence or independence; the first two are meaningless.

36.   Archie Brown and Gordon Wightman, 'Czechoslovakia: Revival and Retreat', in Archie Brown and Jack Gray (eds), *Political Culture and Political Change in Communist States* (London: Macmillan, 1977), pp. 170–172.

37.   Gabriel A. Almond and Sidney Verba, *The Civic Culture: Political Attitudes and Democracy in Five Nations* (Princeton, NJ: Princeton University Press, 1963; abridged edn. Boston: Little, Brown, 1965, repr. Newbury Park, CA and London: Sage, 1989), e.g. at pp. 66, 184f; Ronald Inglehart, *Culture Shift in Advanced Industrial Society* (Princeton, NJ: Princeton University Press, 1990), p. 33.

38.   Stephen White, *Political Culture and Soviet Politics* (London: Macmillan, 1979), p. 20.

39.   Raymond Williams, *Marxism and Literature* (Oxford: Oxford University Press, 1977), pp. 77–80.

5: Political Culture and Stalinism

1.   Robert C. Tucker, 'Communist Revolutions, National Cultures, and the Divided Nations', *Studies in Comparative Communism* 7, 1974, 235–245, p. 236: 'comparativism is built into the very structure of theorizing'.

2.   Robert C. Tucker, 'Communism and Political Culture', *Newsletter on Comparative Studies of Communism* 4, 1971, 3–12, pp. 11f. Tucker has not pursued his suggestion.

3.   Robert Tucker, 'Culture, Political Culture and Communist Studies', in Robert C. Tucker, *Political Culture and Leadership in Soviet Russia: From Lenin To Gorbachev* (Brighton: Wheatsheaf, 1987), p. 5. (First published in a slightly different form as Robert C. Tucker, 'Culture, Political Culture, and Communist Society', *Political Science Quarterly* 88, 1973, 173–190.)

4.   Tucker, 'Culture, Political Culture and Communist Studies', p. 4.

5.   Robert Tucker, 'Lenin's Bolshevism as a Culture in the Making', in Tucker, *Political Culture and Leadership*, pp. 34–36.

6.   Quoted in Tucker, 'Lenin's Bolshevism', p. 45. Original emphasis.

7.   Tucker, 'Lenin's Bolshevism', p. 46.

8.   Tucker, 'Communist Revolutions', p. 245.

9.   A similar view was developed more or less simultaneously by Alfred Meyer, who argued that 'Communism can be described as a deliberate and systematic attempt at culture-building', and also recommended the study of 'communist culture'. Alfred G. Meyer, 'Communist Revolutions and Cultural Change', *Studies in Comparative Communism* 5, 1972, 345–372, p. 365.

10.   Robert Tucker, 'Leadership and Culture in Social Movements', in

Tucker, *Political Culture and Leadership*, p. 20. See also the essay 'On Revolutionary Mass-Movement Regimes' in Robert C. Tucker, *The Soviet Political Mind: Studies in Stalinism and Post-Stalin Change* (London and Dunmow: Pall Mall Press, 1963).

11. Tucker, 'Leadership and Culture', p. 22.
12. Tucker, 'Lenin's Bolshevism', p. 45.
13. Tucker, 'Lenin's Bolshevism', p. 37.
14. Zenovia A. Sochor, *Revolution and Culture: The Bogdanov–Lenin Controversy* (Ithaca, NY and London: Cornell University Press, 1988), pp. 68, 74.
15. Quoted in Sochor, *Revolution and Culture*, p. 148. Original emphasis.
16. Maurice Meisner writes of the priority of the economy in Lenin's conception of cultural revolution; of 'the Leninist emphasis on the need to learn the modern material and technical "culture" of the capitalist West in order to overcome the feudal habits and inertia of the Russian cultural-historical heritage'. Maurice Meisner, 'Iconoclasm and Cultural Revolution in China and Russia', in Abbott Gleason, Peter Kenez and Richard Stites (eds), *Bolshevik Culture: Experiment and Order in the Russian Revolution* (Bloomington, IN: Indiana University Press, 1985), p. 287. Leszek Kolakowski writes similarly of Proletkult's utopianism that it 'seemed to Lenin an idle fantasy unconnected with the party's true objectives. In a country with a huge percentage of illiterates the need was to teach them reading, writing and arithmetic . . . and give them an elementary idea of technology and organization, not to pull civilization up by the roots and start again from zero'. Leszek Kolakowski, *Main Currents of Marxism: Its Rise, Growth, and Dissolution. Volume II: The Golden Age* (trans. P. S. Falla) (Oxford: Oxford University Press, 1978), p. 444. See also Sochor, *Revolution and Culture*, p. 119.
17. Alfred G. Meyer, 'The Use of the Term Culture in the Soviet Union', Appendix B of A. L. Kroeber and Clyde Kluckhohn, *Culture: A Critical Review of Concepts and Definitions* (New York: Vintage Books, n. d.) (originally published as *Papers of the Peabody Museum of American Archaeology and Ethnology, Harvard University* 47, 1952), p. 415.
18. Quoted in Sheila Fitzpatrick, 'Cultural Revolution as Class War', in Sheila Fitzpatrick (ed.), *Cultural Revolution in Russia, 1928–31* (Bloomington, IN and London: Indiana University Press, 1978), p. 9. *Pravda*'s emphasis.
19. Robert Tucker, 'Stalinism as Revolution from Above', in Tucker, *Political Culture and Leadership*, p. 85.
20. Jonathan R. Adelman, 'The Impact of Civil Wars on Communist Political Culture: The Chinese and Russian Cases', *Studies in Comparative Communism* 16, 1983, 25–48, pp. 29f.
21. Sheila Fitzpatrick, 'The Civil War as Formative Experience', in Gleason *et al.*, *Bolshevik Culture*, pp. 60f., 74.

22. Tucker, 'Stalinism', p. 85.
23. Robert Tucker, 'Gorbachev and the Fight for Soviet Reform', in Tucker, *Political Culture and Leadership*, pp. 176–179.
24. Stephen F. Cohen, *Bukharin and the Bolshevik Revolution: A Political Biography 1888–1938* (London: Wildwood House, 1974), p. 126.
25. Robert Tucker, 'Between Lenin and Stalin: The Breakdown of a Revolutionary Culture', in Tucker, *Political Culture and Leadership*, p. 59.
26. Fitzpatrick, 'Cultural Revolution as Class War', p. 32.
27. Gail Warshovsky Lapidus, 'Educational Strategies and Cultural Revolution: The Politics of Soviet Development', in Fitzpatrick, *Cultural Revolution*, pp. 91–94.
28. Robert Sharlet, 'Pashukanis and the Withering Away of the Law in the USSR', in Fitzpatrick, *Cultural Revolution*.
29. Fitzpatrick, 'Cultural Revolution as Class War', p. 11.
30. Moshe Lewin, 'Society, State and Ideology During the First Five-Year Plan', in Moshe Lewin, *The Making of the Soviet System: Essays in the Social History of Interwar Russia* (London: Methuen, 1985), pp. 220f.
31. Donald W. Treadgold, *Twentieth Century Russia* (7th edn) (Boulder, CO: Westview, 1990), p. 245.
32. Moshe Lewin, 'The Immediate Background of Soviet Collectivization', in Lewin, *The Making of the Soviet System*, *passim*.
33. Sheila Fitzpatrick, 'New Perspectives on Stalinism', *Russian Review* 45, 1986, 357–373, p. 364.
34. Robert C. Tucker, 'Stalin and the Uses of Psychology', in Tucker, *The Soviet Political Mind*, p. 98.
35. Tucker, 'Stalin and the Uses of Psychology', pp. 92–94.
36. David Joravsky, 'The Construction of the Stalinist Psyche', in Fitzpatrick, *Cultural Revolution*, pp. 110, 117, 126f.
37. Robert C. Williams, 'The Nationalization of Early Soviet Culture', *Russian History* 9, 1982, 157–172, p. 172.
38. Max Hayward, 'The Decline of Socialist Realism', in Max Hayward, *Writers in Russia: 1917–1978* (London: Harvill, 1983), p. 156.
39. Katerina Clark, *The Soviet Novel: History as Ritual* (Chicago and London: University of Chicago Press, 1981), *passim*.
40. Clark, *The Soviet Novel*, pp. 37–41.
41. Graeme Gill, 'Personality Cult, Political Culture and Party Structure', *Studies in Comparative Communism* 17, 1984, 111–121.
42. Tucker, 'Stalinism', pp. 88–93.
43. Tucker, 'Stalinism', p. 95.
44. Archie Brown, review in *The Times Literary Supplement*, 7 March 1980, p. 273.
45. Edward L. Keenan, 'Muscovite Political Folkways', *Russian Review* 45, 1986, 115–181.
46. Other examples are Frederick Barghoorn, 'Stalinism and the Russian Cultural Heritage', *Review of Politics* 14, 1952, 178–203; Zbigniew

K. Brzezinski, 'Soviet Politics: From the Future to the Past?', in Paul Cocks, Robert V. Daniels and Nancy Whittier Heer (eds), *The Dynamics of Soviet Politics* (Cambridge, MA and London: Harvard University Press, 1976); Stephen R. Burant, 'The Influence of Russian Tradition on the Political Style of the Soviet Elite', *Political Science Quarterly* 102, 1987, 273–293; and Richard Pipes, *Russia Under the Old Regime* (New York: Scribners Sons, 1974).

47. Tucker, 'Stalinism', p. 96.

48. Tucker, 'Stalinism', p. 95. Frederick Barghoorn has made a similar connection between Russian cultural influences and Stalin's personality: 'only those aspects of Russian culture and history with which in some way Stalin identifies himself are permitted to figure significantly in Soviet intellectual activity'. Barghoorn, 'Stalinism and the Russian Cultural Heritage', p. 180.

49. See Robert C. Tucker, *Stalin as Revolutionary 1879–1929: A Study in History and Personality* (New York: W. W. Norton, 1973); Robert C. Tucker, *Stalin in Power: The Revolution from Above 1928–1941* (New York and London: W. W. Norton, 1990).

50. Hannah Arendt, *The Origins of Totalitarianism* (Cleveland, OH: Meridian, 1958), pp. 398, 405. Arendt is speaking of the Nazi regime and Hitler's personality cult, but the point is equally relevant here.

51. T. H. Rigby, 'Stalinism and the Mono-Organizational Society', in Robert C. Tucker (ed.), *Stalinism: Essays in Historical Interpretation* (New York: W. W. Norton, 1977), pp. 55–59. Gill's analysis of the personality cult also has some affinities with this perspective. Arendt's emphasis on organizational confusion distinguishes her approach from that of later theorists of totalitarianism, among whom Carl Friedrich and Zbigniew Brzezinski are pre-eminent, who conceived of totalitarianism in terms of its institutional features. Carl J. Friedrich and Zbigniew K. Brzezinski, *Totalitarian Dictatorship and Autocracy* (2nd edn) (Cambridge, MA: Harvard University Press, 1965), pp. 21–27. Revisionist findings such as Lewin's of the *ad hoc* nature of central planning and J. Arch Getty's of the inadequacy of bureaucratic control procedures within the Party (J. Arch Getty, *Origins of the Great Purges: The Soviet Communist Party Reconsidered, 1933–1938* (Cambridge: Cambridge University Press, 1985), e.g. ch. 3) tell more against the latter conception of totalitarianism than Arendt's.

52. Arendt, *Origins of Totalitarianism*, p. 323.

53. Arendt, *Origins of Totalitarianism*, p. 317.

54. Arendt, *Origins of Totalitarianism*, p. 391. Jerry Hough writes, ostensibly *contra* Arendt, 'The regime's "mobilization" program was really an unprecedented attempt to integrate, not atomize, a vast number of inexperienced workers and former peasants into a rapidly expanding urban sector'. Jerry F. Hough, 'The Cultural Revolution and Western Understanding of the Soviet System', in Fitzpatrick, *Cultural Revolution*, p. 246. This criticism misunderstands Arendt's position, which

precisely argues that atomization is a precondition of integration.

55. Lewin, 'Society, State and Ideology', p. 221; Daniel R. Brower, 'Stalinism and the "View From Below"', *Russian Review* 46, 1987, 379–381, pp. 380f.

56. Geoff Eley, 'History With the Politics Left Out – Again?', *Russian Review* 45, 1986, 385–394, p. 390. Original emphasis.

57. Michael Waller, 'What Is to Count as Ideology in Soviet Politics?', in Stephen White and Alex Pravda (eds), *Ideology and Soviet Politics* (Basingstoke and London: Macmillan, 1988), pp. 29, 31. Emphasis added.

58. Daniel Bell, 'Ten Theories in Search of Soviet Reality', in Alex Inkeles and Kent Geiger (eds), *Soviet Society: A Book of Readings* (London: Constable, 1961), p. 49.

59. Vladimir Andrle, *Workers in Stalin's Russia: Industrialization and Social Change in a Planned Economy* (Hemel Hempstead: Harvester-Wheatsheaf; New York: St. Martin's Press, 1988).

60. Andrle, *Workers in Stalin's Russia*, pp. 116–125.

61. Andrle, *Workers in Stalin's Russia*, p. 168.

62. Andrle accepts that an element of inheritance contributes to the techniques used by workers in navigating through the environment he describes; for instance of the use of *blat* ('pull' or 'connections') he writes, '*blat* networks provided a practical context for the familiar communal virtues of personal reciprocity and loyalty, social settings in which the rules of conduct were understandable and the rewards tangible' (Andrle, *Workers in Stalin's Russia*, p. 55). Nevertheless, such techniques were readily taken up by Western immigrants also, and in a context in which, by 1939, half of the urban population consisted of post-1926 arrivals (p. 32), it is clear, as Andrle argues, that inheritance alone is not a sufficient explanation of such behaviour. His findings here recall those of DiFranceisco and Gitelman, discussed in Chapter 4.

63. Andrle, *Workers in Stalin's Russia*, p. 91.

64. Andrle, *Workers in Stalin's Russia*, p. 99.

65. Andrle reports that F. W. Taylor had the same status as Marx in articles in management journals. Andrle, *Workers in Stalin's Russia*, p. 93.

66. Tucker, 'Stalinism', p. 95.

67. Archie Brown, 'Conclusions', in Archie Brown (ed.), *Political Culture and Communist Studies* (London: Macmillan, 1984), pp. 180f.

68. For further discussion of the relative merits of the notions of 'communist political culture' and 'official political culture' in the Stalin and Brezhnev periods, see Stephen Welch, 'Political Culture and Communism: Definition and Use', *Journal of Communist Studies* 5, 1989, 91–98. See also (on the relativity of political culture to the tasks undertaken by the leadership) Kenneth Jowitt, 'An Organizational Approach to the Study of Political Culture in Marxist–Leninist Systems', *American Political Science Review* 68, 1974, 1171–1191.

69. Michael E. Urban, 'Conceptualizing Political Power in the USSR: Patterns of Binding and Bonding', *Studies in Comparative Communism* 18, 1985, 207–226, pp. 216–220. The *nomenklatura* system enabled Party control of appointments within governmental and other non-Party organizations.

70. Rachel Walker, 'Marxism–Leninism as Discourse: The Politics of the Empty Signifier and the Double Bind', *British Journal of Political Science* 19, 1989, 161–189, pp. 179f.

71. Michael E. Urban, *The Ideology of Administration: American and Soviet Cases* (Albany, NY: State University of New York Press, 1982), p. 129.

72. T. H. Rigby, 'Introduction: Political Legitimacy, Weber and Communist Mono-Organizational Systems', in T. H. Rigby and Ferenc Fehér (eds), *Political Legitimation in Communist States* (London: Macmillan, 1982).

73. Rigby, 'Introduction', p. 15.

74. Christel Lane, 'Legitimacy and Power in the Soviet Union Through Socialist Ritual', *British Journal of Political Science* 14, 1984, 207–217, p. 210.

75. It is worth noticing, however, that Lane's own emphasis on popular legitimation through new Soviet rituals in Christel Lane, *The Rites of Rulers: Ritual in Industrial Society – The Soviet Case* (Cambridge: Cambridge University Press, 1981) cannot ultimately deliver on the promise, made through the contrast Lane draws between her approach and Rigby's, to provide empirical evidence of acceptance by the population: 'Are the official norms and values embodied in the ritual completely absorbed, or do they form no more than an acceptable backcloth against which events of interpersonal relevance are given heightened significance? We just do not have answers and probably never will acquire them.' Lane, 'Legitimacy and Power', pp. 216f.

76. Gordon Smith, 'A Model of the Bureaucratic Culture', *Political Studies* 22, 1974, 31–43, p. 32.

77. Ronald J. Hill, 'Soviet Political Development and the Culture of the Apparatchiki', *Studies in Comparative Communism* 19, 1986, 25–39, p. 33. See also Ronald J. Hill, 'The Cultural Dimension of Communist Political Evolution', *Journal of Communist Studies* 1, 1985, 34–53.

78. The continuity of this concept with the evaluative conception of 'culture' Meyer identified in Marxism and Leninism is clear. See Archie Brown, 'Soviet Political Culture Through Soviet Eyes', in Brown, *Political Culture and Communist Studies*, pp. 103f. for the connection between Soviet usage of '*political* culture' and this evaluative conception.

79. George Yaney, 'Bureaucracy as Culture: A Comment', *Slavic Review* 41, 1982, 104–111, p. 106.

80. Yaney, 'Bureaucracy as Culture', pp. 106f.

81. See Hill, 'Soviet Political Development', pp. 34f.

6:   Political Culture and Interpretation

1.   Their common membership of the category of 'political culture research' is, on the other hand, suggested by this observation of Lucian Pye's: 'Through the works of . . . Hannah Arendt, among others, we know something about the distinctive human or cultural basis of totalitarianism; and through the works of Almond and Verba, among others, we know something about the civic culture basic to stable democracy.' Lucian W. Pye, 'Political Science and the Crisis of Authoritarianism', *American Political Science Review* 84, 1990, 3–19, p. 13.

2.   Archie Brown, 'Conclusion', in Archie Brown (ed.), *Political Culture and Communist Studies* (London: Macmillan, 1984), pp. 149–155.

3.   Quoted in A. L. Kroeber and Clyde Kluckhohn, *Culture: A Critical Review of Concepts and Definitions* (New York: Vintage Books, n. d.) (originally published as *Papers of the Peabody Museum of American Archaeology and Ethnology, Harvard University* 47, 1952), p. 81.

4.   Mead had celebrated sexual freedom in Samoa; Freeman on the other hand wrote of repression, a cult of virginity, and furthermore of claims by the inhabitants that Mead was misled. Subsequent defences of Mead have shown, however, that the issues of fact are by no means straightforward, and this is what makes the argument seem like one over mood. See Ivan Brady (ed.), 'Speaking in the Name of the Real: Freeman and Mead on Samoa', *American Anthropologist* 85, 1983, 908–947.

5.   James A. Boon, *Other Tribes, Other Scribes: Symbolic Anthropology in the Comparative Study of Cultures, Histories, Religions, and Texts* (Cambridge: Cambridge University Press, 1982), p. 16.

6.   Ernest Gellner, *The Concept of Kinship and Other Essays on Anthropological Method and Explanation* (Oxford: Basil Blackwell, 1987) (originally published as *Cause and Meaning in the Social Sciences*, 1973), p. ix; Boon, *Other Tribes, Other Scribes*, p. 8.

7.   Roger M. Keesing, 'Theories of Culture', *Annual Review of Anthropology* 3, 1974, 73–97, p. 73.

8.   Richard Basham and David DeGroot, 'Current Approaches to the Anthropology of Urban and Complex Societies', *American Anthropologist* 79, 1977, 414–440, pp. 430f.

9.   See Edmund Leach, *Social Anthropology* (London: Fontana, 1982), ch. 1 for an account of the differences between social and cultural anthropology.

10.   See the discussion in A. L. Epstein, *Ethos and Identity: Three Studies in Ethnicity* (London: Tavistock; Chicago: Aldine, 1978), pp. 10f.

11.   Epstein, *Ethos and Identity*, ch. 2.

12.   M. Gluckman, 'Anthropological Problems Arising From the African Industrial Revolution', in Aidan Southall (ed.), *Social Change in Modern Africa* (London: Oxford University Press, 1961), pp. 67, 69.

13. Abner Cohen, *Two-Dimensional Man: An Essay on the Anthropology of Power and Symbolism in Complex Society* (London: Routledge & Kegan Paul, 1974), pp. 92–96.
14. Cohen, *Two-Dimensional Man*, p. 124.
15. Anthony P. Cohen, *The Symbolic Construction of Community* (Chichester: Ellis Horwood; London and New York: Tavistock, 1985), p. 44.
16. Cohen, *Symbolic Construction of Community*, p. 47.
17. Cohen, *Symbolic Construction of Community*, pp. 79–81.
18. Nathan Glazer and Daniel P. Moynihan, 'Why Ethnicity?', *Commentary* 58, 1974, 33–39, p. 33. For a survey of recent writing on the political use of ethnicity, see James McKay, 'An Exploratory Synthesis of Primordial and Mobilizationist Approaches to Ethnic Phenomena', *Ethnic and Racial Studies* 5, 1982, 395–420. An interesting example of the earlier confidence about assimilation is provided by Stephen Meyer's account of the Ford Motor Company's attempted Americanization of its substantially immigrant workforce. Ford's 'Sociological Department' aimed to improve workers' domestic environment, attending to matters such as cleanliness, table manners and etiquette. Stephen Meyer, 'Adapting the Immigrant to the Line: Americanization in the Ford Factory, 1914–1921', *Journal of Social History* 14, 1980, 67–82, pp. 71–75. A graduation pageant from the Department's English school featured a model 'melting pot', fifteen feet in diameter. The effort, Meyer reports, was undermined by the erosion of the monetary incentive on which it was predicated, a down-to-earth illustration of the influence of material circumstances on the survival or otherwise of ethnic attachments.
19. Glazer and Moynihan, 'Why Ethnicity?', pp. 35, 37.
20. Epstein, *Ethos and Identity*, p. 122.
21. Clifford Geertz, 'Thick Description: Toward an Interpretive Theory of Culture', in Clifford Geertz, *The Interpretation of Cultures* (London: Hutchinson, 1975), pp. 6f.
22. Geertz, 'Thick Description', p. 13.
23. Geertz, 'Thick Description', p. 14. It is from this position, presumably, that Tucker draws his overstated conclusion that political culture may not explain anything; the kind of understanding that Geertz aims at, however, clearly involves explanation, if in a looser sense – as indeed does Weberian sociology.
24. Clifford Geertz, 'Deep Play: Notes on the Balinese Cockfight', in Geertz, *The Interpretation of Cultures*, pp. 448f.
25. Jonathan Lieberson, 'Interpreting the Interpreter', in *New York Review of Books* 31, 15 March 1985, 39–46, p. 46.
26. See Roy Wagner, *The Invention of Culture* (Englewood Cliffs, NJ: Prentice-Hall, 1975), pp. 26–29.
27. Clifford Geertz, 'Ideology As a Cultural System', in Geertz, *The Interpretation of Cultures*, p. 205.

28. Geertz, 'Ideology As a Cultural System', p. 220.
29. Lance Banning, *The Jeffersonian Persuasion: Evolution of a Party Ideology* (Ithaca, NY and London: Cornell University Press, 1978), p. 15.
30. For a critique of the influence of Geertz on the development of the republican 'paradigm', see Joyce Appleby, 'Republicanism in Old and New Contexts', *William and Mary Quarterly* 43, 1986, 20–34.
31. See, for instance, Richard J. Bernstein, *The Restructuring of Social and Political Theory* (London: Methuen, 1979), pp. 141–146.
32. Peter L. Berger and Thomas Luckmann, *The Social Construction of Reality: A Treatise in the Sociology of Knowledge* (Harmondsworth: Penguin, 1967), pp. 67–75.
33. Alfred Schutz, 'Common-Sense and Scientific Interpretation of Human Action', in Alfred Schutz, *Collected Papers I: The Problem of Social Reality* (The Hague: Martinus Nijhoff, 1973), pp. 7, 19.
34. Schutz, 'Common-Sense and Scientific Interpretation', pp. 11f.
35. Berger and Luckmann, *Social Construction*, p. 85.
36. Clifford Geertz, 'The Impact of the Concept of Culture on the Concept of Man', in Geertz, *The Interpretation of Cultures*, p. 45.
37. Alfred Schutz, 'Concept and Theory Formation in the Social Sciences', in Schutz, *Collected Papers I*, pp. 56–59. See also Maurice Natanson, 'Introduction', in Schutz, *Collected Papers I*, pp. xxvf., and Bernstein, *Restructuring*, pp. 138–140.
38. Berger and Luckmann, *Social Construction*, p. 87.
39. Wes Sharrock and Bob Anderson, *The Ethnomethodologists* (Chichester: Ellis Horwood; London and New York: Tavistock, 1986), pp. 29–32. For the relationship between ethnomethodology and phenomenology see pp. 1–12.
40. The research was by Emmanuel Schegloff. Sharrock and Anderson, *The Ethnomethodologists*, p. 70.
41. David Middleton and Derek Edwards, 'Conversational Remembering: a Social Psychological Approach', in David Middleton and Derek Edwards (eds), *Collective Remembering* (London and Newbury Park, CA: Sage, 1990), quotation from p. 43.
42. William Roseberry, 'Balinese Cockfights and the Seduction of Anthropology', *Social Research* 49, 1982, 1013–1028, p. 1022.
43. Quoted in Maurice Natanson, *Anonymity: A Study in the Philosophy of Alfred Schutz* (Bloomington, IN: Indiana University Press, 1986), pp. 21f.

7: Political Culture and National Identity

1. Brian Girvin, 'Change and Continuity in Liberal Democratic Political Culture', in John R. Gibbins (ed.), *Contemporary Political Culture:*

Politics in a Postmodern Age (London: Sage, 1989), pp. 34f.

2. Claude Lévi-Strauss, 'Social Structure', in *Structural Anthropology* (volume 1) (New York and London: Basic Books, 1963), p. 295.

3. Benedict Anderson, *Imagined Communities: Reflections on the Origins and Spread of Nationalism* (London: Verso, 1983).

4. E. J. Hobsbawm, *Nations and Nationalism Since 1870: Programme, Myth, Reality* (Cambridge: Cambridge University Press, 1990), pp. 3–5.

5. Ernest Gellner, *Nations and Nationalism* (Oxford: Basil Blackwell, 1983), p. 51.

6. Gellner, *Nations and Nationalism*, pp. 54–57.

7. Eric Hobsbawm and Terence Ranger (eds), *The Invention of Tradition* (Cambridge: Cambridge University Press, 1983).

8. Eric Hobsbawm, 'Mass-Producing Traditions: Europe, 1870–1914', in Hobsbawm and Ranger, *Invention of Tradition*, p. 307.

9. Anthony D. Smith, *The Ethnic Origins of Nations* (Oxford: Basil Blackwell, 1986), p. 178.

10. Norman Davies, *God's Playground: A History of Poland* (2 vols) (Oxford: Clarendon Press, 1981). In this section, page references in parentheses are to volumes I and II of this work.

11. The 'fourth' was the creation of the Duchy of Warsaw (II, p. 297), the 'fifth' occurred at the Congress of Vienna, 1815 (II, p. 307), and the 'sixth' was the outcome of the Treaty of Brest-Litovsk, 1918, soon rendered void by the defeat of Germany (II, p. 385).

12. Paul G. Lewis, 'Obstacles to the Establishment of Political Legitimacy in Communist Poland', *British Journal of Political Science* 12, 1982, 125–147, pp. 130f.

13. Jadwiga Staniszkis, 'On Some Contradictions of Socialist Society: The Case of Poland', *Soviet Studies* 31, 1979, 167–187, pp. 175–178. See also Neal Ascherson, *The Polish August: The Self-Limiting Revolution* (Harmondsworth: Penguin, 1981), pp. 38–42.

14. Lech Trzeciakowski, *The Kulturkampf in Prussian Poland* (New York: East European Monographs; distributed by Columbia University Press, 1990), pp. 82f.

15. Trzeciakowski, *The Kulturkampf in Prussian Poland*, p. 140.

16. Trzeciakowski, *The Kulturkampf in Prussian Poland*, ch. 4.

17. Trzeciakowski, *The Kulturkampf in Prussian Poland*, p. 188.

18. Hagen Schulze, 'Europe and the German Question in Historical Perspective', in Hagen Schulze (ed.), *Nation-Building in Central Europe* (Leamington Spa: Berg, 1987), p. 186.

19. Hagen Schulze, 'The Revolution of the European Order and the Rise of German Nationalism', in Schulze, *Nation-Building*, p. 12.

20. Hagen Schulze, *The Course of German Nationalism: From Frederick the Great to Bismarck, 1763–1867* (Cambridge: Cambridge University Press, 1991), pp. 47–50.

21. Smith, *The Ethnic Origins of Nations*, pp. 178–183.

22. Harold James, *A German Identity 1770–1990* (London: Weidenfeld and Nicolson, 1989), p. 51.
23. James, *German Identity*, p. 3.
24. James, *German Identity*, p. 122.
25. In this respect one of the most significant outcomes of Germany's defeat was the largely forced migration of 12 million Germans from their former East European homes to the new East and West Germany. Despite the persistence of small pockets of German nationality in the East, the centuries-old expansionist implications of the romantic *Kulturnation* were eliminated at a stroke. The cost may, however, be yet to pay, in resentment over this 'lost' Germany (Amity Shlaes's term) and over the hardship that the mass emigration involved (over 2 million deaths, Shlaes reports). Amity Shlaes, *Germany: The Empire Within* (New York: Farrar, Straus & Giroux, 1991), p. 6.
26. James, *German Identity*, p. 147–150.
27. Schulze, *The Course of German Nationalism*, pp. 150–164.
28. David D. Laitin and Aaron Wildavsky, 'Political Culture and Political Preferences', *American Political Science Review* 82, 1988, 589–596, p. 592. Another attempt to incorporate the idea of culture as a resource into political culture theory has been made by Lowell Dittmer. Defining political culture as a system of symbols, Dittmer argues that 'symbols exist independently of human beings and may therefore transmit meanings from person to person despite vast distances of space and time'. Lowell Dittmer, 'Political Culture and Political Symbolism: Toward a Theoretical Synthesis', *World Politics*, 29, 1977, 552–583, p. 557. Indeed, Dittmer also recommends a 'process' view of political culture that has some affinity with the phenomenological perspective we have been developing. However, he fails to reconcile the notion of culture as a resource with the process view; a reconciliation, we are arguing, that only phenomenological social theory can achieve. See also Lowell Dittmer, 'Comparative Communist Political Culture', *Studies in Comparative Communism*, 16, 1983, 9–24.

8: New Trends in Political Culture Research

1. See Claude Lévi-Strauss, 'Structural Analysis in Linguistics and Anthropology', in Claude Lévi-Strauss, *Structural Anthropology* (volume 1) (trans. Claire Jacobson and Brooke Grundfest Schoepf) (New York and London: Basic Books, 1963), pp. 31–34.
2. Saussure, quoted in Arthur Asa Berger, *Agitpop: Political Culture and Communication Theory* (New Brunswick, NJ and London: Transaction, 1990), p. 140.
3. Lévi-Strauss, 'The Structural Study of Myth', in Lévi-Strauss, *Structural Anthropology*, pp. 212f.
4. Eloise A. Buker, *Politics Through a Looking Glass: Understanding*

Political Culture Through a Structuralist Interpretation of Narratives (Westport, CT and London: Greenwood Press, 1987).

5. Richard M. Merelman, 'On Culture and Politics in America: A Perspective from Structural Anthropology', *British Journal of Political Science* 19, 1989, 465–493.

6. Michael E. Urban and John McClure, 'The Folklore of State Socialism: Semiotics and the Study of the Soviet State', *Soviet Studies* 35, 1983, 471–486.

7. Sebastiano Timpanaro, *On Materialism* (London: NLB, 1975), p. 187.

8. Merelman asserts, for instance, that 'social identity theorists . . . provide ample experimental support for the postulate of structural opposition in social cognition'. Merelman, 'On Culture and Politics in America', p. 473 and n. 43.

9. Timpanaro, *On Materialism*, pp. 185f.

10. Ernest Gellner, *The Concept of Kinship and Other Essays on Anthropological Method and Explanation* (Oxford: Basil Blackwell, 1987) (originally published as *Cause and Meaning in the Social Sciences*, 1973), p. 153.

11. Merelman, 'On Culture and Politics in America', p. 488. The label 'individualism' is easy enough to understand, but the justification for calling it 'mythologized' is a little puzzling. This refers to the recurrence of individualism in media narratives (p. 485); but its recurrence as metaphor is a necessary condition for its identification as 'deep structure'.

12. 'Corporate house organs *frequently* portray the corporation . . .'; '*Many* television sitcoms tell stories about . . .'; 'American mass media *regularly* disparage . . .': these are the 'statistical' demonstrations (emphasis added). Merelman, 'On Culture and Politics in America', pp. 489f.

13. The label 'culture theory' itself hints at the breadth of the claims made of this approach. In our discussion it will be avoided, since it begs too many questions about the relationship of this theory to its many predecessors in political culture research and elsewhere that might have gone under that name if their authors had been less reticent.

14. Merelman sees no difficulty in drawing on both: his 'individualism' is initially specified in terms of Douglas's typology, which he says 'incorporates the structuralist's principle of contrast'. Merelman, 'On Culture and Politics in America', pp. 485f.

15. Aaron Wildavsky, 'Change in Political Culture', *Politics* 20, 1985, 95–102; Aaron Wildavsky, 'Choosing Preferences by Constructing Institutions: A Cultural Theory of Preference Formation', *American Political Science Review* 81, 1987, 3–21; David D. Laitin and Aaron Wildavsky, 'Political Culture and Political Preferences', *American Political Science Review* 82, 1988, 589–596; Michael Thompson, Richard Ellis and Aaron Wildavsky, *Cultural Theory* (Boulder, CO

and Oxford: Westview, 1990). References to the last work in this section will be in parentheses in the text.

16. Wildavsky, 'Choosing Preferences'.

17. Wildavsky, 'Choosing Preferences', p. 18.

18. Berger, *Agitpop*; Arthur Asa Berger (ed.), *Political Culture and Public Opinion* (New Brunswick, NJ and Oxford: Transaction, 1989).

19. Spurious support for the theory is provided by the arbitrary suggestion that the birds have to move from one 'quadrant' to another. The number four is given almost mystical significance by a footnote reference to the tetrahedron as 'the simplest geometric form capable of structural integrity in three dimensions' (n. 1, p. 99). Is it pedantic to observe that the tetrahedron has no geometric connection with either a flock of starlings or the idea of a 'quadrant'?

20. The last involves the analysis of Almond and Verba's 'case histories'. These were based on a smaller group of in-depth and uncoded interviews used to illustrate the main argument, which, as we saw, was based on quantitative survey data.

21. Daniel J. Elazar, *American Federalism: A View from the States* (New York: Thomas W. Crowell, 1966), pp. 85–97.

22. Wildavsky, 'Choosing Preferences', p. 15.

23. Grounds may therefore be provided for David Laitin's observation that Wildavsky's matrix of preference combinations 'illustrates something important about his own culture'. Laitin and Wildavsky, 'Political Culture and Political Preferences', p. 590. Laitin's own idea of the use of political cultural resources by 'political entrepreneurs', which we mentioned in Chapter 7, is of course vulnerable to the same criticism.

24. Laitin and Wildavsky, 'Political Culture and Political Preferences', p. 593.

25. Richard Hofstadter, *The Idea of a Party System: The Rise of Legitimate Opposition in the United States, 1780–1840* (Berkeley: University of California Press, 1970), pp. viif.

26. Hofstadter, *The Idea of a Party System*, p. 238 and generally ch. 6.

27. Ronald P. Formisano, *The Transformation of Political Culture: Massachusetts Parties, 1790s–1840s* (New York and Oxford: Oxford University Press, 1983).

28. John L. Brooke, *The Heart of the Commonwealth: Society and Political Culture in Worcester County, Massachusetts 1713–1861* (Cambridge: Cambridge University Press, 1989), p. xvi. Emphasis added.

29. Robert Kelley, *Battling the Inland Sea: American Political Culture, Public Policy, and the Sacramento Valley 1850–1986* (Berkeley and London: University of California Press, 1989).

30. Philip R. VanderMeer, *The Hoosier Politician: Officeholding and Political Culture in Indiana 1896–1920* (Urbana and Chicago: Illinois University Press, 1985); Robert M. Weir, *'The Last of American Freemen': Studies in the Political Culture of the Colonial and Revolutionary South* (Macon, GA: Mercer University Press, 1986).

31. Formisano, *The Transformation of Political Culture*, p. 4.
32. Ronald P. Formisano, 'Comment' on Kelley, 'Ideology and Political Culture', *American Historical Review* 82, 1977, 568–577, p. 568.
33. Robert Kelley, *The Cultural Pattern in American Politics: The First Century* (New York: Alfred A. Knopf, 1979), p. 10, citing H. Stuart Hughes.
34. Kenneth S. Greenberg, *Masters and Statesmen: The Political Culture of American Slavery* (Baltimore and London: Johns Hopkins University Press, 1985).
35. Greenberg, *Masters and Statesmen*, chs 2, 4.
36. Greenberg, *Masters and Statesmen*, p. vii.
37. Anne Norton, *Alternative Americas: A Reading of Antebellum Political Culture* (Chicago and London: Chicago University Press, 1986).
38. Louis Hartz, *The Liberal Tradition in America: An Interpretation of American Political Thought Since the Revolution* (New York: Harcourt, Brace, 1955), ch. 7; J. G. A. Pocock, *The Machiavellian Moment: Florentine Political Thought and the Atlantic Republican Tradition* (Princeton, NJ: Princeton University Press, 1975), ch. 15; Norton, *Alternative Americas*, pp. 4 (on Hartz), 117f. (on Pocock).
39. Norton, *Alternative Americas*, p. 140. Norton's account also illustrates the perils of thick description, particularly in her use of the metaphors of masculinity and femininity to describe respectively the cultures of the North and the South. These metaphors are suggestive, but perhaps too loosely so. The prevalence of certain forms of violence, such as duelling, in the South might imply the opposite characterization. In the not unrepresentative spectacle of Southerner Preston Brooks attacking Northerner Charles Sumner on the floor of the Senate one certainly fails to see a clear display of 'feminine' qualities. See Greenberg, *Masters and Statesmen*, ch. 2.
40. Norton, *Alternative Americas*, p. 3.
41. Quoted in John Shelton Reed, *The Enduring South: Subcultural Persistence in Mass Society* (Lexington, MA: Lexington Books–D. C. Heath, 1972), p. 12.
42. Reed, *The Enduring South*, pp. 88f.
43. Weir, *'The Last of American Freemen'*, p. 71.
44. Daniel Walker Howe, *The Political Culture of the American Whigs* (Chicago and London: University of Chicago Press, 1979); Jean H. Baker, *Affairs of Party: The Political Culture of Northern Democrats in the Mid-Nineteenth Century* (Ithaca, NY and London: Cornell University Press, 1983). Baker's study extends also into the period of the 'third party system'.
45. Howe, *The Political Culture of the American Whigs*, esp. ch. 3 and Conclusion.
46. Baker, *Affairs of Party*, p. 12.
47. Baker, *Affairs of Party*, p. 289.
48. Hartz, *The Liberal Tradition in America*, ch. 5.

49. See in particular Robert Kelley, 'Ideology and Political Culture from Jefferson to Nixon', *American Historical Review* 82, 1977, 531–562 and the book for which that article was an appetizer, Kelley, *The Cultural Pattern in American Politics*. See also Kelley, *Battling the Inland Sea*.

50. Kelley, 'Ideology and Political Culture', pp. 532f.

51. Formisano, 'Comment', p. 568.

52. Kelley, *Battling the Inland Sea*, p. xv.

53. For an example see Samuel J. Patterson, 'The Political Cultures of the American States', *Journal of Politics* 30, 1968, 187–209.

Bibliography

Abercrombie, Nicholas and Bryan S. Turner, 'The Dominant Ideology Thesis', *British Journal of Sociology* 29, 1978, 149–170.

Adelman, Jonathan R., 'The Impact of Civil Wars on Communist Political Culture: The Chinese and Russian Cases', *Studies in Comparative Communism* 16, 1983, 25–48.

Almond, Gabriel A., 'Comparative Political Systems', *Journal of Politics* 18, 1956, 391–409.

Almond, Gabriel A., 'Communism and Political Culture Theory', *Comparative Politics* 15, 1983, 127–138.

Almond, Gabriel A., *A Discipline Divided: Schools and Sects in Political Science* (Newbury Park, CA and London: Sage, 1990).

Almond, Gabriel A. and James S. Coleman (eds), *The Politics of the Developing Areas* (Princeton, NJ: Princeton University Press, 1960).

Almond, Gabriel A. and Sidney Verba, *The Civic Culture: Political Attitudes and Democracy in Five Nations* (Princeton, NJ: Princeton University Press, 1963; abridged edn Boston: Little, Brown, 1965, repr. Newbury Park, CA and London: Sage, 1989).

Almond, Gabriel A. and Sidney Verba (eds), *The Civic Culture Revisited* (Boston: Little, Brown, 1980, repr. Newbury Park, CA and London: Sage, 1989).

Anderson, Benedict, *Imagined Communities: Reflections on the Origins and Spread of Nationalism* (London: Verso, 1983).

Andrle, Vladimir, *Workers in Stalin's Russia: Industrialization and Social Change in a Planned Economy* (Hemel Hempstead: Harvester-Wheatsheaf; New York: St. Martin's Press, 1988).

Appleby, Joyce, 'Republicanism in Old and New Contexts', *William and Mary Quarterly* 43, 1986, 20–34.

Archer, Margaret S., 'Theory, Culture and Post-Industrial Society', in Mike Featherstone (ed.), *Global Culture: Nationalism, Globalism and Modernity* (A *Theory, Culture and Society* special issue) (London and Newbury Park, CA: Sage, 1990).

Arendt, Hannah, *The Origins of Totalitarianism* (Cleveland, OH: Meridian, 1958).

Ascherson, Neal, *The Polish August: The Self-Limiting Revolution* (Harmondsworth: Penguin, 1981).

Baker, Jean H., *Affairs of Party: The Political Culture of Northern Democrats in the Mid-Nineteenth Century* (Ithaca, NY and London: Cornell University Press, 1983).

Banning, Lance, *The Jeffersonian Persuasion: Evolution of a Party Ideology* (Ithaca, NY and London: Cornell University Press, 1978).

193

Barghoorn, Frederick, 'Stalinism and the Russian Cultural Heritage', *Review of Politics* 14, 1952, 178–203.

Barghoorn, Frederick C. and Thomas F. Remington, *Politics in the USSR* (3rd edn) (Boston: Little, Brown, 1986).

Barnard, F. M., 'Culture and Political Development: Herder's Suggestive Insights', *American Political Science Review* 63, 1969, 379–397.

Barry, Brian M., *Sociologists, Economists and Democracy* (Chicago: University of Chicago Press, 1978).

Basham, Richard and David DeGroot, 'Current Approaches to the Anthropology of Urban and Complex Societies', *American Anthropologist* 79, 1977, 414–440.

Bell, Daniel, 'Ten Theories in Search of Soviet Reality', in Alex Inkeles and Kent Geiger (eds), *Soviet Society: A Book of Readings* (London: Constable, 1961).

Berend, Iván T. and György Ránki, *Economic Development in East-Central Europe in the 19th and 20th Centuries* (New York: Columbia University Press, 1974).

Berger, Arthur Asa, *Agitpop: Political Culture and Communication Theory* (New Bruswick, NJ and London: Transaction, 1990).

Berger, Arthur Asa (ed.), *Political Culture and Public Opinion* (New Brunswick, NJ and Oxford: Transaction, 1989).

Berger, Peter L. and Thomas Luckmann, *The Social Construction of Reality: A Treatise in the Sociology of Knowledge* (Harmondsworth: Penguin, 1967).

Bernstein, Richard J., *The Restructuring of Social and Political Theory* (London: Methuen, 1979).

Bialer, Seweryn, *The Soviet Paradox: External Expansion, Internal Decline* (London: I. B. Tauris, 1986).

Bill, James A. and Robert L. Hardgrave, Jr, *Comparative Politics: The Quest for Theory* (Lanham, MD: University Press of America, 1981).

Black, Cyril E., *Understanding Soviet Politics: The Perspective of Russian History* (Boulder, CO: Westview, 1986).

Boon, James A., *Other Tribes, Other Scribes: Symbolic Anthropology in the Comparative Study of Cultures, Histories, Religions, and Texts* (Cambridge: Cambridge University Press, 1982).

Brady, Ivan (ed.), 'Speaking in the Name of the Real: Freeman and Mead on Samoa', *American Anthropologist* 85, 1983, 908–947.

Brooke, John L., *The Heart of the Commonwealth: Society and Political Culture in Worcester County, Massachusetts 1713–1861* (Cambridge: Cambridge University Press, 1989).

Brower, Daniel R., 'Stalinism and the "View From Below"', *Russian Review* 46, 1987, 379–381.

Brown, Archie, review of White, *Political Culture and Soviet Politics* in *The Times Literary Supplement*, 7 March 1980.

Brown, Archie, 'Ideology and Political Culture', in Seweryn Bialer (ed.), *Politics, Society, and Nationality Inside Gorbachev's Russia* (Boulder, CO: Westview, 1989).

Brown, Archie (ed.), *Political Culture and Communist Studies* (London: Macmillan, 1984).

Brown, Archie and Jack Gray (eds), *Political Culture and Political Change in Communist States* (London: Macmillan, 1977).

Brzezinski, Zbigniew K., 'Soviet Politics: From the Future to the Past?', in Paul Cocks, Robert V. Daniels and Nancy Whittier Heer (eds), *The Dynamics of Soviet Politics* (Cambridge, MA and London: Harvard University Press, 1976).

Buker, Eloise A., *Politics Through a Looking Glass: Understanding Political Culture Through a Structuralist Interpretation of Narratives* (Westport, CT and London: Greenwood Press, 1987).

Burant, Stephen R., 'The Influence of Russian Tradition on the Political Style of the Soviet Elite', *Political Science Quarterly* 102, 1987, 273–293.

Chilton, Stephen, *Defining Political Development* (Boulder, CO and London: Lynne Reiner, 1988).

Clark, Katerina, *The Soviet Novel: History as Ritual* (Chicago and London: University of Chicago Press, 1981).

Cohen, Abner, *Two-Dimensional Man: An Essay on the Anthropology of Power and Symbolism in Complex Society* (London: Routledge & Kegan Paul, 1974).

Cohen, Anthony P., *The Symbolic Construction of Community* (Chichester: Ellis Horwood; London and New York: Tavistock, 1985).

Cohen, Stephen F., *Bukharin and the Bolshevik Revolution: A Political Biography 1888–1938* (London: Wildwood House, 1974).

Collier, David, 'The Comparative Method: Two Decades of Change', in Dankwart A. Rustow and Kenneth Paul Erickson (eds), *Comparative Political Dynamics: Global Research Perspectives* (New York: HarperCollins, 1991).

Crick, Bernard, *The American Science of Politics: Its Origins and Conditions* (Berkeley: University of California Press, 1964).

Czudnowski, Moshe M., 'A Salience Dimension of Politics for the Study of Political Culture', *American Political Science Review* 62, 1968, 878–888.

Dahl, Robert A., 'The Behavioral Approach in Political Science: Epitaph for a Monument to a Successful Revolution', *American Political Science Review* 55, 1961, 763–772.

Davies, Norman, *God's Playground: A History of Poland* (2 vols) (Oxford: Clarendon Press, 1981).

Dawisha, Karen, *Eastern Europe, Gorbachev, and Reform: The Great Challenge* (2nd edn) (Cambridge: Cambridge University Press, 1990).

Devine, Donald J., *The Political Culture of the United States: The Influence of Member Values on Regime Maintenance* (Boston: Little, Brown, 1972).

DiFranceisco, Wayne and Zvi Gitelman, 'Soviet Political Culture and "Covert Participation" in Policy Implementation', *American Political Science Review* 78, 1984, 603–621.

Dittmer, Lowell, 'Political Culture and Political Symbolism: Toward a Theoretical Synthesis', *World Politics* 29, 1977, 552–583.

Dittmer, Lowell, 'Comparative Communist Political Culture', *Studies in Comparative Communism* 16, 1983, 9–24.

Easton, David, *A Systems Analysis of Political Life* (New York: John Wiley and Sons, 1965).

Eckstein, Harry, 'A Culturalist Theory of Political Change', *American Political Science Review* 82, 1988, 789–804.

Elazar, Daniel J., *American Federalism: A View from the States* (New York: Thomas W. Crowell, 1966).

Elazar, Daniel and Joseph Zikmund III (eds), *The Ecology of American Political Culture: Readings* (New York: Thomas W. Crowell, 1975).

Eley, Geoff, 'History With the Politics Left Out – Again?', *Russian Review* 45, 1986, 385–394.

Elkins, David J. and Richard E. B. Simeon, 'A Cause in Search of its Effect, or What Does Political Culture Explain?', *Comparative Politics* 11, 1979, 127–145.

Epstein, A. L., *Ethos and Identity: Three Studies in Ethnicity* (London: Tavistock; Chicago: Aldine, 1978).

Fagen, Richard R., *The Transformation of Political Culture in Cuba* (Stanford: Stanford University Press, 1969).

Fitzpatrick, Sheila (ed.), *Cultural Revolution in Russia, 1928–31* (Bloomington, IN and London: Indiana University Press, 1978).

Fitzpatrick, Sheila, 'New Perspectives on Stalinism', *Russian Review* 45, 1986, 357–373.

Formisano, Ronald P., 'Comment' on Kelley, 'Ideology and Political Culture', *American Historical Review* 82, 1977, 568–577.

Formisano, Ronald P., *The Transformation of Political Culture: Massachusetts Parties, 1790s-1840s* (New York and Oxford: Oxford University Press, 1983).

Frentzel-Zagorska, Janina, 'The Dominant Political Culture in Poland', *Politics* 20, 1985, 82–98.

Friedrich, Carl J. and Zbigniew K. Brzezinski, *Totalitarian Dictatorship and Autocracy* (2nd edn) (Cambridge, MA: Harvard University Press, 1965).

Garton Ash, Timothy, 'Does Central Europe Exist?', *New York Review of Books* 33, 9 October 1986, 45–52.

Gati, Charles, *The Bloc That Failed: Soviet–East European Relations in Transition* (Bloomington, IN: Indiana University Press, 1990).

Gati, Charles (ed.), *The Politics of Modernization in Eastern Europe: Testing the Soviet Model* (New York: Praeger, 1974).

Geertz, Clifford, *The Interpretation of Cultures* (London: Hutchinson, 1975).

Gellner, Ernest, *Nations and Nationalism* (Oxford: Basil Blackwell, 1983).

Gellner, Ernest, *The Concept of Kinship and Other Essays on Anthropological Method and Explanation* (Oxford: Basil Blackwell, 1987) (originally published as *Cause and Meaning in the Social Sciences*, 1973).

Gerner, Kristian, *The Soviet Union and Central Europe in the Post-War Era: A Study in Precarious Security* (Aldershot: Gower, 1985).

Getty, J. Arch, *Origins of the Great Purges: The Soviet Communist Party*

Reconsidered, 1933–1938 (Cambridge: Cambridge University Press, 1985).

Gibbins, John R. (ed.), *Contemporary Political Culture: Politics in a Postmodern Age* (London: Sage, 1989).

Giddens, Anthony, *The Constitution of Society: Outline of the Theory of Structuration* (Cambridge: Polity Press, 1984).

Gill, Graeme, 'Personality Cult, Political Culture and Party Structure', *Studies in Comparative Communism* 17, 1984, 111–121.

Gitelman, Zvi, 'Soviet Political Culture: Insights from Jewish Emigrés', *Soviet Studies* 29, 1977, 543–564.

Glazer, Nathan and Daniel P. Moynihan, 'Why Ethnicity?', *Commentary* 58, 1974, 33–39.

Gleason, Abbott, Peter Kenez and Richard Stites (eds), *Bolshevik Culture: Experiment and Order in the Russian Revolution* (Bloomington, IN: Indiana University Press, 1985).

Gluckman, M., 'Anthropological Problems Arising From the African Industrial Revolution', in Aidan Southall (ed.), *Social Change in Modern Africa* (London: Oxford University Press, 1961).

Greenberg, Kenneth S., *Masters and Statesmen: The Political Culture of American Slavery* (Baltimore and London: Johns Hopkins University Press, 1985).

Grew, Raymond, 'More on Modernization', *Journal of Social History* 14, 1980, 179–187.

Hahn, Jeffrey W., 'Continuity and Change in Russian Political Culture', *British Journal of Political Science* 21, 1991, 393–421.

Hartz, Louis, *The Liberal Tradition in America: An Interpretation of American Political Thought Since the Revolution* (New York: Harcourt, Brace, 1955).

Havel, Václav, 'The Power of the Powerless', in Václav Havel *et al.*, *The Power of the Powerless* (London: Hutchinson, 1985).

Hayward, Max, *Writers in Russia: 1917–1978* (London: Harvill, 1983).

Hill, Ronald J., 'The Cultural Dimension of Communist Political Evolution', *Journal of Communist Studies* 1, 1985, 34–53.

Hill, Ronald J., 'Soviet Political Development and the Culture of the Apparatchiki', *Studies in Comparative Communism* 19, 1986, 25–39.

Hobsbawm, E. J., *Nations and Nationalism Since 1870: Programme, Myth, Reality* (Cambridge: Cambridge University Press, 1990).

Hobsbawm, Eric and Terence Ranger (eds), *The Invention of Tradition* (Cambridge: Cambridge University Press, 1983).

Hofstadter, Richard, *The Idea of a Party System: The Rise of Legitimate Opposition in the United States, 1780–1840* (Berkeley: University of California Press, 1970).

Hofstede, Geert, *Culture's Consequences: International Differences in Work-Related Values* (Beverly Hills, CA and London: Sage, 1980).

Howe, Daniel Walker, *The Political Culture of the American Whigs* (Chicago and London: University of Chicago Press, 1979).

Huntington, Samuel P. and Jorge Domínguez, 'Political Development', in Fred I. Greenstein and Nelson W. Polsby (eds), *Handbook of Political Science Volume 3: Macropolitical Theory* (Reading, MA: Addison-Wesley, 1975).

Inglehart, Ronald, *The Silent Revolution: Changing Values and Political Styles Among Western Publics* (Princeton, NJ: Princeton University Press, 1977).

Inglehart, Ronald, 'The Renaissance of Political Culture', *American Political Science Review* 82, 1988, 1203–1230.

Inglehart, Ronald, *Culture Shift in Advanced Industrial Society* (Princeton, NJ: Princeton University Press, 1990).

Inkeles, Alex and Raymond A. Bauer, *The Soviet Citizen: Daily Life in a Totalitarian Society* (Cambridge, MA: Harvard University Press; London: Oxford University Press, 1959).

James, Harold, *A German Identity 1770–1990* (London: Weidenfeld and Nicolson, 1989).

Jancar, Barbara, 'Political Culture and Political Change', *Studies in Comparative Communism* 17, 1984, 69–82.

Jessop, Bob, *Social Order, Reform and Revolution: A Power, Exchange and Institutionalization Perspective* (London: Macmillan, 1972).

Jessop, Bob, *Traditionalism, Conservatism and British Political Culture* (London: George Allen and Unwin, 1974).

Jessop, R. D., 'Civility and Traditionalism in English Political Culture', *British Journal of Political Science* 1, 1971, 1–24.

Jowitt, Kenneth, 'An Organizational Approach to the Study of Political Culture in Marxist–Leninist Systems', *American Political Science Review* 68, 1974, 1171–1191.

Kavanagh, Dennis, *Political Science and Political Behaviour* (London: George Allen & Unwin, 1983).

Keenan, Edward L., 'Muscovite Political Folkways', *Russian Review* 45, 1986, 115–181.

Keesing, Roger M., 'Theories of Culture', *Annual Review of Anthropology* 3, 1974, 73–97.

Kelley, Robert, 'Ideology and Political Culture from Jefferson to Nixon', *American Historical Review* 82, 1977, 531–562.

Kelley, Robert, *The Cultural Pattern in American Politics: The First Century* (New York: Alfred A. Knopf, 1979).

Kelley, Robert, *Battling the Inland Sea: American Political Culture, Public Policy, and the Sacramento Valley 1850–1986* (Berkeley and London: University of California Press, 1989).

Kolakowski, Leszek, *Main Currents of Marxism: Its Rise, Growth, and Dissolution. Volume II: The Golden Age* (trans. P. S. Falla) (Oxford: Oxford University Press, 1978).

Konrád, George, *Antipolitics: An Essay* (trans. Richard E. Allen) (New York and London: Harcourt Brace Jovanovich, 1984).

Krisch, Henry, 'Changing Political Culture and Political Stability in the

German Democratic Republic', *Studies in Comparative Communism* 19, 1986, 41–53.

Kroeber, A. L. and Clyde Kluckhohn, *Culture: A Critical Review of Concepts and Definitions* (New York: Vintage Books, n.d.) (originally published as *Papers of the Peabody Museum of American Archaeology and Ethnology, Harvard University* 47, 1952).

Kundera, Milan, *The Book of Laughter and Forgetting* (Harmondsworth: Penguin, 1983).

Laitin, David D. and Aaron Wildavsky, 'Political Culture and Political Preferences', *American Political Science Review* 82, 1988, 589–596.

Lane, Christel, *The Rites of Rulers: Ritual in Industrial Society – The Soviet Case* (Cambridge: Cambridge University Press, 1981).

Lane, Christel, 'Legitimacy and Power in the Soviet Union Through Socialist Ritual', *British Journal of Political Science* 14, 1984, 207–217.

Leach, Edmund, *Social Anthropology* (London: Fontana, 1982).

Lehman, Edward W., 'On the Concept of Political Culture: A Theoretical Reassessment', *Social Forces* 50, 1972, 361–370.

Lemke, Christiane, 'New Issues in the Politics of the German Democratic Republic: A Question of Political Culture?', *Journal of Communist Studies* 2, 1986, 351–358.

Lévi-Strauss, Claude, *Structural Anthropology* (volume 1) (trans. Claire Jacobson and Brooke Grundfest Schoepf) (New York and London: Basic Books, 1963).

Lewin, Moshe, *The Making of the Soviet System: Essays in the Social History of Interwar Russia* (London: Methuen, 1985).

Lewis, Paul G., 'Obstacles to the Establishment of Political Legitimacy in Communist Poland', *British Journal of Political Science* 12, 1982, 125–147.

Lewis, Paul G., 'Legitimation and Political Crises: East European Developments in the Post-Stalin Period', in Paul G. Lewis (ed.), *Eastern Europe: Political Crisis and Legitimation* (New York: St Martin's Press, 1984).

Lieberson, Jonathan, 'Interpreting the Interpreter', *New York Review of Books* 31, 15 March 1985, 39–46.

Lijphart, Arend, 'Comparative Politics and Comparative Method', *American Political Science Review* 65, 1971, 682–693.

McKay, James, 'An Exploratory Synthesis of Primordial and Mobilizationist Approaches to Ethnic Phenomena', *Ethnic and Racial Studies* 5, 1982, 395–420.

Mann, Michael, 'The Social Cohesion of American Liberal Democracy', *American Sociological Review* 35, 1970, 423–439.

Merelman, Richard M., 'On Culture and Politics in America: A Perspective from Structural Anthropology', *British Journal of Political Science* 19, 1989, 465–493.

Meyer, Alfred G., 'Communist Revolutions and Cultural Change', *Studies in Comparative Communism* 5, 1972, 345–372.

Meyer, Alfred G., 'The Use of the Term Culture in the Soviet Union',

Appendix B of Kroeber and Kluckhohn, *Culture: A Critical Review of Concepts and Definitions*.

Meyer, Stephen, 'Adapting the Immigrant to the Line: Americanization in the Ford Factory, 1914–1921', *Journal of Social History* 14, 1980, 67–82.

Middleton, David and Derek Edwards, 'Conversational Remembering: a Social Psychological Approach', in David Middleton and Derek Edwards (eds), *Collective Remembering* (London and Newbury Park, CA: Sage, 1990).

Millar, James R. (ed.), *Politics, Work, and Daily Life in the USSR: A Survey of Former Soviet Citizens* (Cambridge: Cambridge University Press, 1987).

Moreno, Fransisco José, *Legitimacy and Stability in Latin America: A Study of Chilean Political Culture* (New York: New York University Press; London: University of London Press, 1969).

Natanson, Maurice, 'Introduction', in Schutz, *Collected Papers I*.

Natanson, Maurice, *Anonymity: A Study in the Philosophy of Alfred Schutz* (Bloomington, IN: Indiana University Press, 1986).

Norton, Anne, *Alternative Americas: A Reading of Antebellum Political Culture* (Chicago and London: Chicago University Press, 1986).

Nowak, Stefan, 'Values and Attitudes of the Polish People', *Scientific American* 245, 1981, 23–31.

Pateman, Carole, 'Criticizing Empirical Theorists of Democracy: A Comment on Skinner', *Political Theory* 2, 1974, 215–218.

Patrick, Glenda M., 'Political Culture', in Giovanni Sartori (ed.), *Social Science Concepts: A Systemic Analysis* (Beverly Hills, CA and London: Sage, 1984).

Pateman, Carole, 'Political Culture, Political Structure and Political Change', *British Journal of Political Science* 1, 1971, 291–305.

Patterson, Samuel J., 'The Political Cultures of the American States', *Journal of Politics* 30, 1968, 187–209.

Paul, David W., *The Cultural Limits of Revolutionary Politics* (Boulder, CO: East European Quarterly; distributed by Columbia University Press, New York, 1979).

Pipes, Richard, *Russia Under the Old Regime* (New York: Scribners Sons, 1974).

Pocock, J. G. A., *The Machiavellian Moment: Florentine Political Thought and the Atlantic Republican Tradition* (Princeton, NJ: Princeton University Press, 1975).

Putnam, Robert D., 'Studying Elite Political Culture: The Case of Ideology', *American Political Science Review* 65, 1981, 651–681.

Pye, Lucian W., 'Culture and Political Science: Problems in the Evaluation of the Concept of Political Culture', in Louis Schneider and Charles M. Bonjean (eds), *The Idea of Culture in the Social Sciences* (Cambridge: Cambridge University Press, 1973).

Pye, Lucian W., 'Political Science and the Crisis of Authoritarianism', *American Political Science Review* 84, 1990, 3–19.

Pye, Lucian W. with Mary W. Pye, *Asian Power and Politics: The Cultural*

Dimension of Authority (Cambridge, MA and London: Belknap Press of Harvard University Press, 1985).

Pye, Lucian W. and Sidney Verba (eds), *Political Culture and Political Development* (Princeton, NJ: Princeton University Press, 1965).

Pynsent, Robert B. (ed.), *T. G. Masaryk (1850–1937)*. Volume 2: *Thinker and Critic* (London: Macmillan, 1989).

Reed, John Shelton, *The Enduring South: Subcultural Persistence in Mass Society* (Lexington, MA: Lexington Books–D. C. Heath, 1972).

Richardson, Bradley M., *The Political Culture of Japan* (Berkeley: University of California Press, 1974).

Rigby, T. H., 'Stalinism and the Mono-Organizational Society', in Robert C. Tucker (ed.), *Stalinism: Essays in Historical Interpretation* (New York: W. W. Norton, 1977).

Rigby, T. H., 'Introduction: Political Legitimacy, Weber and Communist Mono-Organizational Systems', in T. H. Rigby and Ferenc Fehér (eds), *Political Legitimation in Communist States* (London: Macmillan, 1982).

Roberts, Geoffrey K., '"Normal" or "Critical"?: Progress Reports on the Condition of West Germany's Political Culture', *European Journal of Political Research* 12, 1984, 423–431.

Roseberry, William, 'Balinese Cockfights and the Seduction of Anthropology', *Social Research* 49, 1982, 1013–1028.

Rosenbaum, Walter A., *Political Culture* (London: Thomas Nelson & Sons, 1975).

Rothschild, Joseph, *Return to Diversity: A Political History of East Central Europe Since World War II* (New York and Oxford: Oxford University Press, 1989).

Runciman, W. G., 'Some Recent Contributions to the Theory of Democracy', *European Journal of Sociology* 6, 1965, 174–185.

Rusinow, Dennison (ed.), *Yugoslavia: A Fractured Federalism* (Washington DC: Wilson Center Press, 1988).

Schulze, Hagen (ed.), *Nation-Building in Central Europe* (Leamington Spa: Berg, 1987).

Schulze, Hagen, *The Course of German Nationalism: From Frederick the Great to Bismarck, 1763–1867* (Cambridge: Cambridge University Press, 1991).

Schutz, Alfred, *Collected Papers I: The Problem of Social Reality* (The Hague: Martinus Nijhoff, 1973).

Sharrock, Wes and Bob Anderson, *The Ethnomethodologists* (Chichester: Ellis Horwood; London and New York: Tavistock, 1986).

Shklar, Judith N., *Montesquieu* (Oxford: Oxford University Press, 1987).

Shlaes, Amity, *Germany: The Empire Within* (New York: Farrar, Straus and Giroux, 1991).

Skilling, H. Gordon, 'Sixty-eight in Historical Perspective', *International Journal* 33, 1978, 678–701.

Skinner, Quentin, 'The Empirical Theorists of Democracy and Their Critics: A Plague on Both Their Houses', *Political Theory* 1, 1973, 287–306.

Smith, Anthony D., *The Ethnic Origins of Nations* (Oxford: Basil Blackwell, 1986).

Smith, Gordon, 'A Model of the Bureaucratic Culture', *Political Studies* 22, 1974, 31–43.

Sochor, Zenovia A., *Revolution and Culture: The Bogdanov–Lenin Controversy* (Ithaca, NY and London: Cornell University Press, 1988).

Solomon, Richard H., *Mao's Revolution and the Chinese Political Culture* (Berkeley: University of California Press, 1971).

Staniszkis, Jadwiga, 'On Some Contradictions of Socialist Society: The Case of Poland', *Soviet Studies* 31, 1979, 167–187.

Taylor, Charles, 'Interpretation and the Sciences of Man', *Review of Metaphysics* 25, 1971, 3–51.

Thompson, Michael, Richard Ellis and Aaron Wildavsky, *Cultural Theory* (Boulder, CO and Oxford: Westview, 1990).

Timpanaro, Sebastiano, *On Materialism* (London: NLB, 1975).

Treadgold, Donald W., *Twentieth Century Russia* (7th edn) (Boulder, CO: Westview, 1990).

Trzeciakowski, Lech, *The Kulturkampf in Prussian Poland* (New York: East European Monographs; distributed by Columbia University Press, 1990).

Tucker, Robert C., *The Soviet Political Mind: Studies in Stalinism and Post-Stalin Change* (London and Dunmow: Pall Mall, 1963).

Tucker, Robert C., 'Communism and Political Culture', *Newsletter on Comparative Studies of Communism* 4, 1971, 3–12.

Tucker, Robert C., 'Culture, Political Culture, and Communist Society', *Political Science Quarterly* 88, 1973, 173–190.

Tucker, Robert C., *Stalin as Revolutionary 1879–1929: A Study in History and Personality* (New York: W. W. Norton, 1973).

Tucker, Robert C., 'Communist Revolutions, National Cultures, and the Divided Nations', *Studies in Comparative Communism* 7, 1974, 235–245.

Tucker, Robert C., *Political Culture and Leadership in Soviet Russia: From Lenin To Gorbachev* (Brighton: Wheatsheaf, 1987).

Tucker, Robert C., *Stalin in Power: The Revolution from Above 1928–1941* (New York and London: W. W. Norton, 1990).

Urban, Michael E., *The Ideology of Administration: American and Soviet Cases* (Albany, NY: State University of New York Press, 1982).

Urban, Michael E., 'Conceptualizing Political Power in the USSR: Patterns of Binding and Bonding', *Studies in Comparative Communism* 18, 1985, 207–226.

Urban, Michael E. and John McClure, 'The Folklore of State Socialism: Semiotics and the Study of the Soviet State', *Soviet Studies* 35, 1983, 471–486.

VanderMeer, Philip R., *The Hoosier Politician: Officeholding and Political Culture in Indiana 1896–1920* (Urbana and Chicago: Illinois University Press, 1985).

Wagner, Roy, *The Invention of Culture* (Englewood Cliffs, NJ: Prentice-Hall, 1975).

Waller, Michael, 'What Is to Count as Ideology in Soviet Politics?', in Stephen White and Alex Pravda (eds), *Ideology and Soviet Politics* (London: Macmillan, 1988).

Walker, Rachel, 'Marxism–Leninism as Discourse: The Politics of the Empty Signifier and the Double Bind', *British Journal of Political Science* 19, 1989, 161–189.

Wei, Yung, 'A Methodological Critique of Current Studies on Chinese Political Culture', *Journal of Politics* 38, 1976, 114–140.

Weir, Robert M., *'The Last of American Freemen': Studies in the Political Culture of the Colonial and Revolutionary South* (Macon, GA: Mercer University Press, 1986).

Welch, Stephen, 'Issues in the Study of Political Culture: The Example of Communist Party States', *British Journal of Political Science* 17, 1987, 479–500.

Welch, Stephen, 'Political Culture and Communism: Definition and Use', *Journal of Communist Studies* 5, 1989, 91–98.

White, Stephen, 'Political Socialization in the USSR: A Study in Failure?', *Studies in Comparative Communism* 10, 1977, 328–342.

White, Stephen, 'Continuity and Change in Soviet Political Culture: An Emigré Study', *Comparative Political Studies* 11, 1978, 391–395.

White, Stephen, *Political Culture and Soviet Politics* (London: Macmillan, 1979).

White, Stephen, 'Political Culture in Communist States: Some Problems of Theory and Method' (Research Note), *Comparative Politics* 16, 1984, 351–365.

White, Stephen, 'Propagating Communist Values in the USSR', *Problems of Communism* 34, 1985, 1–17.

Wildavsky, Aaron, 'Change in Political Culture', *Politics* 20, 1985, 95–102.

Wildavsky, Aaron, 'Choosing Preferences by Constructing Institutions: A Cultural Theory of Preference Formation', *American Political Science Review* 81, 1987, 3–21.

Williams, Raymond, *Marxism and Literature* (Oxford: Oxford University Press, 1977).

Williams, Robert C., 'The Nationalization of Early Soviet Culture', *Russian History* 9, 1982, 157–172.

Winters, Stanley B. (ed.), *T. G. Masaryk (1850–1937). Volume 1: Thinker and Politician* (London: Macmillan, 1989).

Yaney, George, 'Bureaucracy as Culture: A Comment', *Slavic Review* 41, 1982, 104–111.

Index